Disobedience Without the Jail Time

Guerrilla Tactics for the Surveillance Age

Dillinger Press

Dillinger Publishing

© 2025 by Dillinger Publishing. All rights reserved.

Content Warning

This publication contains real-world tactics, historical references, and technical methods related to civil disobedience, surveillance evasion, and digital activism. Some material may be considered sensitive, controversial, or unsuitable for younger audiences.

For mature readers.

Recommended for individuals age 16 and older with the capacity to evaluate risk and ethical responsibility.

This book is a nonfiction guide that draws from historical records, open-source activist materials, academic research, and publicly available tactical frameworks. It is intended for educational and informational purposes only.

Use of any tactic, tool, or method described herein is undertaken at the reader's sole discretion and risk. The author and publisher do not encourage or condone illegal activity and accept no responsibility for outcomes resulting from any real-world application of this material.

Readers are urged to consult legal counsel and understand applicable laws in their region before engaging in any form of protest, civil disobedience, or direct action.

E-Book ISBN: 979-8-9926341-5-0
Print (Paperback) ISBN: 979-8-9926341-6-7
Printed in the United States of America
First Edition

Legal Notice

All rights reserved. No part of this book may be reproduced, distributed, or transmitted in any form or by any means, including photocopying, recording, or other electronic or mechanical methods, without the prior written permission of the publisher, except in the case of brief quotations embodied in critical reviews and specific other noncommercial uses permitted by copyright law. The digital edition may not be re-sold, shared, or altered without written permission, except where expressly allowed by license. For permission requests, write to the publisher at the address below.

Dillinger Publishing
Attn: General Inquiry
620 SW 5th Avenue
Suite 900 #224
Portland, OR 97204
USA
E: general.inquiry@adamantholdingsllc.com

Trademark Notice

All trademarks, service marks, product names, and logos appearing in this book are the property of their respective owners. Use of these marks does not imply affiliation with or endorsement by them.

By reading this book, you agree to the terms of this disclaimer and legal notice.

Disclaimer Notice

This publication explores civil disobedience, protest strategy, and digital self-defense through a historical, psychological, and tactical lens. It is intended solely for educational, informational, and expressive purposes protected under the United States Constitution, including but not limited to the rights granted in *Brandenburg v. Ohio*, 395 U.S. 444 (1969), which affirms that speech may not be prohibited unless it is directed to inciting imminent lawless action and is likely to incite or produce such action.

This book does not encourage or incite unlawful activity. It presents knowledge, context, and tools so that readers may make informed, ethical decisions, particularly in environments where civil liberties may be under threat.

Neither the author nor the publisher assumes any liability for legal, civil, or personal consequences resulting from the use, misuse, or interpretation of this content. Readers are solely responsible for understanding the laws, regulations, and risks applicable in their jurisdiction and are urged to seek legal counsel before engaging in any form of protest, resistance, or related activity.

Examples, tactics, and case studies described herein are for illustrative purposes only. Their inclusion does not constitute legal instruction, operational endorsement, or a guarantee of legality in any location or circumstance.

FOREWORD

This book isn't written for one generation, one ideology, or one kind of rebel.

It's for the schoolteacher who won't stay silent in the face of injustice.
The delivery driver watching their city reshape without consent.
The student told to behave while the world burns.
The veteran organizer fluent in the old tools; and hungry for new ones.
The protester who doesn't seek martyrdom, only momentum.

In an age of surveillance capitalism, algorithmic control, and vanishing civil liberties, resistance demands more than outrage. It demands clarity. What you do must matter.

But it must also be smart.
Secure.
Sustainable.

You don't have to break windows.
You don't have to burn out or break down.
You need precision tools. This book provides them.

Inside, you'll find:

- Mesh networks that function where cell towers fall silent

- Guerrilla projection tactics that transform cities into canvases

- Augmented reality that resurrects erased narratives

- Drones, zines, encryption, and everything in between

This isn't theory. This is practice.
You don't need permission to be powerful.
You don't have to be young, tech-savvy, or part of any movement to matter.

Whether you're stepping into dissent for the first time or leading your hundredth action, this book was built to put real tools into real hands.

No violence. No gatekeeping. No excuses.
Just the means to disrupt what demands disruption, and to walk away free.

This book is not illegal.
But it is dangerous… to the right people.

— *Dillinger Publishing*

Contents

Quick Start Page & Navigation Guide ... X
Two ways to use this book

Part I ... 1
The Why: Foundations of Disobedience

1. The Spirit of Rebellion ... 2
2. Historical Mavericks ... 9
3. The Psychology of Resistance ... 14
4. The Ethics of Radical Action ... 19
5. The Myth of the "Good Protest" ... 24
6. Disobedience in the Age of Surveillance ... 30

Part II ... 37
The Who: Becoming a Modern Dissenter

7. Critical Thinking and Skepticism ... 38
8. Embracing Risk and Uncertainty ... 46
9. Breaking Boundaries ... 52
10. Networking and Fellow Mavericks ... 60
11. Choosing Your Line: Tactical Ethics for Protestors ... 69
12. Resilience Without Burnout ... 75

Part III ... 83
The How: Disruption Modules

Disruption Module A	84
Mesh Networking for Off-Grid Coordination	
Disruption Module B	90
Privacy & Routing with Raspberry Pi	
Disruption Module C	97
Guerrilla Projection and Light Tactics	
Disruption Module D	103
AR Activism – Augmented Reality for Social Justice	
Disruption Module E	110
Anonymous Broadcast Messaging in Blackouts	
Disruption Module F	118
Zine Warfare – Physical and Digital Subversion	
Disruption Module G	125
Drone-Based Messaging and Aerial Tactics	
Disruption Module H	135
Bonus Tools and References	
Part IV	143
Staying Smart, Staying Safe	
13. Real-Time Rescue: Emergency Legal Tactics and Contacts	144
14. Legal Considerations and Risks	149
15. Funding the Fight: Economics of Resistance	156
16. Knowing More, Risking Less: Tactical Intelligence for Resistance	164
17. Security and Anonymity in Activism	170
Part V	177
For the Future: Sustaining the Spark	
18. Being Disappeared	178
19. Education as a Revolutionary Act	184
20. Art as a Weapon	190
21. Sustaining the Spark: A Call to Future Disobedients	194
Glossary	200

Index	202
QR Code Reference Pages	210
Navigate to QR Code Sections	

Quick Start Page & Navigation Guide

Two ways to use this book

Follow a path (recommended below).
Jump by need (use the legend + parts / chapters listed).

Note: *All hyperlinks in this entire work have QR Codes listed in the QR Code Reference Page.*

Pick your lane

If you're new to protesting → Part II, then Part III.

If you're returning and need tactics now → Part III, then Part I.

If you need off-grid communications → Disruption Module A + Disruption Module D.

If you're under surveillance / need OPSEC → Chapter 6, Chapter 17, Disruption Module G.

If you're choosing your ethical line → Chapter 11.

If burnout is already here → Chapter 12.

If you just got detained / rights violated → Chapter 13 + 14.

If you organize groups/trust cells → Chapter 10 + Disruption Module G.

If you want creative disruption tactics → Chapter 9 + Disruption Modules B–F.

If you're digital-first → Disruption Module D + Chapter 9.

If you're an academic / educator → Part I + Part IV.

If you want the long view / future forecasts → Part V.

Legend

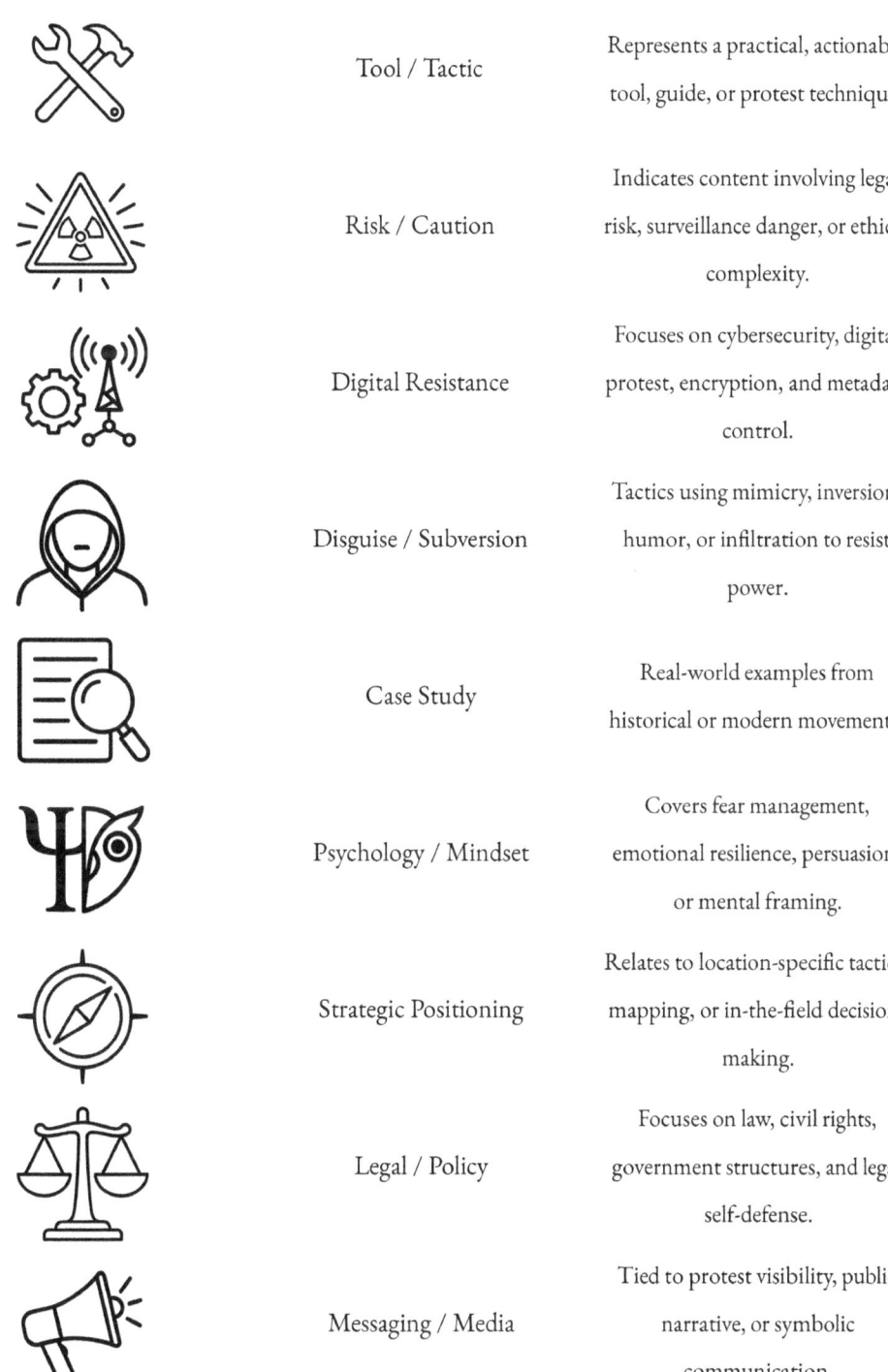

	Tool / Tactic	Represents a practical, actionable tool, guide, or protest technique.
	Risk / Caution	Indicates content involving legal risk, surveillance danger, or ethical complexity.
	Digital Resistance	Focuses on cybersecurity, digital protest, encryption, and metadata control.
	Disguise / Subversion	Tactics using mimicry, inversion, humor, or infiltration to resist power.
	Case Study	Real-world examples from historical or modern movements.
	Psychology / Mindset	Covers fear management, emotional resilience, persuasion, or mental framing.
	Strategic Positioning	Relates to location-specific tactics, mapping, or in-the-field decision-making.
	Legal / Policy	Focuses on law, civil rights, government structures, and legal self-defense.
	Messaging / Media	Tied to protest visibility, public narrative, or symbolic communication.

Quick Start Legend Cross-Reference

Tool / Tactic

- Chapters: 1, 7, 9, 10, 11, 12, 13, 14, 15, 16, 17, 18, 19, 20, 21
- Modules: A, B, C, D, E, F, G, H

Risk / Caution

- Chapters: 7, 10, 13, 14, 16, 17, 18
- Modules: B, E, H

Digital Resistance

- Chapters: 7, 9, 10, 13, 16, 17, 18
- Modules: A, B, C, D, E, F, H

Disguise / Subversion

- Chapters: 9, 10, 12, 20
- Modules: C, F

Case Study

- Chapters: 1, 7, 9, 13, 14, 16, 17
- Modules: A, C, E, G

Psychology / Mindset

- Chapters: 7, 9, 11, 12, 21
- Modules: —

Strategic Positioning

- Chapters: 7, 9, 11, 13, 14, 16, 21
- Modules: A, B, D, E, G, H

Legal / Policy

- Chapters: 1, 13, 14, 15, 16, 18
- Modules: B, H

Messaging / Media

- Chapters: 1, 7, 9, 20
- Modules: C, D, F

Part I

The Why: Foundations of Disobedience

"The first act of resistance is not protest; it is awareness."
— Unknown

Chapter One

The Spirit of Rebellion

Legal Notice (read first)

This chapter discusses principles of disobedience and resistance. The material is intended for educational and historical analysis only. It does not constitute legal advice, nor does it encourage unlawful conduct. Readers must consider the laws of their jurisdiction and act at their own risk. Neither author nor publisher assumes liability for misuse.

Field Note: Your Arrest Is Already Scheduled

You don't have to throw a brick to get put on a list anymore. Just show up. Hold a sign. Turn off your phone in a protest zone. Refuse a police order and speak to a journalist instead.

In 2020, over 10,000 people were arrested during Black Lives Matter protests in the U.S. alone. Some faced felony rioting charges for simply being there. Others were targeted later through phone metadata, facial recognition, or social media surveillance (ACLU, 2021; Zuboff, 2019).

If you think rebellion is safe, romantic, or rhetorical—stop reading.

If you're still reading, here's what you need to know:

Disobedience today means learning how to encrypt, mask, hide, and reappear.

It means recording cops while protecting others, setting up fallback communication plans, and knowing what to say when they cuff you.

It means having the right to remain silent—and knowing that won't always protect you.

Philosophy matters. But only if it's followed by action.
This book offers both.

Rebellion has long been the crucible in which transformative change is forged. From peasant uprisings to labor strikes, from suffrage marches to civil rights sit-ins, the act of disobedience has challenged the legitimacy of oppressive systems and reshaped society's moral compass (Graeber, 2013). Rebellion is not mere chaos, it is a rational, often moral response to institutional failure (Thoreau, 1849).

> "Throughout history, it was not obedience, but disobedience that brought about progress. Those who defied the rules of their time pushed humanity forward."
> — Unknown

The spirit of rebellion arises not from anarchy, but from agency. It asserts that authority, when unchecked, must be interrogated. As Howard Zinn wrote:

> "Protest beyond the law is not a departure from democracy; it is absolutely essential to it."
> — Howard Zinn, *Declarations of Independence* (1990)

Rebellion, then, becomes the responsibility of the governed when governance ceases to serve the people.

The Role of the Individual

Defiance often begins with one voice. Rosa Parks did not incite a riot, she quietly refused to comply. Yet her singular action ignited a movement (Theoharis, 2013). Mohamed Bouazizi's self-immolation in Tunisia became a catalyst for the Arab Spring, proving that rebellion can emerge from despair just as much as from conviction (Ryan, 2011). Thoreau, decades earlier, practiced tax resistance as a rejection of war and slavery.

What links these moments is individual agency, an internal decision that the cost of silence outweighs the consequences of action. This transformation of personal conviction into public resistance is the seed from which movements grow.

The following tactics were not improvisations: they were strategic, deliberate, and continue to inform modern resistance. Each tool listed here is rooted in historical action but points toward real-world tactics available now.

- **Tax Resistance**
  Henry David Thoreau refused to fund the state. His stance laid the groundwork for modern forms of fiscal withdrawal, boycott, and coordinated legal obstruction.
  Learn more: https://nwtrcc.org (National War Tax Resistance Coordinating Committee)

See also Chapter 11: Tactical Ethics.

- **Coordinated Disruption**
  Rosa Parks did not act in isolation. The Montgomery Bus Boycott depended on transportation alternatives, community messaging, and disciplined action networks.
  Learn more: https://meshpoint.me
  See also Chapter 10: Networking and Fellow Mavericks and Disruption Module A: Building a Mesh Network.

- **Flash Mobilization**
  Mohamed Bouazizi's self-immolation lit a fire, but peer-to-peer texting, SMS rally chains, and social media flash coordination enabled the wildfire of dissent.
  Learn more: https://signal.org, https://briarproject.org
  See also Disruption Module D: AR Activism and Disruption Module E: Anonymous Broadcast Messaging in Blackouts.

- **Court Disruption and Jail Support**
  Angela Davis disrupted carceral systems through legal defense coordination, court disruption, and jail support organizing.
  Learn more: https://www.nlg.org/know-your-rights/
  See also Chapter 14: Legal Considerations and Risks.

- **Anonymous Symbolic Action**
  The Boston Tea Party was masked, timed, and symbolic. Its legacy continues in guerrilla projection, anonymous messaging drops, and light vandalism.
  Learn more: https://beautifultrouble.org/toolbox/tool/light-projection/
  See also Disruption Module C: Guerrilla Projection & Light Tactics.

- **Organizing Structures**
  Zinn and Graeber remind us that rebellion is not improvisation, it's logistical. From labor strikes to mutual aid pods, structure sustains resistance.
  Learn more: https://mutualaiddisasterrelief.org/resources/
  See also Part III: The How.

Rejecting Norms as Constructive Praxis

Norms are the invisible scaffolding of society, guidelines of behavior, speech, and obedience (Cialdini, 2007). But norms are not immutable. They reflect the dominant narrative, and when that narrative favors power over justice, rebellion becomes an ethical act.

> "I am no longer accepting the things I cannot change. I am changing the things I cannot accept."
> — Angela Davis

To reject norms is not to destroy society, but to remake it.

Popular culture romanticizes rebellion but rarely examines its cost. True rebellion is neither safe nor glamorous. It risks arrest, surveillance, and exile. The Boston Tea Party, now enshrined in American mythos, was considered vandalism and insurrection in its time (Raphael, 2001). The same is true for countless liberation movements around the globe, later sanitized in hindsight.

The rebel, therefore, is not an outcast but a historian in motion, rewriting the record not with ink, but with interruption.

Toward Purposeful Defiance

In a surveillance society where dissent is algorithmically flagged and criminalized by design, rebellion must be more intentional (Zuboff, 2019). It is no longer enough to simply say "no." Rebellion today demands strategic planning, coalition building, and digital literacy. It is both a posture and a praxis: a stance and a strategy.

Henry David Thoreau, writing in 1849, understood that submission to unjust systems corrodes the soul of democracy. His essay *Civil Disobedience* remains a foundation of modern resistance philosophy:

> "All men recognize the right of revolution; that is, the right to refuse allegiance to and to resist the government when its tyranny or its inefficiency are great and unendurable."
> — Henry David Thoreau, *Civil Disobedience* (1849)

Thoreau's legacy echoes in every act of purposeful defiance, reminding us that to obey unjust authority is to betray one's conscience.
This book is built for that spirit, not to glorify rebellion, but to equip it.

End Note: *Want to communicate rebellion safely? See Disruption Module A (Building a Mesh Network), Disruption Module D (AR Activism), and Disruption Module E (Anonymous Broadcast Messaging in Blackouts) for secure communication strategies used in modern uprisings. See Chapter 10 for movement-building tactics and Chapter 13 for survival under legal duress.*

Selected References

American Civil Liberties Union (ACLU). (2021). *Free speech under attack: Protesters at risk.* Retrieved from https://www.aclu.org/news/free-speech/free-speech-under-attack-protesters-at-risk

Beautiful Trouble. (n.d.). *Light projection.* Retrieved from https://beautifultrouble.org/toolbox/tool/light-projection/

Briar Project. (n.d.). *Briar: Secure messaging, anywhere.* Retrieved from https://briarproject.org

Cialdini, R. B. (2007). *Influence: The Psychology of Persuasion* (Rev. ed.). Harper Business.

Davis, A. (n.d.). Quote attributed; authorship widely accepted though precise source unclear.

Graeber, D. (2013). *The Democracy Project: A History, a Crisis, a Movement.* Spiegel & Grau.

MeshPoint.me. (n.d.). *Mesh networks for crisis response and community organization.* Retrieved from https://meshpoint.me

Mutual Aid Disaster Relief. (n.d.). *Resources.* Retrieved from https://mutualaiddisasterrelief.org/resources/

National Lawyers Guild (NLG). (n.d.). *Know Your Rights.* Retrieved from https://www.nlg.org/know-your-rights/

National War Tax Resistance Coordinating Committee (NWTRCC). (n.d.). *National War Tax Resistance.* Retrieved from https://nwtrcc.org

Raphael, R. (2001). *Founding Myths: Stories That Hide Our Patriotic Past.* New Press.

Ryan, Y. (2011, January 20). Tunisia's bitter cyberwar. *Al Jazeera*. Retrieved from https://www.aljazeera.com/

Signal Foundation. (n.d.). *Signal – Private Messenger*. Retrieved from https://signal.org

Theoharis, J. (2013). *The Rebellious Life of Mrs. Rosa Parks*. Beacon Press.

Thoreau, H. D. (1849). *Civil Disobedience*. Various editions.

Zinn, H. (1990). *Declarations of Independence: Cross-Examining American Ideology*. Harper Perennial.

Zuboff, S. (2019). *The Age of Surveillance Capitalism*. Public Affairs.

Chapter Two

Historical Mavericks

Legal Notice (read first)

This chapter examines historical figures such as Emma Goldman, Mahatma Gandhi, and Malcolm X, and the tactics they employed in their struggles. The material is presented for educational and historical purposes only. References to strategies used by these figures are not instructions for action and may be unlawful if applied today. Readers are responsible for understanding and complying with the laws of their jurisdiction. Neither the author nor publisher accepts liability for misuse of the information herein.

Field Note: They Will Call You Dangerous

The names in this chapter are carved into monuments and textbooks, but in their time, they were branded subversives, traitors, or terrorists.

Emma Goldman was jailed and deported. Gandhi was beaten and vilified. Malcolm X was surveilled and assassinated. They didn't resist for aesthetics. They resisted because injustice thrives when people stay quiet.

Want to carry their legacy? Then carry their risk, and their tools.

Mavericks and the Mechanisms of Rebellion

Every era is shaped by those unwilling to wait. Mavericks, whether labeled agitators or prophets, disrupted the status quo through coordinated defiance. Their legacies weren't just moral; they were *mechanical*. Each used specific tactics to weaponize ideology into action. The same applies today.

> "The reasonable man adapts himself to the world: the unreasonable one persists in trying to adapt the world to himself. Therefore all progress depends on the unreasonable man."
> —George Bernard Shaw, *Man and Superman* (1903)

These weren't just rebels. They were strategists. Architects. Organizers.

Emma Goldman: Educator of Dissent

Once called *the most dangerous woman in America*, Goldman challenged the structures of capitalism, carceral systems, and patriarchal control—but always through literacy, oratory, and print.

- **Tactics Used**:
    - Independent printing presses and radical publications (see Disruption Module F: Zine Warfare)
    - Traveling lecture circuits under surveillance (see Chapter 7: Critical Thinking and Skepticism)
    - Civil disobedience tied to women's health access and labor justice (see Chapter 4: The Ethics of Radical Action."

> "The most violent element in society is ignorance."
> —Emma Goldman, *Living My Life* (1931)

Her refusal to dilute her beliefs cost her citizenship—but empowered generations of radical educators.

Mahatma Gandhi: Architect of Coordinated Refusal

Gandhi's Satyagraha ("truth-force") campaign was not passive. It was a full-spectrum resistance strategy—part spiritual philosophy, part insurgent logistics.

- **Tactics Used**:
    - Consumer strikes and targeted boycotts (see Chapter 8: Embracing Risk and Uncertainty)
    - Media-synchronized protest spectacles like the Salt March (see Chapter 5: The Myth of the "Good Protest")
    - Decentralized organizing across rural communities (see Chapter 10: Networking and Fellow Mavericks)

> "You may never know what results come of your actions. But if you do nothing, there will be no result."
> —Mahatma Gandhi, *The Story of My Experiments with Truth* (1927)

His techniques echo today in climate marches, indigenous sovereignty actions, and economic disruptions.

Malcolm X: Precision in Public Disruption

Malcolm X's rhetorical force and grassroots organizing weren't accidents. He studied the press, leveraged confrontation, and built a message that could not be co-opted.

- **Tactics Used**:
  - Strategic use of media to provoke controlled outrage (see Chapter 5)
  - Religious and cultural community organizing as resistance platforms (see Chapter 9: Breaking Boundaries)
  - Surveillance countermeasures and disciplined self-defense training (see Disruption Module G: Drone-Based Messaging and Disruption Module H: Bonus Tools for detection counter-strategies)

"If you're not ready to die for it, put the word 'freedom' out of your vocabulary."
—Malcolm X, *The Autobiography of Malcolm X* (1965)

His influence remains not just in speeches, but in mutual aid pods, know-your-rights training, and community-led justice efforts.

Lessons for the Modern Resistor

These figures did not agree on ideology. They didn't survive to see their revolutions fulfilled. But each of them *moved the line*...and taught others how to do the same.

Today's dissenters build on their legacy, often unconsciously. But rebellion is not inherited. It is *reconstructed*, piece by piece, tool by tool.

This book is your blueprint.

Even historical movements built on moral clarity required tactical sharpness. The following tools, drawn from the legacies of prominent dissenters, remain applicable for those navigating modern disobedience.

- **Consequence Mapping**
  Before committing to action, outline personal and societal consequences. This helps prevent reactive missteps and allows realignment when conditions shift. Malcolm X's life illustrates how adaptable framing can make a message endure. (Marable, 2011)

Learn more: https://beautifultrouble.org/toolbox/tool/consequence-scanning/
This link leads to a tactical explanation of how to forecast consequences of activist actions, framed accessibly.

- **Micro-Ritual Resistance**

    Embed subversive meaning into daily routines. Gandhi's spinning practice transformed a symbol into a habit of defiance. Modern equivalents might include clothing choices, digital signatures, or routine refusals. (Dalton, 2012)

    Learn more: https://www.opendemocracy.net/en/microresistance-political-rituals-power/
    This article explains how habitual micro-resistance can shape public discourse.

- **Symbol Saturation**

    Repetition of gestures, colors, or messages strengthens movement coherence. Think of the clenched fist, color-coded protests, or recurring slogans that make resistance unmistakable, even when silent.

    Learn more: https://beautifultrouble.org/toolbox/tool/meme-warfare/
    This expands the concept to meme warfare and persistent symbolic visuals in protest.

- **Legacy Documentation**

    Maintain a record of personal acts, whether public-facing or private. These reflections can become the future's tactical guides, just as past letters, manifestos, and memoirs shaped current strategy.

    Learn more: https://crimethinc.com/zines
    CrimethInc's underground zine archive reflects legacy documentation practices in modern activism.

End Note: *Want to reproduce Emma Goldman's underground publishing tactics? See Disruption Module F: Zine Warfare. Want to coordinate resistance actions across space using secure comms? See Disruption Module A: Mesh Networking, Disruption Module E: Anonymous Broadcast Messaging, and Disruption Module G: Drone-Based Messaging. To carry out Gandhi's decentralized organizing model, read Chapter 10. To understand Malcolm's information disruption strategy, revisit Chapter 5 and Disruption Module H: Bonus Tools.*

Selected References

Beautiful Trouble. (n.d.). *Consequence Scanning*. Retrieved from https://beautifultrouble.org/toolbox/tool/consequence-scanning/

Beautiful Trouble. (n.d.). *Meme Warfare*. Retrieved from https://beautifultrouble.org/toolbox/tool/meme-warfare/

CrimethInc. (n.d.). *Zines Archive*. Retrieved from https://crimethinc.com/zines

Dalton, D. (2012). *Mahatma Gandhi: Nonviolent Power in Action*. Columbia University Press.

Gandhi, M. (1958). *The Story of My Experiments with Truth*. Navajivan Trust.

Goldman, E. (1931). *Living My Life*. Alfred A. Knopf.

Haley, A. (1965). *The Autobiography of Malcolm X*. Grove Press.

Joseph, P. E. (2020). *The Sword and the Shield: The Revolutionary Lives of Malcolm X and Martin Luther King Jr.*. Basic Books.

Marable, M. (2011). *Malcolm X: A Life of Reinvention*. Penguin Books.

openDemocracy. (n.d.). *Microresistance: How small acts of political ritual shift power*. Retrieved from https://www.opendemocracy.net/en/microresistance-political-rituals-power/

Shaw, G. B. (1903). *Man and Superman*. Archibald Constable & Co.

Zinn, H. (1990). *Declarations of Independence: Cross-Examining American Ideology*. Harper Perennial.

Chapter Three

The Psychology of Resistance

Legal Notice (read first)

This chapter explores psychological dynamics of fear, resistance, and moral courage. It includes references to protest scenarios and role-play exercises. These are presented as educational illustrations and should not be construed as legal or clinical advice. Readers assume full responsibility for their actions and decisions. Neither the author nor publisher bears liability for application of the material.

Field Note: The Real War Is Psychological

You can jail a body. You can censor a post. But the most effective tool of authoritarian control is psychological: fear, helplessness, the creeping voice that says, *"Why bother?"*

Before they silence you, they convince you to silence yourself.

They teach you to mistrust your outrage, dismiss your instincts, and wait for permission. They tell you the time isn't right, the method is flawed, or the problem isn't yours.

That's the battlefield.

Your job isn't just to resist the system. It's to resist the internalized obedience it planted in your mind.

If your rage feels irrational, it isn't. If your fear feels overwhelming, it's expected.
But neither has to be permanent. Rebellion begins the moment fear becomes fuel.

You're not broken. You're being broken. Stop cooperating with the process.

Resistance is rarely born from comfort; it is the product of psychological tension, of unbearable dissonance between lived reality and moral conviction. While laws and institutions frame the battlefield, the true war for justice begins in the mind.

> "The most common way people give up their power is by thinking they don't have any."
> — Alice Walker (source uncertain)

Fear is the first weapon of authoritarian control. It paralyzes individuals, isolates dissenters, and manufactures compliance (Seligman, 1972). But fear can also clarify. It forces people to confront the cost of inaction, the danger of silence. Movements arise not when fear is eliminated, but when it is reframed, as fuel rather than a cage.

The Anatomy of Resistance

What makes a person defy orders, challenge power, or step into danger when others stay silent? Psychologists call it *moral courage:* the willingness to act ethically despite risk (Greitemeyer et al., 2006). Studies of whistleblowers, protest leaders, and revolutionaries reveal common traits: empathy, autonomy, and a strong sense of injustice. These are not abnormal qualities, but suppressed ones.

> "When we are no longer able to change a situation, we are challenged to change ourselves."
> — Viktor E. Frankl, *Man's Search for Meaning* (1946)

Collective resistance often begins with a single defector. The first marcher, the first refusal, the first breach in the wall. That act becomes a psychological permission slip for others. Social scientists refer to this as the threshold model of collective behavior (Granovetter, 1978); movements gain momentum as individuals see others take action. Resistance is contagious.

Fear, Control, and the Crowd

Authoritarian regimes thrive not only on fear, but on learned helplessness—a psychological condition in which people believe their actions have no effect (Seligman, 1972). Over time, this perceived powerlessness becomes cultural. What breaks the spell is often a moment of moral clarity: a murder caught on camera, a neighbor wrongfully detained, a ballot box removed in broad daylight.

These flashpoints galvanize collective identity. Crowds do not move randomly; they respond to patterns, stories, and symbols. As Gustave Le Bon observed in *The Crowd: A Study of the Popular Mind*, individuals in groups adopt a shared identity; one capable of courage they may not possess alone (Le Bon, 1895).

> "It is not rebellion itself which is noble, but the demands it makes on us."
> — Albert Camus, *The Rebel* (1951)

This is the psychology of the tipping point: when enough people recognize their shared pain and convert it into shared purpose.

Rewiring Resistance

Understanding the psychological mechanics of resistance allows activists to build movements that are emotionally resonant and neurologically persuasive. Protest music, slogans, memes, and rituals aren't decorative; they are anchoring mechanisms that stabilize identity in volatile situations (Tajfel & Turner, 1979). They calm the fearful, empower the hesitant, and unify the isolated.

Digital repression, via surveillance, de-platforming, and censorship, is not only technical but psychological warfare (Zuboff, 2019). The antidote is emotional literacy: recognizing that fear is expected, trauma is real, and hope is a learned behavior. Sustainable resistance requires care, reflection, and solidarity.

In the end, rebellion is not just a political act. It is a psychological reclamation of agency.

> "Revolution begins in the mind before it ever takes to the streets."
> — Unknown

Resistance begins in the mind. But knowledge alone isn't enough to counteract years of internalized compliance, fear conditioning, and crowd-driven reflex. Below are practical techniques designed to help dissenters break the psychological bonds described in this chapter: training tools, not just insights.

- **Narrative Reversal Log**
  Keep a personal log of moments when you felt pressured to comply; socially, professionally, politically. For each, write down what you wish you had said or done. This rewires behavioral scripts and builds active recall of disobedient alternatives.
  Learn more: https://www.nonviolent-conflict.org/resource/strategic-nonviolent-conflict/

- **Stress Inoculation Roleplay**
  Practice scenarios like police stops, employer threats, or bystander shaming in low-stakes environments. Role rehearsals lower your panic threshold and give your nervous system a rehearsal for the real thing (Meichenbaum, 1977).
  Learn more: https://www.apa.org/pubs/journals/releases/ccp-ccp0000239.pdf

- **Symbolic Anchoring**
  Choose a physical or verbal ritual to reassert agency: a bracelet, a phrase, a gesture. Use it before entering contested space or during confrontation. These anchors help reinforce identity under pressure.
  Learn more: https://positivepsychology.com/anchoring-nlp/

- **Controlled Digital Exposure**
  In short, timed bursts, intentionally expose yourself to fear-inducing media (e.g., bodycam footage, surveillance articles). Narrate your internal reactions aloud. This builds tolerance and trains response over reactivity (Wolpe, 1958).
  Learn more: https://www.ncbi.nlm.nih.gov/pmc/articles/PMC5799053/

- **Breach Story Bank**
  Collect stories of people who acted first: whistleblowers, lone sign-carriers, recorders of injustice. Review these stories regularly. Social proof from others lowers your brain's perception of risk (Cialdini, 2006).
  Learn more: https://www.whistleblowers.org

- **Tactical Exit Planning**
  Prepare psychological fallback plans. Know when you'll exit a protest, log off, or shut down engagement. Predetermined escape points reduce dread and increase clarity during stress.
  Learn more: https://mentalhealthfirstaid.org/external/2022/12/developing-a-self-care-plan/

End Note: *For strategies on psychological resilience in digital environments, see Chapter 12 on burnout avoidance and Disruption Module E on digital subversion through media.*

Selected References

Camus, A. (1951). *The Rebel*. Alfred A. Knopf.

Cialdini, R. B. (2006). *Influence: The psychology of persuasion*. Harper Business.

Frankl, V. E. (1946). *Man's Search for Meaning*. Beacon Press.

Granovetter, M. (1978). Threshold models of collective behavior. *American Journal of Sociology*, 83(6), 1420–1443.

Greitemeyer, T., Fischer, P., Kastenmüller, A., & Frey, D. (2006). Civil courage and helping behavior. *Journal of Applied Social Psychology*, 36(1), 198–209.

Le Bon, G. (1895). *The Crowd: A Study of the Popular Mind*. Viking Press.

Meichenbaum, D. (1977). *Cognitive-behavior modification: An integrative approach*. Springer.

Seligman, M. E. P. (1972). Learned helplessness. *Annual Review of Medicine*, 23, 407–412.

Tajfel, H., & Turner, J. C. (1979). An integrative theory of intergroup conflict. In W. G. Austin & S. Worchel (Eds.), *The Social Psychology of Intergroup Relations* (pp. 33–47). Brooks/Cole.

Walker, A. (n.d.). Quote attributed; source unverified.

Wolpe, J. (1958). *Psychotherapy by reciprocal inhibition*. Stanford University Press.

Zuboff, S. (2019). *The Age of Surveillance Capitalism*. Public Affairs.

Chapter Four

The Ethics of Radical Action

Legal Notice (read first)

This chapter examines ethical debates around escalation, sabotage, and radical action. These examples are historical and theoretical in nature, not instructions for conduct. Certain tactics discussed may be unlawful under local, state, or federal law. The material is provided solely for educational purposes. Neither the author nor publisher assumes responsibility for misuse.

Field Note: The Ethics of Broken Windows

Ask yourself this: If the government poisons your water, cages your neighbor, sterilizes your sister, or leaves your community to drown, how long must you obey its rules?

Radical action isn't about chaos. It's about escalation *after* exhaustion. It begins when every sanctioned path to change has been blocked, co-opted, or criminalized.

You don't have to like broken windows or street blockades. But you do have to ask:
What conditions made them feel necessary? And who benefits when the conversation stays focused on "property damage" instead of human harm?

> *When the law protects injustice, disruption becomes a form of truth-telling.*

This book won't tell you what line to cross. But it will help you understand where the lines came from, and who they were built to contain.

Radical action exists at the tension point between morality and necessity. While peaceful protest is often idealized, history offers countless instances where marginalized groups turned to sabotage, disruption, or even violence—not out of malice, but desperation. The question is not whether these actions occurred, but whether they were justified.

> "Those who make peaceful revolution impossible will make violent revolution inevitable."
> — John F. Kennedy, *Address on the First Anniversary of the Alliance for Progress* (1962)

Every movement faces a moral crossroads. When institutions suppress speech, rig elections, or enforce inequality through violence, the oppressed are left with constrained options. Should they maintain nonviolent discipline in the face of brutality? Or escalate to confront injustice on its own terms?

The Moral Threshold

Philosopher Judith Butler argues that all ethical action is situated: the morality of resistance cannot be divorced from the structures it challenges. In oppressive contexts, legality and morality often diverge. Slavery was once legal. Apartheid was once constitutional. Resistance, in these cases, required violating the law to uphold a higher ethical principle.

Similarly, Frantz Fanon, in The Wretched of the Earth (1961), argued that colonial violence begets resistance violence, not as a choice, but as an inevitable mirror. He did not glorify violence, but he recognized it as a symptom of systemic dehumanization.

> "When we revolt it's not for a particular culture. We revolt simply because, for many reasons, we can no longer breathe."
> — Frantz Fanon, *The Wretched of the Earth* (1961)

To understand radical action is not to condone all of it, but to examine the context in which moderation fails.

Strategic Escalation vs. Moral Absolutism

Some thinkers, like Gene Sharp, advocate absolute nonviolence as both ethical and strategic, citing long-term legitimacy and reduced backlash. Others, like Malcolm X or the Weather Underground, believed that in certain conditions, radical action was not only justified but required.

Modern activists navigate this terrain cautiously. Pipeline sabotage, digital hacks, and direct action campaigns all walk the line between civil disobedience and criminality. What defines them is not just their methods, but their intent, transparency, and proportionality.

> "Justice too long delayed is justice denied."
> — Martin Luther King Jr., *Letter from Birmingham Jail* (1963)

The line between radical and reckless often lies in accountability. Are actions aimed at systems or at innocents? Are they a last resort or a first impulse?

When the System Is the Violence

Governments often frame dissent as extremism to discredit movements. But as legal scholar Michelle Alexander points out, the real extremism may lie in mass incarceration, economic disenfranchisement, or militarized policing. If the system itself perpetuates violence, can radical resistance be framed as self-defense?

This ethical inversion is uncomfortable, yet necessary. True ethical inquiry asks not only "what action is taken," but "what conditions made this action necessary?"

Disruption in the Modern Era

In recent years, the Black Lives Matter movement has employed civil disruption to great effect. From freeway shutdowns in major U.S. cities to mass die-ins and coordinated economic boycotts, BLM has forced the public and media to confront uncomfortable truths about racial violence. Freeway blockades, in particular, sparked fierce debate: critics called them reckless and dangerous, while supporters defended them as nonviolent but disruptive acts aimed at a system that otherwise ignores quiet pleas.

These shutdowns follow a historical logic of inconvenience as resistance: when power refuses to listen, the streets become a megaphone.

Toward an Ethics of Disruption

Radical action, when rooted in justice and guided by restraint, can function as a moral imperative. It reminds society that comfort is not a universal experience, and that progress often requires unsettling the status quo.

Today's activists must assess not just the morality of their cause, but the impact of their methods. Ethics does not require passivity. It demands discernment.

Radical action isn't reckless, it's often strategic. While this chapter explores the ethical dilemmas of escalation, many resistance efforts require pragmatic preparation, not just moral resolve. The following tools are designed to support movements operating near or beyond the boundary of sanctioned protest:

- **Escalation Decision Frameworks**
  Use structured ethical decision trees (e.g., the "Spectrum of Allies" or NVDA readiness scales) to evaluate timing, proportionality, and potential backlash before undertaking high-risk actions (see Chapter 11).
  Learn more: Michael Albert's Thought Dreams and tools at Beautiful Trouble.

https://www.beautifultrouble.org/toolbox/tool/escalation-spectrum

- **Signal Encryption Tools**
  Apps like Signal, Briar, and Session offer encrypted communication for planning direct actions while minimizing digital exposure (EFF, 2023).
  How-to guides available from the Electronic Frontier Foundation:
  https://ssd.eff.org/en/module/introduction-encryption

- **Emergency Protocol Templates**
  Pre-written arrest plans, jail support trees, and legal observation assignments ensure accountability and rapid response if escalated action results in detention (NLG, 2021).
  Template sources: National Lawyers Guild and local support collectives.
  https://www.nlg.org/legalobservers/

- **Decentralized Disruption Models**
  Adopt tactics like "swarm protests," flash convergence, or digital sabotage that rely on distributed coordination with minimal central leadership (Feldman, 2020).
  Recommended read: Zeynep Tufekci's Twitter and Tear Gas.
  https://yalebooks.yale.edu/book/9780300234176/twitter-and-tear-gas/

- **Ethical Risk Assessment Matrices**
  Some affinity groups use customized matrices to assess actions along axes like visibility, potential harm, moral justification, and symbolic value.
  Framework examples from CrimethInc and decentralized organizing zines.
  https://crimethinc.com

- **Deplatforming & Tactical Sabotage**
  In rare cases, cyber-activist groups disrupt oppressive systems through temporary service takedowns or targeted leaks. These actions require high ethical scrutiny and cybersecurity training (Ackerman & Sandoval-Ballesteros, 2017).
  More context: Hacking//Hustling network and the Hacktivist's Field Manual (see Disruption Module E and H).
  https://hackinghustling.org

These are not endorsements, they are options, developed through necessity, employed with discernment. Disruption may begin with a broken window, but it requires a clear vision of what justice should replace it.

End Note: *For frameworks on decision-making in high-risk protest scenarios, see Chapter 11 on tactical ethics and Disruption Module E on narrative framing through DIY media.*

Selected References

Ackerman, J., & Sandoval-Ballesteros, I. (2017). *Cyberactivism and the End of Information Control.* Journal of Democracy, 28(2), 71–85.

Alexander, M. (2010). *The New Jim Crow: Mass Incarceration in the Age of Colorblindness.* The New Press.

Butler, J. (2005). *Giving an Account of Oneself.* Fordham University Press.

Electronic Frontier Foundation (EFF). (2023). *Surveillance Self-Defense Guide.* https://ssd.eff.org

Fanon, F. (1961). *The Wretched of the Earth.* Grove Press.

Feldman, B. (2020). The Swarm Protest Model: Leaderless Resistance in the Digital Age. Mobilization: An International Quarterly, 25(3), 291–310.

Kennedy, J. F. (1962). *Address on the First Anniversary of the Alliance for Progress.*

King, M. L. Jr. (1963). *Letter from Birmingham Jail.* Various editions.

National Lawyers Guild (NLG). (2021). *Know Your Rights and Legal Observer Manual.* https://www.nlg.org/know-your-rights/

Rickford, R. (2016). *Black Lives Matter: Toward a Modern Practice of Mass Struggle.* New Labor Forum, 25(1), 34–42.

Sharp, G. (1973). *The Politics of Nonviolent Action.* Porter Sargent Publishers.

Chapter Five

The Myth of the "Good Protest"

Legal Notice (read first)

This chapter analyzes media framing of protest movements and references disruptive tactics used in history. The material is educational and interpretive, not operational guidance. Engaging in protest may lead to legal consequences. Readers are responsible for compliance with applicable law. The author and publisher disclaim liability for any misuse.

Field Note: Whose Protest Gets Remembered?

You don't get to control how your protest is seen. But you *can* decide what story you're forcing the world to reckon with.

Peaceful protests get ignored. Angry ones get vilified. And no matter what, someone will call you dangerous—because you are. Not to people, but to power.

> *The truth won't trend unless you hack the frame.*

If you wear a suit, you're dismissed as performative. If you wear a mask, you're called a terrorist. If you kneel, they say you hate your country. And if you burn something? They forget what you were even angry about.

There is no "good protest" under a bad regime. Only visibility... or silence.

Legitimacy is not earned through moral clarity, it is granted or denied by those who control the narrative. In every era, protest movements have been divided into the "reasonable" and the "radical," with legitimacy hinging less on ethics than on optics. What makes a protest acceptable to the public is rarely the justice of its cause, but the frame through which it is delivered.

As political scientist Robert Entman explained, framing is the act of selecting "some aspects of a perceived reality and making them more salient in a communicating text" (Entman, 1993). This subtle shaping determines whether protesters are seen as defenders of democracy, or as dangerous agitators.

> "The revolution will not be televised."
> — Gil Scott-Heron, *Small Talk at 125th and Lenox* (1970)

The Myth of the Respectable Dissenter

Movements are judged not by their goals, but by their methods. The civil rights movement is now romanticized, but at the time, Martin Luther King Jr. was widely condemned. According to a 1966 Gallup poll, 63% of Americans held a negative view of him during his final years. Sit-ins were called disruptive. Marches were seen as inciting unrest. The state sanctioned violence not by disproving the cause, but by portraying the movement as unruly and dangerous.

Decades later, Colin Kaepernick would kneel silently during the national anthem, only to be vilified as anti-American. Despite his peaceful posture, political media reframed his action as a threat to patriotism, deliberately ignoring the original protest against police brutality. This is the double bind of dissent: to be heard, one must disrupt, but disruption becomes the excuse to dismiss the message entirely.

Framing, Fear, and Manufactured Consent

The myth of the "good protester" is not accidental, it's manufactured. Media gatekeepers and political elites shape public discourse using tools of agenda-setting and priming (McCombs & Shaw, 1972), deciding what gets covered, how often, and in what tone. Peaceful protests are ignored. Riots are broadcast in loops. The exception becomes the narrative.

In the wake of George Floyd's murder, global uprisings filled the streets. In some cities, activists shut down major freeways to demand attention. These were deliberate, nonviolent acts of disruption. Yet news outlets focused on looting at the margins, casting the entire movement in a criminal light. The moral urgency was lost in the obsession with property damage.

The same dynamic unfolded in Ferguson, Standing Rock, and beyond. Protesters were treated not as citizens exercising rights, but as threats to stability. "Order" became the value prioritized, not justice, not truth.

> "There may be times when we are powerless to prevent injustice, but there must never be a time when we fail to protest."
> — Elie Wiesel, *Nobel Lecture* (1986)

The State as Narrator: COINTELPRO and Manufactured Illegitimacy

Long before algorithmic manipulation and bot armies, the U.S. government weaponized perception through covert operations aimed at delegitimizing protest. Chief among these was COINTELPRO (Counter Intelligence Program), a secret FBI initiative from 1956 to 1971 that targeted civil rights groups, antiwar activists, Indigenous sovereignty movements, and Black liberation organizations, especially the Black Panther Party and Dr. Martin Luther King Jr.

The goal was not surveillance alone, but disruption. Internal FBI memos outlined strategies to "neutralize" leaders by sowing division, planting false media narratives, spreading disinformation, and provoking violence. The program deliberately blurred dissent with criminality, portraying legitimate protest as extremism in order to fracture public support.

According to the 1976 Church Committee Report:

> "Many of the techniques used would be intolerable in a democratic society even if all the targets had been involved in violent activity, but COINTELPRO went far beyond that. The Bureau conducted a sophisticated vigilante operation aimed squarely at preventing the exercise of First Amendment rights."
> — *Final Report of the Select Committee to Study Governmental Operations with Respect to Intelligence Activities, Book II* (1976)

Though officially dismantled, COINTELPRO's legacy echoes in modern surveillance, infiltration of protest spaces, and strategic framing of dissent as disorder. Understanding this history is crucial: framing is not always passive or organic, it is sometimes an intentional act of state repression.

Bots, Social Media, and Weaponized Perception

In the digital age, perception warfare is no longer the exclusive domain of traditional media. Social platforms, often viewed as democratizing tools, are increasingly polluted by political bots, coordinated disinformation, and algorithmic bias.

As reported by NBC's The Rachel Maddow Show (2025), bot networks deployed by unknown actors have begun to contradict themselves within minutes, amplifying posts that simultaneously support and oppose issues like the Epstein investigation. These aren't accidents; they are precision-engineered to sow confusion, dilute outrage, and fracture solidarity.

Scholars such as Woolley and Howard (2016) have detailed how computational propaganda uses automation to distort political discourse. During the 2016 and 2020 U.S. elections, botnets promoted disinformation designed to discredit movements like Black Lives Matter while amplifying messages of "law and order." The target isn't the truth, it's perception itself.

The Global Frame

Framing is not constrained by borders. During the 2019–2020 Hong Kong protests, demonstrators were labeled "rioters" in Chinese state media while Western outlets portrayed them as heroes of democracy. In Palestine, protesters are often framed through a lens of terrorism, whereas in Ukraine, similar acts of resistance are framed as valor. Who is seen as legitimate depends not on action, but on alignment with global interests.

Legitimacy is a currency minted by power.

Refusing the Frame

Movements cannot always control their image, but they can disrupt the framing. Visual storytelling, direct messaging, decentralized leadership, and strategic disruption are tools that force the narrative to shift. The Montgomery bus boycott didn't just change laws, it changed the story Americans told themselves about justice.

To resist effectively, modern protestors must understand that every sign, chant, and disruption will be reinterpreted. The question is not whether the protest is right, but how it will be remembered.

> "The master's tools will never dismantle the master's house."
> — Audre Lorde, *Sister Outsider* (1984)

In an era where truth is fragmented and dissent is branded as disloyalty, protest must be not only righteous, but media-literate.

The following tools help activists recognize, resist, and reframe dominant narratives. These are not just media literacy tools—they are weapons for reclaiming reality.

Framing Forensics

Understanding the structure of a news story, press release, or social media campaign is critical to spotting hidden agendas. Tools like *Media Bias Chart* or *NewsGuard* help map a source's ideological leanings and financial incentives. But activists should go further: analyze what's left *unsaid*, who is quoted, and what terms are repeated. Framing forensics empowers dissenters to identify the emotional priming, scapegoating, or dog whistles in political discourse. This skill can be taught using real examples from local media.
Learn more: https://mediabiasfactcheck.com, https://www.newsguardtech.com
See Disruption Module F: Zine Warfare.

Counter-Narrative Seeding

Authoritarian or corporate entities often control the "first story," and first stories stick. Seeding counter-narratives—short, credible, emotionally resonant stories—can challenge this dominance. Visual storytelling (memes, posters, reels) works well, but even a thread or quote retweet with a reframed caption can shift perception. Tools like Canva and CapCut make it easy to produce content.

Learn more: https://knowyourmeme.com, https://canva.com, https://capcut.com

See also Disruption Module C: Guerrilla Projection & Light Tactics.

Digital Disinfo Detection

Tools like *Bot Sentinel*, *Hoaxy*, or *CrowdTangle* help identify coordinated influence campaigns. These tools track suspicious accounts, retweet chains, or repeated links from disinformation sources. They help uncover astroturfing (fake grassroots), sockpuppets, or botnets. These patterns often precede anti-protest crackdowns or policy pushes.

Learn more: https://botsentinel.com, https://hoaxy.osome.iu.edu, https://www.crowdtangle.com

Amplification Clusters

When one voice is silenced, others can echo. Form amplification pods (also known as "retweet circles" or "mutual boost crews")—small groups who commit to resharing and defending messages from one another. Tools like Signal groups or Matrix rooms can coordinate real-time push strategies. These clusters amplify authentic voices and reduce the spread of bad actors.

Learn more: https://matrix.org, https://signal.org

See also Chapter 10: Networking and Fellow Mavericks.

Screenshot Layering for Truth Anchoring

In the face of deleted posts or retracted statements, screenshots are armor. But screenshot *layering*—juxtaposing a quote, image, and source across a single panel—adds permanence and context. These composites freeze narratives before they're "cleaned up." Apps like InShot or Preview let users arrange and timestamp layers. Use it to expose contradictions, capture public sentiment, or protect disappearing stories.

Learn more: https://inshot.com, https://thepreviewapp.com

See also Disruption Module D: AR Activism.

End Note: *For techniques on decentralized messaging and counter-framing, see Disruption Module F. For infrastructure tools used in digital resistance, see Disruption Module A or Disruption Module D.*

Selected References

Church Committee. (1976). *Final Report of the Select Committee to Study Governmental Operations with Respect to Intelligence Activities, Book II*. U.S. Senate.

Entman, R. M. (1993). *Framing: Toward Clarification of a Fractured Paradigm*. Journal of Communication, 43(4), 51–58.

Gallup. (1966). *Public Opinion on Civil Rights Leaders*. Gallup Archives.

Lorde, A. (1984). *Sister Outsider: Essays and Speeches*. Crossing Press.

McCombs, M. E., & Shaw, D. L. (1972). *The Agenda-Setting Function of Mass Media*. Public Opinion Quarterly, 36(2), 176–187.

Scott-Heron, G. (1970). *Small Talk at 125th and Lenox*. Flying Dutchman.

Theoharis, A. (1989). *The FBI & American Democracy: A Brief Critical History*. University Press of Kansas.

Wiesel, E. (1986). *Nobel Peace Prize Acceptance Speech*. NobelPrize.org.

Woolley, S. C., & Howard, P. N. (2016). *Computational Propaganda Worldwide*. Oxford Internet Institute.

The Rachel Maddow Show. (2025, July 22). *NBC News segment on political bots and disinformation* [TV broadcast]. NBC News.

Chapter Six

Disobedience in the Age of Surveillance

Legal Notice (read first)

This chapter explores surveillance technology and countermeasures such as metadata scrubbing, burner phones, and mesh networking. These descriptions are educational examples only. Attempting such measures may be regulated or illegal in some jurisdictions. Readers must assess risks independently. The author and publisher accept no liability for misuse.

Field Note: If They Can't Predict You, They Can't Stop You

You're being watched—but that doesn't mean you have to be seen.
They expect slogans, not silence. Outrage, not adaptation.
Confuse the algorithm. Scramble the pattern. Reclaim unpredictability as your camouflage.

They made surveillance the new battlefield. So be the thing they can't track, tag, or profile. Not because you're hiding—but because you're evolving.

> *Visibility got attention. Invisibility gets results.*

Rebellion once depended on visibility. Now, survival may depend on vanishing.

Today's dissidents navigate a landscape shaped not only by power, but by omnipresent observation. Surveillance is no longer a tool of last resort, it is the operating system of modern governance. Through cameras, metadata, predictive algorithms, and biometric scanners, states and corporations have achieved what centuries of informants could not: real-time omniscience.

The Architecture of Control

The old world relied on fences and guards. The new world builds systems: autonomous, decentralized, and quietly permanent. From public transit turnstiles logging your entry to traffic cameras scanning license plates across cities, passive data collection defines modern life. Facial recognition programs once considered Orwellian now power everyday policing in London, New York, and Beijing.

In many countries, surveillance powers expanded dramatically under the justification of counterterrorism. The USA PATRIOT Act, passed just weeks after 9/11, loosened legal standards for wiretaps, secret searches, and mass data collection. Programs like PRISM, revealed by whistleblower Edward Snowden, showed how governments collect internet communications directly from tech giants (Greenwald, 2014). Surveillance is no longer targeted. It is ambient.

> "Arguing that you don't care about the right to privacy because you have nothing to hide is no different than saying you don't care about free speech because you have nothing to say."
> — Edward Snowden, *Permanent Record* (2019)

Protesters as Data Points

Attending a protest can now trigger a chain of digital flags. Your phone pings cell towers. Cameras scan your gait and compare it to stored biometric profiles. Faceprints captured at an airport may match images scraped from social media. Surveillance is retroactive—data collected now can be weaponized later.

Even encrypted apps are not immune. In 2020, the NYPD subpoenaed Signal metadata during racial justice protests (ACLU, 2021). Protesters in Iran and Myanmar were tracked using mobile phone triangulation. In many countries, it is not the protest that is illegal, it is the presence at one.

> "Big Brother isn't watching you. He's making sure you're watching him."
> — Unknown

Case Study: ICE and the New Face of Surveillance

U.S. Immigration and Customs Enforcement (ICE) has expanded its use of facial recognition, rolling out a mobile application called Mobile Fortify. The app enables agents to identify individuals in real time by scanning faces or contactless fingerprints and matching them against massive DHS biometric databases (Wired, 2025). What was once a slow, back-office process is now a handheld tool in the field, collapsing the distance between suspicion and identification. For immigrant communities, this has turned everyday spaces into checkpoints.

But as state surveillance intensifies, dissenters have not remained passive. Activists have developed counter-strategies that mirror the very technologies turned against them. One effort, known as the ICE List Project, has used artificial intelligence to reconstruct the partially masked faces of ICE officers from public videos, then applied reverse-image searches to unmask them (Washington Post, 2025; WebProNews, 2025). The logic is simple: if state agents can strip away anonymity from civilians, then the public can hold state agents accountable by denying them invisibility behind badges. This tactic has exposed dozens of officers and forced debate over transparency, ethics, and retaliation.

Still, countersurveillance requires caution. Unlike anonymity tools that protect protestors, unmasking opponents treads a more dangerous line. Doxxing exposes not just officials but their families, and risks undermining broader solidarity if used recklessly. As with all high-stakes tools, the question isn't only whether it works; it's whether its use can be defended ethically and strategically.

Corporate Surveillance and Data Capitalism

Not all surveillance is state-driven. In fact, private companies often outpace governments. Social media platforms monitor behavior, preferences, and networks. Data brokers compile dossiers from purchase histories, search terms, location trails, and facial scans. These profiles are sold, traded, and used to algorithmically predict and shape behavior.

Corporations may not build prisons, but they build the maps that tell police where to patrol. They don't arrest, but they filter job applications, loan approvals, and insurance rates. The line between profit and punishment is thin.

Adapting the Tactics

Dissenters must evolve faster than the systems pursuing them. This doesn't mean hiding forever, it means disrupting predictability.

- Ditch the phone when attending high-risk actions. Or use burner phones purchased with cash and discarded after one use.

- Obscure your identity using masks, hats, and clothing that doesn't signal affiliations.

- Scrub metadata from images, videos, and documents before uploading or sharing them. Metadata is invisible data attached to files, such as when and where a photo was taken, what device was used, or which software saved a file. It can include usernames, GPS coordinates, camera IDs, and even editing history. Police, corporate platforms, and surveillance tools can use this hidden information to trace the origin of a file, link it to your device, or connect you to other activists.

Free tools like MAT2 or ExifTool can strip this metadata clean before sharing, reducing your digital fingerprint. This step is critical if you're filming police, documenting abuse, or posting under a pseudonym.
- Avoid tagging or naming others in photos and posts related to activism.

- Mesh networks allow devices to communicate directly with each other without internet or cell towers. They're ideal for protest zones where access is blocked or monitored. Offline routers (like Raspberry Pi relays) can act as local hubs for sharing maps, messages, or updates among trusted users, even without connectivity (see Disruption Module A).

    Learn more:
    https://gotenna.com/pages/mesh
    https://meshtastic.org/
    https://pimylifeup.com/raspberry-pi-wi-fi-extender/

- Practice strong OPSEC (Operational Security) to protect yourself and your network.
    OPSEC is the habit of protecting information by limiting what is shared, who knows what, and how systems can be breached. Good OPSEC means separating your personal identity from your activist role. Use different devices, names, emails, and accounts for organizing work. Avoid crossing streams; never check your activist email from your personal phone, and never log into personal accounts while using organizing tools.

    OPSEC also means staying cautious even within trusted groups. Many surveillance operations work by infiltrating groups or exploiting loose talk. Share only what others truly need to know. Trust your crew, but lock your doors.

    Learn more:
    https://ssd.eff.org/en/module/introduction-operational-security
    https://ssd.eff.org/en/playlist/activist-privacy-and-digital-security

The Psychological Toll

Living under constant watch isn't only a technical challenge, it's a psychological one. Surveillance chills dissent. It whispers, You are alone. You are exposed. You are foolish to resist. The power of surveillance is not merely in what it sees, but in what it prevents you from doing.

The antidote is solidarity. Surveillance isolates; collective strategy unites. Knowledge-sharing, shared tools, and informed consent within activist communities are more powerful than encryption alone. You are not a lone node in the system. You are part of a swarm.

The following tactics aren't abstract—they're used by real activists navigating the realities of surveillance. These tools are especially critical for resisting digital tracking, profiling, and predictive policing.

Burner Phones and Phone Discipline

Use temporary, prepaid phones purchased with cash and never linked to your name or accounts. Avoid bringing your everyday device to high-risk actions. If possible, leave all phones behind during direct action. Learn more:
Learn more: https://ssd.eff.org/en/module/how-use-phone-safely-protest

MAC Address Randomization and Device Spoofing

Phones and laptops broadcast unique identifiers that can be used to track you. Modern devices sometimes allow MAC address randomization, but tools like Tails OS and specialized Wi-Fi spoofers offer stronger protection. Tails OS is a secure, amnesiac operating system that runs from a USB stick and leaves no trace on your device.
Learn more: https://tails.net

Faraday Bags

Store your devices in Faraday pouches to block cellular, Wi-Fi, and Bluetooth signals when not in use. These bags prevent real-time tracking but do not erase metadata already collected.
Learn more: https://www.wired.com/story/faraday-bags-digital-privacy/

Facial Recognition Obfuscation Tools

Use anti-recognition tactics like IR LED arrays, face paint disrupting landmark points, or accessories designed to foil AI recognition systems. This field is rapidly evolving; monitor civil liberties organizations for updates. Some facial recognition obfuscation tools may not work in jurisdictions where face coverings are restricted by law. Research your local protest laws before relying on them. Also note that newer surveillance cameras may filter out IR interference.
Learn more: https://www.cnet.com/news/privacy/this-face-paint-can-fool-ai-surveillance-systems/

Secure Communication and Metadata Scrubbing

(See earlier metadata section above for full explanation.)

Decentralized and Offline Tools

Where possible, switch to mesh networks (like goTenna or Meshtastic) or Raspberry Pi-based local relays for coordination. These tools bypass cell towers and reduce central points of failure.
(See Disruption Module A and D for full setup guides)

Operational Security (OpSec) Habits

Compartmentalize identities. Never cross personal and activist usernames, email addresses, or devices. Practice need-to-know discipline even in trusted groups.
Learn more: https://ssd.eff.org

Parting Reflections: From Watched to Watchful

The first act of rebellion is to see clearly. The second is to act anyway.

Throughout Part I, we've seen how disobedience emerges from conscience, conviction, and historical necessity. But theory alone cannot withstand surveillance. Movements fail not only because they are crushed—but because they are discouraged into silence. Visibility, once a strength, now comes with risk. But invisibility cannot become a prison.

The answer is not to retreat from activism, but to adapt it. To become cleverer. Quieter. Sharper. Dissent must be engineered with the same precision as the systems that monitor it.

Part II will explore what it takes to become a modern dissenter, not in abstract terms, but in lived realities. Who resists? How do they survive it? What skills matter more than ideology? These questions mark the next step, not only toward resistance, but toward transformation.

Your name may never appear in history books. But if the system never saw you coming, you're already winning.

> "Surveillance is the enemy of imagination."
> — Naomi Wolf, *The End of America* (2007)

End Note: *For tools to resist digital surveillance, see Disruption Module D on Raspberry Pi protest tech and Disruption Module G for encryption and safe-distance tactics. For legal protections when operating under surveillance, see Chapter 13. See Chapter 11 for a deeper discussion on tactical ethics, and Disruption Module H for additional tools on digital countersurveillance.*

Selected References

ACLU. (2021). *Surveillance of Protesters and Legal Challenges*. ACLU Reports.

Greenberg, A. (2019). Hackers' Delight: Testing Faraday Bags for Digital Privacy. Wired. https://www.wired.com/story/faraday-bags-digital-privacy/

Greenwald, G. (2014). *No Place to Hide: Edward Snowden, the NSA, and the U.S. Surveillance State*. Metropolitan Books.

Snowden, E. (2019). *Permanent Record*. Metropolitan Books.

The Washington Post. (2025). "Activists Are Using AI to Track and Expose ICE Officers."

WebProNews. (2025). "Activists Use AI to Unmask ICE Officers, Igniting Privacy Debates."

Wired. (2025). "ICE Rolls Facial Recognition Tools Out to Officers' Phones."

Wolf, N. (2007). *The End of America: Letter of Warning to a Young Patriot*. Chelsea Green.

Part II

The Who: Becoming a Modern Dissenter

"Guerrilla warfare is not simply a military strategy; it is a way of thinking—resilient, adaptive, and informed."
—Unknown

Chapter Seven

Critical Thinking and Skepticism

Legal Notice (read first)

This chapter discusses methods of critical analysis, skepticism, and evaluation of information. While it references activist contexts, the material is intended for educational purposes only. It does not constitute legal, professional, or operational advice. Readers bear full responsibility for how the information is applied.

The Armor of Thought

Obedience thrives on unexamined assumptions. Systems of control depend not just on fear, but on passivity, the kind that accepts slogans as truth and silence as wisdom. To dissent effectively, one must first learn to think critically and question relentlessly. Dissent without discernment is just noise. But dissent grounded in analysis becomes strategy.

Critical thinking is not merely a skill; it is a form of protection. When narratives are shaped by governments, corporations, and algorithms, the ability to separate evidence from opinion becomes survival. Propaganda doesn't require lies, it only needs a flood of emotionally charged half-truths. Skepticism is the filter that holds that flood at bay.

The rise of deep-fakes, AI-generated articles, and partisan media echo chambers has created a landscape where perception is manipulated at scale. In this environment, believing nothing is just as dangerous as believing everything. The goal isn't cynicism, it's discernment.

These threats are explored in depth by West (2021), who details how synthetic media and algorithmic targeting are reshaping truth and trust in democratic systems.

Cognitive Traps and Mental Shortcuts

Human minds crave efficiency. We rely on cognitive shortcuts like confirmation bias (favoring evidence that supports our beliefs), groupthink (suppressing dissent to maintain social harmony), and the Dunning-Kruger effect (overestimating our knowledge). These mental traps are not failures, they are defaults. But unchecked, they are exploitable by every bad actor in power.

These effects have been documented extensively, most notably by Kruger and Dunning (1999), and popularized by Kahneman's work on human decision-making.

To resist, one must deliberately break these patterns: read beyond headlines, seek out opposing perspectives, ask who benefits from the narrative being pushed.

Skepticism ≠ Paralysis

Skepticism must not lead to inaction. When every source feels compromised and every fact is suspect, the temptation is to disengage entirely. That is precisely what authoritarian systems hope for. The answer is to triangulate—verify claims from multiple sources, follow money trails, and trust patterns, not personalities.

Cultivating a Maverick Mindset

Radical thinking begins with radical humility: knowing what you don't know. It involves asking uncomfortable questions:

- What am I assuming to be true?

- Who constructed this narrative?

- What voices are missing from this version of events?

Historical dissenters, whether Emma Goldman, James Baldwin, or Rachel Carson, were not just brave. They were intellectually relentless.

Applied Resistance: Tools for Today

In the age of manufactured consent and algorithmic manipulation, critical thinking is tactical. These tools are used by modern dissenters, investigative journalists, and digital skeptics to **resist manipulation**, expose falsehoods, and reclaim cognitive sovereignty.

- **Lateral Reading**

    Instead of accepting the first source you see, lateral reading means *leaving the site* to see what other trusted sources say about it. It's what professional fact-checkers do: open multiple tabs, compare information, and investigate the *publisher's credibility* before believing a claim. It disrupts siloed thinking and combats misinformation spread through emotionally charged headlines.

Learn more:

https://guides.lib.uw.edu/research/evaluate/lateralreading

https://checkology.org

- **Source Vetting**

    Not all news outlets or influencers operate from a place of transparency. Vetting means asking: Who funds this outlet? What's its editorial history? Is it left, right, or corporate-aligned? Understanding a source's bias helps you separate reporting from spin and can guide how you weight or compare claims across ideological lines.

    Learn more:

    https://www.allsides.com/media-bias/media-bias-ratings

    https://adfontesmedia.com

- **Fallacy Spotting**

    Authoritarian rhetoric often relies on fallacies—logical errors designed to manipulate, distract, or overwhelm. Examples include *ad hominem* attacks (attacking the person, not the idea), *false dilemmas* (either-or framing), or *appeals to authority* without evidence. Recognizing these tactics helps you resist persuasion by force of emotion or social pressure.

    Learn more:

    https://yourlogicalfallacyis.com

    https://nizkor.org/features/fallacies/

- **Reverse Image and Video Verification**

    Online content is often repurposed, miscaptioned, or artificially generated. Tools like Google Reverse Image Search or InVID allow you to trace where an image or video *actually* came from—whether it's authentic, altered, or taken from a different context entirely. This is essential during unfolding events or in conflict zones where propaganda spreads rapidly.

    Learn more:

    https://www.invid-project.eu/tools-and-services/invid-verification-plugin/

    https://images.google.com

- **Cognitive Fallibility Awareness**

    Know your own limits. The Dunning-Kruger effect explains how people with the least knowledge often feel the most confident. This isn't a flaw—it's a default. Cultivating a "beginner's mind" helps keep you flexible, humble, and open to new evidence, which is exactly what authoritarian systems fear.

    Learn more:

    https://www.ncbi.nlm.nih.gov/pmc/articles/PMC7757655/

    https://www.psychologytoday.com/us/articles/200310/confidence-the-illusion-competence

- **Disinformation Pattern Recognition**
  QAnon, deepfake campaigns, and fake grassroots movements often share markers: anonymous sources, emotional urgency, calls to "do your own research" without real data, and shape-shifting narratives. Spotting the structure of disinfo campaigns helps neutralize them before they radicalize others—or you.
  Learn more:
  https://datasociety.net/library/oxygen-of-amplification/
  https://www.cisa.gov/news-events/news/cisa-insight-disinformation-stop-its-spread

- **Digital Hygiene for the Mind**
  Overexposure to constant news, outrage, and doomscrolling degrades attention and heightens emotional susceptibility. Tactical resistance requires *mental stamina*. Set consumption boundaries, take breaks from algorithm-driven platforms, and prioritize longform sources with editorial review.
  Learn more:
  https://centerforhumantechnology.org
  https://reboot.fm/research-attention-resistance/

- **Confirmation Bias Checks**
  Your brain wants to be right. It subconsciously seeks out facts that support what you already believe and dismisses those that don't. Actively look for *disconfirming* evidence to test your own views. This isn't disloyalty to your cause, it's intellectual integrity, and it prevents echo chambers from becoming traps.
  Learn more:
  https://thedecisionlab.com/biases/confirmation-bias
  https://www.psychologytoday.com/us/basics/confirmation-bias

- **Claim Triangulation**
  Single sources can be manipulated or mistaken. Triangulation means comparing **three or more** credible sources to identify consistencies and anomalies. Focus on what's corroborated across ideologically diverse outlets or independent experts. This method is slower—but it creates clarity in the fog of propaganda.
  Learn more:
  https://www.factcheck.org
  https://www.snopes.com
  https://www.poynter.org/fact-checking/

In the digital age, thinking clearly is an act of defiance.

"The most common way people give up their power is by thinking they don't have any."
— Alice Walker, *unknown source*

The Machinery of Belief

From McCarthyism to the War on Terror, mass consensus has often been manufactured. During the lead-up to the 2003 Iraq War, U.S. officials promoted the idea that Saddam Hussein possessed weapons of mass destruction. Despite conflicting reports from weapons inspectors and international watchdogs, the media amplified the claim. Fear eclipsed scrutiny. The war was launched. No weapons were found.

Investigative accounts by Isikoff and Corn (2006) reveal how intelligence was manipulated and dissenting voices downplayed in the rush to war.

This wasn't just a policy failure, it was a public critical thinking failure.

Manufactured consent, as described in Manufacturing Consent by Noam Chomsky and Edward Herman (1988), relies on repetition, emotional salience, and selective framing. When governments and media collude, even the absurd can sound inevitable.

Learn more:
https://nsarchive2.gwu.edu/NSAEBB/NSAEBB80/iraq02.pdf
(Declassified U.S. intelligence documents on Iraq's WMD claims – National Security Archive)

https://www.cia.gov/library/reports/general-reports-1/iraq_wmd_2004/index.html
(Iraq Survey Group Final Report – CIA, 2004)

https://www.pbs.org/wgbh/frontline/film/newswar/
(Frontline documentary: News War – Role of media in shaping public consent)

https://presswatchers.org/2020/06/the-real-story-of-how-the-media-failed-on-iraq/
(Dan Froomkin's analysis on press failures before the Iraq War)

https://www.pbs.org/moyers/journal/btw/watch.html
(Bill Moyers Journal: Buying the War – Media complicity in the Iraq invasion narrative)

https://press.princeton.edu/books/paperback/9780691006001/many-are-the-crimes
(Book page: Ellen Schrecker's Many Are the Crimes: McCarthyism in America)

Case Study: QAnon and the Collapse of Skepticism

Few recent movements reveal the dangers of uncritical belief like **QAnon**. Emerging from anonymous message boards in 2017, QAnon posited that a shadowy elite engaged in satanic child trafficking was being secretly opposed by Donald Trump. There was no verifiable evidence—only cryptic posts, digital speculation, and emotionally charged claims.

Yet QAnon metastasized. Social media algorithms helped it spread through Facebook, YouTube, TikTok, and Telegram, bypassing traditional editorial filters. Followers felt empowered, even enlightened. When reality contradicted the prophecy, the narrative merely shifted. Failed predictions didn't collapse belief, they strengthened it.

QAnon weaponized confirmation bias, pattern-seeking, and cognitive dissonance. Its appeal wasn't logic, it was *identity*, *belonging*, and the *illusion of control*. It offered a mythology where followers were cast as soldiers in a cosmic battle of good and evil, while any mainstream rejection only confirmed its "truth" in the eyes of believers.

The **January 6th insurrection** was not just a violent political outburst—it was a tragic culmination of myth overtaking fact, of tribal identity replacing verifiable truth. QAnon didn't merely deceive, it reshaped how its adherents *defined reality*.

The lesson is simple: unchallenged narratives, no matter how absurd, can grow into action. Skepticism isn't a luxury; it's a civic duty.

Learn more:

https://www.theatlantic.com/magazine/archive/2020/06/qanon-nothing-can-stop-what-is-coming/610567/
https://www.technologyreview.com/2020/10/23/1010944/how-qanon-went-mainstream-election/
https://www.pewresearch.org/fact-tank/2020/09/16/most-americans-have-heard-of-qanon-but-few-have-positive-views-of-it/
https://counterhate.com/research/the-disinformation-dozen/
https://intelligence.house.gov/uploadedfiles/qanon_and_domestic_terrorism.pdf
https://doi.org/10.1177/14614448211019856

End Note: *For frameworks on evaluating information threats and misinformation tactics, see Chapter 15 on security and deception. For real-time tools to verify sources and resist manipulation, consult Disruption Module G.*

Selected References

Chomsky, N., & Herman, E. S. (1988). Manufacturing consent: The political economy of the mass media. Pantheon Books.

Hofstadter, R. (1964). The paranoid style in American politics. Harper's Magazine.

Isikoff, M., & Corn, D. (2006). Hubris: The inside story of spin, scandal, and the selling of the Iraq War. Crown Publishing.

Kahneman, D. (2011). Thinking, fast and slow. Farrar, Straus and Giroux.

Kruger, J., & Dunning, D. (1999). Unskilled and unaware of it: How difficulties in recognizing one's own incompetence lead to inflated self-assessments. Journal of Personality and Social Psychology, 77(6), 1121–1134. https://doi.org/10.1037/0022-3514.77.6.1121

Marwick, A., & Partin, W. C. (2021). QAnon and the emergence of the unreal. New Media & Society. https://doi.org/10.1177/14614448211019856

Sunstein, C. R. (2009). On rumors: How falsehoods spread, why we believe them, what can be done. Farrar, Straus and Giroux.

Walker, A. (n.d.). "The most common way people give up their power is by thinking they don't have any." Quotation attribution unclear; included per common usage.

West, D. M. (2021). Airwaves, algorithms, and democracy: Artificial intelligence in the battle against disinformation. Brookings Institution Press.

Williams, R. (1989). Resources of hope: Culture, democracy, socialism. Verso.

Additional Public Source References:

- The Atlantic. (2020). *Nothing can stop what is coming*. https://www.theatlantic.com/magazine/archive/2020/06/qanon-nothing-can-stop-what-is-coming/610567/

- MIT Technology Review. (2020). *How QAnon went mainstream*. https://www.technologyreview.com/2020/10/23/1010944/how-qanon-went-mainstream-election/

- Pew Research Center. (2020). *Most Americans have heard of QAnon, but few have positive views*. https://www.pewresearch.org/fact-tank/2020/09/16/most-americans-have-heard-of-qanon-but-few-have-positive-views-of-it/

- Center for Countering Digital Hate. (2021). *The disinformation dozen*. https://counterhate.com/research/the-disinformation-dozen/

- U.S. House Intelligence Committee. (2021). *QAnon and domestic terrorism.* https://intelligence.house.gov/uploadedfiles/qanon_and_domestic_terrorism.pdf

- Data & Society. (2018). *The oxygen of amplification: Better practices for reporting on extremists, antagonists, and manipulators online.* https://datasociety.net/library/oxygen-of-amplification/

Chapter Eight

Embracing Risk and Uncertainty

Legal Notice (read first)

This chapter explores risk-taking and uncertainty in activism. While it draws on historical and modern examples, it is presented for educational purposes only. Readers must understand that engaging in risky action may carry legal or personal consequences. Neither the author nor publisher accepts liability for misuse of these ideas.

Disobedience is not safe. Movements that matter are rarely easy or predictable. The cost of pushing against injustice is often paid in surveillance, isolation, legal threat...or worse. But without risk, there is no rupture. Without uncertainty, there is no evolution.

Learning to face these conditions, without paralysis, bravado, or burnout, is central to the dissenting life.

The Illusion of Safety

Systems of control promise comfort. Obey, and you'll be left alone. Keep your head down, and things might stay the same. But for many, that comfort was never real to begin with. For the oppressed, the marginalized, the surveilled: uncertainty is already the baseline.

The activist's task is not to escape risk, but to engage with it consciously, tactically, and with purpose.

Fear is a teacher. Not an enemy.

The Psychology of Danger

Research shows that humans tend to overestimate immediate dangers and underestimate long-term threats. We also fear ambiguity more than pain. This cognitive bias, called "ambiguity aversion", can stall even the most principled plans. Why? Because acting under uncertainty feels like losing control.

Movements that thrive under pressure develop what psychologists call "hardiness": the ability to remain committed, flexible, and purposeful amid stress (Kobasa, 1979).

In short, you don't eliminate fear, you repurpose it.

Lessons from High-Risk Movements

Freedom Riders faced beatings and imprisonment on segregated buses, but their strategy depended on consistency under chaos, what McAdam (1986) described as "high-risk activism," driven by deeply internalized commitments and strong group identity.

Hong Kong's Umbrella Movement relied on adaptability, rotating tactics, roles, and communication tools daily to withstand surveillance (Schoenfeld, 2020)

The Zapatistas built entire communities under the shadow of military threat, embracing autonomy not as an ideal but as daily practice (Hayden, 2002).

Each movement succeeded not by removing uncertainty, but by learning to move with it.

The Danger of Overconfidence

Uncertainty can be terrifying, but certainty can be fatal.

Movements that cling to fixed ideologies, fail to adapt, or assume invincibility are vulnerable to disruption. Certainty makes you rigid. Risk makes you awake.

Embracing uncertainty means accepting that plans will fail, allies will falter, and moments will turn. Resilience depends not on a single strategy, but on a living, evolving relationship with conditions.

Practicing Strategic Discomfort

To grow more resilient, build your capacity to operate at the edge of discomfort.

- Train under stress: Conduct drills or simulations under time pressure or with limited information.

- Vary your tactics: Practice flexibility, not just repetition.

- Challenge your assumptions: Invite critique before the opposition forces it upon you.

- Rest before collapse: Recovery is not retreat—it is ammunition.

The goal is not to feel brave. The goal is to remain clear-headed, responsive, and committed in conditions others flee.

Fear as Compass

The presence of fear often signals the importance of the work. If your actions don't carry risk, they may not carry meaning.

But there's a difference between boldness and recklessness.

Boldness is measured, informed, and intentional.

Recklessness is reactive, ego-driven, and contagious.

The challenge is to build internal barometers: ***What level of risk is acceptable? When does action serve the cause, and when does it serve pride?***

Anchoring Through Chaos

Uncertainty will test your values. Moments of crisis reveal what you believe, and whether you believe it alone. Anchor yourself in:

- Community: not just affinity, but trust and accountability.

- Vision: not rigid plans, but purpose-driven direction.

- Process: small steps that affirm your agency when the future feels too big.

Disobedience requires not just courage, but continuity. What matters most is not the absence of fear, but the decision to act with it, through it, and despite it.

Tactics for Operating Under Uncertainty

It's one thing to accept that danger exists—it's another to train for it. Movement organizers, direct action participants, and even solo dissenters benefit from simple but deliberate practices that increase readiness under volatile conditions. These are not elite or militarized strategies. They are accessible tools to keep your head clear, your risks intentional, and your courage sustainable.

Here are practical methods for strengthening your relationship with uncertainty:

- **Stress Drills**
  Simulate chaos before it finds you. Practice decision-making under time pressure, emotional overload, or partial information.
  Example: Set a timer to make a protest-day decision in 90 seconds—without your usual contacts available. Try navigating a blackout without phone service for one hour.
  Learn more: https://trainingforchange.org/training_tools/scenario-drills/
  Learn more: https://www.psychologytools.com/resource/grounding-techniques/

- **Tactical Flexing**

    Avoid becoming predictable. Change tactics, locations, tools, or leadership structures often enough to stay agile.

    Example: Instead of holding weekly meetings at the same café, rotate venues and organizers. If you always use Signal, try Briar for one week.

    Learn more: https://beautifultrouble.org/tactic/tactic-star/

    Learn more: https://ssd.eff.org/

- **Red Teaming**

    Proactively find the flaws before someone else does. Assign someone to challenge your plan from the outside, like a "devil's advocate for resistance."

    Example: Before launching a campaign, invite a trusted skeptic to list five ways it might fail—then build those answers into your prep.

    Learn more: https://www.lesswrong.com/posts/Bn8jbmxF7ZRL8KQWa/red-teaming-101

    Learn more: https://commonslibrary.org/using-pre-mortems-to-avoid-campaign-failures/

- **Risk Laddering**

    Create personal and group "risk tiers" in advance. What level of danger are you willing to face, and where do you draw the line?

    Example: You might accept public exposure but not physical risk. Someone else might be okay with arrest, but not losing custody or immigration status. These ladders differ—but must be known.

    Learn more: https://www.activistsecurity.org/

    Learn more: https://www.frontlinedefenders.org/en/resource-publication/security-risk-assessment-planning

- **Psychological Anchoring**

    Fear will rise. Build rituals that bring you back to purpose.

    Example: A grounding phrase before a protest. A shared gesture with a comrade. A tea ritual, prayer, or breath cycle that connects you to your "why."

    Learn more: https://www.humanrightsconnected.org/activist-toolkit/grounding-and-centering-for-activists/

    Learn more: https://www.mindful.org/mindfulness-and-protesting-how-to-show-up-without-burning-out/

These tools are not just survival tactics. They are discipline under uncertainty, designed to keep movements responsive, not reactive. You do not eliminate risk. But you can prepare for it in ways that sharpen clarity, not panic.

End Note: *For frameworks on navigating psychological risk, see Chapter 3 on resistance psychology. For burnout prevention and sustainability planning, see Chapter 12 and Disruption Module E on resilience tactics.*

Selected References

Beautiful Trouble. (n.d.). Tactic Star. Retrieved August 8, 2025, from https://beautifultrouble.org/tactic/tactic-star/

Chenoweth, E., & Stephan, M.J. (2011). *Why Civil Resistance Works: The Strategic Logic of Nonviolent Conflict*. Columbia University Press.

Commons Library. (n.d.). Using Pre-Mortems to Avoid Campaign Failures. Retrieved August 8, 2025, from https://commonslibrary.org/using-pre-mortems-to-avoid-campaign-failures/

Electronic Frontier Foundation. (n.d.). Surveillance Self-Defense. Retrieved August 8, 2025, from https://ssd.eff.org/

Frontline Defenders. (n.d.). Security Risk Assessment & Planning Workbook. Retrieved August 8, 2025, from https://www.frontlinedefenders.org/en/resource-publication/security-risk-assessment-planning

Hayden, T. (Ed.). (2002). *The Zapatista Reader*. Thunder's Mouth Press.

Human Rights Connected. (2020). Grounding and Centering for Activists. Retrieved August 8, 2025, from https://www.humanrightsconnected.org/activist-toolkit/grounding-and-centering-for-activists/

Kessler, R. (2020, July 21). Mindfulness and Protesting: How to Show Up Without Burning Out. Mindful.org. Retrieved August 8, 2025, from https://www.mindful.org/mindfulness-and-protesting-how-to-show-up-without-burning-out/

Kobasa, S. C. (1979). Stressful life events, personality, and health: An inquiry into hardiness. *Journal of Personality and Social Psychology, 37*(1), 1–11.

McAdam, D. (1986). Recruitment to high-risk activism: The case of Freedom Summer. *American Journal of Sociology, 92*(1), 64–90.

Schoenfeld, D. J. (2020). Tactical adaptation and movement endurance: Lessons from Hong Kong. *Journal of Social Movement Studies, 19*(4), 555–573.

Scott, J. C. (1990). *Domination and the Arts of Resistance*. Yale University Press.

Training for Change. (n.d.). Scenario Drills. Retrieved August 8, 2025, from https://trainingforchange.org/training_tools/scenario-drills/

Chapter Nine

Breaking Boundaries

Legal Notice (read first)

This chapter examines innovation and cross-boundary organizing within movements. Some examples may describe actions that could be unlawful if attempted today. The material is provided for informational purposes only and does not constitute legal advice. Readers are solely responsible for evaluating risks.

Resistance is not just confrontation, it is innovation. In oppressive environments, creativity becomes a survival trait. When direct action is blocked, subversive imagination breaks paths around the obstacle. The most powerful dissenters are often not the loudest, but the most unpredictable.

From encrypted memes to misused algorithms, today's dissidents leverage surprise as a strategy. Constraint becomes canvas.

Tactical Toolkit: Creative Resistance Methods

To innovate under pressure, dissenters must think like designers: adaptive, curious, and irreverent. Below are examples of real-world tactics that have broken boundaries, many of which can be remixed or reimagined for your own context:

Digital Subversion Tactics

Modern dissenters operate in digital spaces that are heavily policed. But those same tools can be turned inward.

- **Meme warfare**: Humorous, viral content can bypass censors and deliver sharp critique. A 2021 study by Phillips & Milner highlights how memetic language allows subversive ideas to flourish under cover of humor (Phillips & Milner, 2021).
  Implementation: Use widely recognized formats with satirical or emotionally disarming overlays. Pair

visual irony with minimal text. Use image-hosting sites or ephemeral platforms like Instagram Stories to increase reach while minimizing traceability.
Why it works: Humor lowers defenses and allows dissent to travel in disguise. Memes also move fast, often faster than censorship can keep up.
Learn more: https://knowyourmeme.com/
Learn more: https://ssd.eff.org/

- **Hashtag cloaking**: Using innocuous or misleading tags to evade content suppression.
  Implementation: Post content under tags that are trending but unrelated (e.g., cooking, fitness), then embed visual or textual resistance inside the media. Rotate tags often and use subtle signals recognizable only to your community.
  Why it works: Algorithmic moderation often fails to grasp context—using unrelated tags can buy visibility while confusing automated systems.
  Learn more: https://citizenlab.ca/
  Learn more: https://beautifultrouble.org/tactic/hashtag-hijack/

- **Geo-misdirection**: Using VPNs, GPS spoofing, and masked metadata to confuse digital surveillance systems.
  Implementation: Use mobile spoofing apps like Mock Location (Android) or Xcode-based simulators (iOS) to generate false GPS trails. Always pair this with anonymized browsers and encrypted messaging apps like Signal.
  Why it works: Modern surveillance depends on location and metadata more than content. Misdirection disrupts profiling and live tracking.
  Ethical note: These tools can be powerful but may violate terms of service or local laws. Use with caution and legal awareness.
  Learn more: https://privacyguides.org/
  Learn more: https://github.com/ValleZ/PokemonGoLocationFeeder

The aim is not just to speak, but to stay heard and untraceable.

Disguise and Subversion

- **Invisible Ink Messaging**: Activists in Belarus wrote chalk messages using lemon juice, revealing the message only under heat.
  Implementation: Use common household acids (e.g., lemon juice or vinegar) on porous surfaces. Messages can be revealed with a lighter, iron, or warm surface later. Works well on paper, cardboard, or concrete under specific lighting.
  Why it works: Covert messages can be planted without drawing attention, then revealed later in trusted spaces.

Learn more: https://science.howstuffworks.com/innovation/inventions/invisible-ink.htm

- **QR Code Hijacking**: Protesters replaced restaurant QR menus with links to resistance literature or encryption guides (Poell et al., 2022).
  Implementation: Generate redirect QR codes using open-source tools, then print stickers or transparencies to overlay real ones. Use link shorteners or self-hosted URLs for redirection, and test thoroughly on mobile.
  Why it works: QR codes appear benign, but allow hidden access to dissenting ideas—especially when placed where phones are already scanning.
  Learn more: https://qrd.by/tools
  Learn more: https://www.privacyguides.org/tools/

- **Fashion as Camouflage**: Hong Kong protesters used clothing and umbrellas not just to shield identities but to signal roles and coordinate movement (Schoenfeld, 2020).
  Implementation: Assign dress codes to roles (e.g., red for medics, black for scouts). Use accessories to indicate intent (a sunflower pin = media observers). Use umbrellas or scarves to break facial recognition.
  Why it works: Clothing is both a defense and a language. It protects anonymity while communicating within the group.
  Learn more: https://beautifultrouble.org/tactic/fashion-as-camouflage/
  Learn more: https://frontlinedefenders.org/en/resource-publication/security-in-a-box

Symbolic Infiltration

- **Barcode Graffiti**: Used to represent surveillance capitalism and make public spaces feel watched, prompting dialogue.
  Implementation: Use 3D-printed or papier-mâché statues for mobility and low cost. Mock plaques can be attached magnetically or with adhesive. Use solemn fonts and passive-voice language to mimic official tone for credibility.
  Why it works: Familiar symbols—like barcodes—become uncanny when repurposed. They invoke questions with minimal explanation.
  Learn more: https://tacticaltech.org/
  Learn more: https://www.theglassroom.org/

- **Hijacked Holidays**: Marking "Independence" or "Thanksgiving" with somber vigils, die-ins, or satirical celebration exposes the narrative.
  Implementation: Plan peaceful actions tied to the holiday's public meaning. Use props (flags at half-mast, funeral attire) to invert the expected tone. Document and distribute media to challenge dominant framing.
  Why it works: Co-opting familiar events adds tension and contrast, creating resonance with those who

might otherwise ignore protests.

Learn more: https://beautifultrouble.org/tactic/hijacking-traditions/

Digital Rewiring

- **Noise Injection**: Groups flood surveillance algorithms with false positives: random names, faces, keywords, to dilute data pools.

  Implementation: Use scripts or manual posting to repeatedly insert fake "targets" into monitored systems. Avoid patterns. Share toolkits for generating synthetic content or recycled metadata.

  Why it works: Surveillance systems depend on signal-to-noise ratios. Flooding them with garbage reduces effectiveness and raises analyst fatigue.

  Ethical note: This tactic risks triggering false alarms or targeting innocent profiles. Use only when your group understands the risks.

  Learn more: https://www.tacticaltech.org/resources/data-and-activism/

  Learn more: https://exposingtheinvisible.org/en/guides/data-shadow/

- **Scraping the Scrapers**: Using bots to overwhelm data-harvesting systems with junk data or looped redirects.

  Implementation: Deploy scraper bots of your own to interact with known surveillance crawlers. Redirect them to decoy sites or endless loops using ".htaccess" or reverse proxies.

  Why it works: Web crawlers are automated. Redirect loops or honeytraps waste their bandwidth and introduce false positives into the system.

  Clarification: .htaccess is a server configuration file that can be used to control access and URL behavior.

  Learn more: https://github.com/stamparm/maltrail

  Learn more: https://null-byte.wonderhowto.com/how-to/set-up-honeypot-trap-spam-bots-your-website-0175476/

- **"Google Bombing"**: Tying a phrase to search engine results via mass hyperlinking (e.g., linking political names to satirical websites).

  Implementation: This technique gained attention in the early 2000s when "miserable failure" was linked to political biographies (Naughton, 2004). Coordinate posts with consistent anchor text across forums and blogs.

  Why it works: Search engine ranking algorithms can be gamed with repetition and links. When coordinated, even satirical phrases can surface in serious contexts.

  Learn more: https://en.wikipedia.org/wiki/Google_bomb

  Learn more: https://beautifultrouble.org/tactic/google-bombing/

Performance and Absurdity

- **Flash Rituals**: Protesters hold mock weddings, funerals, or tea parties in front of embassies or banks to draw attention while confusing security forces.
  Implementation: Choose rituals that are easily recognizable but contextually bizarre. Plan short, mobile actions that don't require permits. Costumes and props should fit in backpacks and be easily discarded if needed.
  Why it works: Rituals lend emotional power and legitimacy. Absurd combinations cause pause, confusion, and press coverage.
  Learn more: https://beautifultrouble.org/tactic/mock-funerals/
  Learn more: https://howlround.com/how-resistance-performs

- **Clown Brigades**: Used to mock militarized police response and create cognitive dissonance for onlookers. Groups like the Clandestine Insurgent Rebel Clown Army (CIRCA) have used this technique effectively in Europe and the UK (Jordan, 2007).
  Implementation: Organize trained "clown units" that act confused, exaggerated, or overly helpful. Practice physical comedy and use megaphones or musical instruments. The goal is to disarm tension and gather attention.
  Why it works: Laughter and ridicule break fear. When authority figures appear ridiculous, their power is psychologically diminished.
  Learn more: https://beautifultrouble.org/tactic/clown-army/
  Learn more: https://crimethinc.com/2003/07/10/clowning-as-resistance

- **Silent Choirs**: Groups appear in public spaces mouthing resistance chants with no sound: disruptive, legal, unforgettable.
  Implementation: Choreograph movements and use placards or hand gestures to coordinate silent participation. Film for later release with dubbed audio or captions.
  Why it works: Silence disrupts expectation. It avoids legal triggers while still delivering emotional weight, especially when documented for media.
  Learn more: https://beautifultrouble.org/tactic/silent-protest/
  Learn more: https://nonviolence.wagingpeace.org/

System Gaming

Authoritarian systems run on rules. When you follow those rules in unexpected ways, you reveal their absurdity, and sometimes, you break them.

- **Bureaucratic Flooding**: File paperwork *en masse* under public record laws or permit procedures. This technique was used by the Yes Men and other activist groups to overwhelm legal bottlenecks (Boyle, 2011).
  Implementation: Use open-source templates to submit dozens or hundreds of minor-but-legal requests.

Share instructions and scripts for automation. The goal is not to get answers; it's to slow the machine.
Why it works: Authoritarian systems are often rule-bound. Too many requests force them to show their hand—or collapse under their own weight.
Learn more: https://logicmag.io/security/bureaucracy-as-resistance/
Learn more: https://crimethinc.com/tools/system-jamming

- **Rule-Literalism**: Obey repressive laws to the point of parody.
  Implementation: If a protest requires standing exactly 100 meters from a monument, use tape measures and GPS to highlight the absurdity. If curfews exist, hold synchronized "bed-ins" right before enforcement.
  Why it works: When rules are enforced blindly, complying to an extreme can reveal their ridiculousness, making the system look foolish.
  Learn more: https://beautifultrouble.org/tactic/rule-following/

- **Feedback Exploits**: Use reporting mechanisms against themselves.
  Implementation: Mass-report harmful misinformation that is state-approved. Overwhelm moderation systems with competing narratives. Use satire and legal mimicry to blur intent.
  Why it works: Platforms are vulnerable to their own systems. Turning them inward reveals their inconsistency and bias.
  Learn more: https://citizenlab.ca/
  Learn more: https://eff.org/issues/censorship

Cognitive Jamming

Power depends on predictability. When your actions violate expectation, they jam the system, not physically, but mentally.

- **Pattern Disruption**: Never repeat the same route, tool, or phrase. Civil resistance literature identifies this as a key component of avoiding suppression (Sharp, 2010).
  Implementation: Vary protest routes, slogans, and attire to resist modeling. Assign roles to create intentional "noise" in surveillance systems; each member performs different visual or verbal behaviors.
  Why it works: Predictability is the enemy of dissent. Chaos creates resilience and forces systems to adapt inefficiently.
  Learn more: https://beautifultrouble.org/tactic/pattern-disruption/
  Learn more: https://exposingtheinvisible.org/

- **Emotional Ambiguity**: Use contradiction, smiles in riot gear, solemnity in satire, to confuse expectations.
  Implementation: Train to shift emotional tone rapidly. Combine props or symbols with opposing affect

(e.g., carrying flowers while dressed in riot helmets).
Why it works: Mixed signals disrupt narrative certainty. Audiences and opponents alike hesitate, unsure how to respond.
Learn more: https://howlround.com/how-resistance-performs

- **Assumption Violation**: Show up where you're least expected. Speak in forums that usually host your opposition.
  Implementation: Publish op-eds in unlikely outlets. Use formal language or credentials to gain access, then shift tone inside. Appear to "play along" until the critical moment.
  Why it works: Subversion is strongest when it plays inside enemy terrain. Discomfort=impact.
  Learn more: https://beautifultrouble.org/tactic/assumption-violation/
  Learn more: https://tacticaltech.org/

Cognitive Jamming Prompts

- Ask: What assumptions is the system making about us? Then violate them.
  Example: If the system assumes physical resistance, respond with silence or irony. If it assumes disorganization, become hyper-structured.

- Ask: How can this law or rule be followed in a way that makes it useless?
  Example: Obey a no-signs rule by printing messages on clothing, umbrellas, or tattoos. Use the letter of the law to reveal its fragility.

- Ask: If I couldn't speak, how would I still dissent? (Gestures, color, pattern, or rhythm.)
  Example: Use synchronized movement, flash colors, or even dance as forms of nonverbal protest. Create symbols or rhythms that signal coordination without sound.

End Note: *For techniques related to misdirection, covert signaling, and coordination under pressure, see Chapter 8 on risk and resilience. For encryption, metadata, and anonymity tools, consult Disruption Module G on digital resistance frameworks.*

Selected References

Boyle, M. (2011). *Creative Protest: Culture Jamming and the Anti-Corporate Movement.* Peter Lang Publishing.

Jordan, J. (2007). "The Art of Clowning: Disobedience, Performance, and Subversion." In *Art and Activism.* Pluto Press.

Naughton, J. (2004). "Google and the miserable failure." *The Observer,* UK.

Phillips, W., & Milner, R.M. (2021). *You Are Here: A Field Guide for Navigating Polarized Speech, Conspiracy Theories, and Our Polluted Media Landscape.* MIT Press.

Poell, T., Rajagopalan, S., & Zimmer, M. (2022). *Platforms and Cultural Production.* Polity Press.

Schoenfeld, D. J. (2020). Tactical adaptation and movement endurance: Lessons from Hong Kong. *Journal of Social Movement Studies, 19*(4), 555–573.

Sharp, G. (2010). *From Dictatorship to Democracy: A Conceptual Framework for Liberation.* Albert Einstein Institution.

Chapter Ten

Networking and Fellow Mavericks

Legal Notice (read first)

This chapter addresses networking among activists and building movement infrastructure. Such organizing activities may be subject to surveillance or legal restrictions in some jurisdictions. The information is provided for educational purposes only. Neither the author nor publisher assumes liability for real-world application or misuse.

In dissent, isolation is not a safeguard, it is a silencer. Authoritarian systems thrive when opponents remain scattered, uncoordinated, and easily dismissed. But connection, when built with care and intention, becomes a form of resistance in itself. Networks grounded in trust, not hierarchy, can adapt, recover, and grow stronger under pressure. These are not echo chambers; they are ecosystems of subversion.

When you find the others, you begin to remember your strength.

Trust Cells in Practice

The trust cell model is decentralized by design. Instead of large, visible movements vulnerable to disruption, these cells consist of small, secure groups (3–7 people) bonded through mutual trust, shared goals, and protective boundaries (CrimethInc., 2020; Scott, 1990).

Each cell operates semi-autonomously, linked by minimal but essential contact with other cells. This prevents cascading collapse while enabling strategic coordination.

Implementation:

- Form cells through observation over time; behavior, not claims, determine trust.

- Use non-digital vetting methods: shared physical experiences, past collaborations, or witnessed solidarity.

- Limit sensitive information to "need to know" levels, even within the cell.

This strategy mirrors successful models used by resistance groups in 20th-century Europe (Gerlach, 1971), post-9/11 whistleblower networks, and modern hacktivist enclaves (Braybrooke & Jordan, 2017).

Infiltration and Disruption: Proactive Defense

Infiltration is inevitable once a group becomes effective. But infiltration is often less about brute surveillance and more about disruption of trust: sowing paranoia, provoking division, or capturing narrative control (Mitrano, 2022).

<u>Common Red Flags</u>:

- Sudden ideological purity tests or factionalism.
- Excessive charisma with no real contribution.
- Obsession with documentation, planning, or weapons.
- Abrupt escalations to high-risk proposals without consensus.

Implementation:

- Practice rotational leadership or facilitation to prevent hierarchy calcification (Polletta, 2002).
- Establish "red line" protocols: how to respond when sabotage, suspicion, or harm emerges.
- Conduct routine internal check-ins: not to enforce control, but to surface tension early.

> "The best infiltrators don't disagree—they agree too easily."
> — Unknown

Rituals of Trust: Building the Invisible Backbone

Strong networks aren't formed through apps or slogans, they're formed through rituals. Shared actions, habits, and practices strengthen relational bonds beyond ideology (Duncombe, 2007).

<u>Examples of Trust-Building Rituals</u>:

- Shared meals or skill exchanges.
- Collective reading of banned texts.
- Co-creation projects: mapping injustice, mutual aid drives, digital art (Costanza-Chock, 2020).

Implementation:

Design rituals that are low-cost, replicable, and symbolic. Encourage periodic story-sharing or vulnerability exercises. These activities build not just cohesion but psychological safety, essential for taking risks together (Edmondson, 1999).

Solidarity ≠ Sameness

Effective networks allow for disagreement. Uniformity is not a virtue, it's a liability. What holds mavericks together is not tactical consensus but value alignment and mutual respect. The principle: fight different battles, but watch each other's backs.

Implementation:

- Use "shared core, diverse limbs" models: agree on 3–5 inviolable principles, allow flexible methods.
- Formalize a code of respect, not rules of speech or affiliation.
- Celebrate ideological edges when they sharpen shared vision, not fracture it.

Visibility Without Vulnerability

Sometimes solidarity must become visible to inspire others or shift public narrative. But visibility carries risk. Smart cells manage their signal: what is shown, who shows it, and when (Zuboff, 2019).

Implementation:

- Use pseudonyms or avatars for outward-facing work.
- Share stories through intermediaries (e.g., sympathetic journalists, artist collectives).
- Train one person in the group as "signal bearer" while the others remain less exposed (e.g., handles press contacts, maintains social feeds, or gives public statements).

"A well-fed fire does not always roar—it radiates."
— Unknown

Momentum through Mutual Aid

The surest way to sustain a movement isn't through rhetoric, but reciprocity. Sharing food, covering rent, fixing gear, holding grief, these are not side acts. They are the revolution (Spade, 2020).

Implementation:

- Map local needs: housing, safety, transport, mental health.

- Create an "offer/ask" board shared within or between cells.

- Document successes anonymously to uplift morale and attract aligned allies.

When your network supports life, people fight harder to protect it.

Applied Resistance: Tools for Building Resilient Networks

Modern dissent depends not only on courage, but also on the ability to organize without leaving easy trails for adversaries. This requires both social resilience and technical safeguards. The following tools and practices have been field-tested in activist movements, disaster response scenarios, and communities operating under surveillance-heavy conditions.

Encrypted Messaging & Group Coordination

Ordinary text messages and many chat apps store your conversations on company servers, where they may be visible to employees, hackers, or government agencies. They also keep records of who you talked to and when — called metadata — which can be as revealing as the conversation itself (Zuboff, 2019).

Signal is a free app that uses end-to-end encryption to scramble messages so that only you and the recipient can read them. Not even Signal's own servers can see your conversations. It also supports private group chats, which can be paired with a cell structure approach — splitting large groups into smaller ones so that if one person is compromised, the rest are less exposed.

When to use: Planning events, sharing sensitive information, or communicating with trusted contacts during risky actions.

Risks/limits: Encryption doesn't prevent someone from taking screenshots or photographing the screen. You still need to trust your contacts.

Learn more:

https://signal.org

https://ssd.eff.org/module-categories/messaging

Secure Document Sharing

Mainstream cloud storage (Google Drive, Dropbox) can see your files and will comply with legal requests to hand them over. For dissenters, that's a serious risk.

CryptPad and Proton Drive use zero-knowledge encryption, meaning files are encrypted before they ever leave your device (Braybrooke & Jordan, 2017). Even the hosting company cannot read or scan them. These platforms support collaborative editing, making them ideal for drafting joint statements, storing research, or maintaining organizational records without tying them to your personal account.

When to use: Working on plans, archiving sensitive documents, or collecting photos/videos that must remain private.
Risks/limits: If you lose your password, you lose the data permanently — there's no recovery option with true zero-knowledge services.
Learn more:
https://cryptpad.org
https://proton.me/drive

Metadata Scrubbing Tools

Photos, videos, and documents often contain metadata — hidden information like GPS coordinates, the camera model, timestamps, or even your username. This data can identify where and when a file was created and sometimes who created it.

Free tools like ExifTool (advanced) or MAT2 (Metadata Anonymisation Toolkit) can remove this data before sharing. On mobile, apps like Scrambled Exif (Android) or built-in "Remove Location" settings (iOS) can do the same. This practice has been critical in past movements, such as Hong Kong's 2019 protests, where activists removed metadata before posting images online to avoid arrests.

When to use: Before uploading media from protests, meetings, or private spaces.
Risks/limits: Removing metadata doesn't hide what's visible in the photo itself; be mindful of faces, landmarks, or signs in the image.
Learn more:
https://exiftool.org
https://0xacab.org/mat/mat2

Password & Account Security

Weak or reused passwords make it easy for hostile actors to compromise your accounts. A password manager like Bitwarden or KeePassXC generates and stores long, unique passwords for every service you use, encrypted with one strong master password.

Pair this with two-factor authentication (2FA), preferably using an app like Authy or Aegis instead of SMS, to make account breaches much harder (Zuboff, 2019).

When to use: For all activism-related accounts, email, and cloud logins.
Risks/limits: If you lose your master password, you lose all stored logins. Always back up encrypted password databases securely.
Learn more:
https://bitwarden.com
https://keepassxc.org
https://authy.com

Anonymous Browsing & Counter-Surveillance Skills

Your internet provider (ISP) and websites you visit can log your browsing history and location. Tools like Tor Browser route your traffic through multiple encrypted relays, hiding your IP address and making it far harder to trace activity back to you. For everyday browsing that still needs privacy, a reputable no-log VPN (like Mullvad or Proton VPN) encrypts your traffic and masks your IP from your ISP.

Beyond digital protection, activists benefit from counter-surveillance skills: varying routes to meetings, monitoring for suspicious observers, and using disguises when appropriate (Mitrano, 2022).

When to use: Researching sensitive topics, reading banned content, moving through monitored areas, or communicating in high-surveillance environments.

Risks/limits: VPNs require trust in the provider, and Tor can be slower than normal browsing. Counter-surveillance can raise suspicion if performed too obviously.

Learn more:

https://www.torproject.org

https://mullvad.net

https://protonvpn.com

Secure Offline Communication

In some scenarios — such as during internet blackouts — online tools won't work. Mesh networking apps like Briar (Android) or hardware-based tools like goTenna Mesh allow phones to connect directly to each other via Bluetooth or radio frequencies, creating a local communication network without central servers.

These tools can pass encrypted messages between devices without touching the internet, making them valuable for protests, disaster zones, or authoritarian shutdowns (Jordan, 2002).

When to use: When you expect connectivity disruptions, or need a private backchannel during in-person events.

Risks/limits: Range is limited; devices must be within Bluetooth or radio range, or connected through intermediate devices acting as relays.

Learn more:

https://briarproject.org

https://gotenna.com

Mutual Aid Networks

Mutual aid is the practice of building systems of reciprocal care and support within a community. Instead of relying on hierarchical or state-run aid systems, mutual aid networks distribute resources, labor, and knowledge horizontally. During crises — such as natural disasters or police crackdowns — these networks can mobilize faster and reach people traditional relief ignores (Spade, 2020; Graeber, 2013).

When to use: In preparation for, during, and after crises where traditional aid is delayed or absent.

Risks/limits: Requires trust and coordination; infiltration can damage effectiveness if security is not considered.

Learn more:

https://mutualaidhub.org
https://crimethinc.com

Decentralized Information Distribution

Peer-to-peer networks and decentralized hosting tools like IPFS (InterPlanetary File System) or Secure Scuttlebutt allow content to be shared without a central server. By distributing files across many independent nodes, these systems make it far harder for adversaries to remove or censor information (Braybrooke & Jordan, 2017).

When to use: Sharing large or sensitive datasets, maintaining archives, or bypassing government censorship.

Risks/limits: Requires technical setup and may not be accessible to non-technical allies without training.

Learn more:

https://ipfs.tech
https://scuttlebutt.nz

Psychological Safety Practices

Movements collapse when members fear punishment for speaking up. Creating an environment of "psychological safety" — where people can express dissent and share ideas without retaliation — improves adaptability, trust, and innovation (Edmondson, 1999).

When to use: In organizing meetings, training sessions, and strategy discussions where diverse perspectives are valuable.

Risks/limits: Requires strong facilitation; can be abused by bad-faith actors if no accountability exists.

Learn more:

https://www.psychsafety.co.uk
https://hbr.org/2014/01/building-a-culture-of-candor

Operational Security (OPSEC) Discipline

OPSEC is the practice of controlling information about your plans, movements, and capabilities so adversaries can't exploit them. It's not just about tools — it's about habits.

This includes separating personal and activist identities, limiting what you share even with trusted contacts, and assuming that any channel could be compromised (Scott, 1990; Polletta, 2002). Good OPSEC treats information as a resource that must be protected; once it leaks, it can't be recalled.

Practical steps: Use code names, separate devices, avoid predictable routines, and never discuss sensitive matters in insecure spaces.

When to use: Always — OPSEC is a mindset, not a one-time task.

Risks/limits: Over-restriction can harm group cohesion; balance secrecy with the need for coordination.

Learn more:

https://www.eff.org/issues/security
https://ssd.eff.org

These are not abstract suggestions, they are battle-tested strategies. From Hong Kong's 2019 protests to disaster relief coordination in Puerto Rico, these tools have allowed dissenters to organize, communicate, and survive against technologically advanced opposition.

End Note: *For strategies related to navigating uncertainty and ideological risk, see Chapter 8. For ethical decision-making in collective action, see Chapter 11. To understand burnout risks and regenerative practices in activist networks, see Chapter 12. For secure digital communications, metadata shielding, and encryption tools, refer to Disruption Module G.*

Selected References

Braybrooke, K., & Jordan, T. (2017). *Hacking Protest: Technology, Resistance, and Activism*. Routledge.

Costanza-Chock, S. (2020). *Design Justice: Community-Led Practices to Build the Worlds We Need*. MIT Press.

CrimethInc. (2020). *From Democracy to Freedom*. CrimethInc Ex-Workers Collective.

Duncombe, S. (2007). *Dream: Re-imagining Progressive Politics in an Age of Fantasy*. New Press.

Edmondson, A. (1999). "Psychological safety and learning behavior in work teams." *Administrative Science Quarterly*, 44(2), 350–383.

Gerlach, L. P., & Hine, V.H. (1971). *People, Power, Change: Movements of Social Transformation*. Bobbs-Merrill.

Graeber, D. (2013). *The Democracy Project: A History, a Crisis, a Movement*. Spiegel & Grau.

Jordan, T. (2002). *Activism!: Direct Action, Hacktivism and the Future of Society*. Reaktion Books.

Mitrano, T. (2022). "Infiltration and the Politics of Disruption." *Journal of Civic Trust and Security*, 8(2), 103–119.

Polletta, F. (2002). *Freedom Is an Endless Meeting: Democracy in American Social Movements*. University of Chicago Press.

Scott, J. C. (1990). *Domination and the Arts of Resistance: Hidden Transcripts*. Yale University Press.

Spade, D. (2020). *Mutual Aid: Building Solidarity During This Crisis (and the Next)*. Verso Books.

Zuboff, S. (2019). *The Age of Surveillance Capitalism*. Public Affairs.

Chapter Eleven

Choosing Your Line: Tactical Ethics for Protestors

Legal–Ethical Use Notice (read first)

This chapter discusses ethical decision-making in protest and civil disobedience. It is not legal advice. Every individual is solely responsible for understanding and complying with the laws in their jurisdiction. Nothing here authorizes illegal conduct; it is intended to help readers think critically about risk, morality, and tactics. Consult a qualified attorney or trusted legal resource before taking any action that could involve legal consequences.

There is no resistance without lines. Some you will cross. Others you must not. Every act of dissent tests the boundary between strategy and conviction, and those who participate in radical action must constantly ask: *What am I willing to do? What am I unwilling to become?*

When the stakes escalate, when violence erupts, when others are watching, when silence becomes complicity, you will need answers to these questions. They are not theoretical. They are survival tools. And if you don't choose your line, someone else will draw it for you.

> "There may be times when we are powerless to prevent injustice, but there must never be a time when we fail to protest."
> — Elie Wiesel, *Night* (1956)

Personal Conviction vs. Group Strategy

Movements fracture when values go unspoken. A person who is ready to chain themselves to a gate may clash with someone who believes even property damage is a betrayal of message. That tension is natural, but dangerous if left unexamined.

<u>Ethical dissent demands two kinds of awareness:</u>

    1. Inward: What you personally believe is necessary, defensible, and morally just.

    2. Outward: What the group has agreed to do, and what the group will be perceived to have done.

You may disagree with your group's chosen tactic. The ethical choice isn't always to fall in line, but it's also not always to go rogue. If you violate the collective ethic, you risk endangering not just yourself, but others. If you obey without reflection, you risk moral collapse.

The Consent Principle in Collective Action

Tactical decisions, especially those involving risk, require consent. No one should be dragged into higher-risk or higher-visibility roles without clear agreement. This principle, rooted in both liberatory ethics and trauma-informed organizing, ensures that people retain autonomy even inside collective movements (Spade, 2020; INCITE!, 2007; CrimethInc., 2020).

Implementation:

- Break actions into risk tiers (e.g., "support," "presence," "frontline") and allow self-selection.
- Use color-coded systems or role tags during live protest (e.g., green = legal observer, red = marshals, black = direct action participants).
- Debrief openly afterward. No moral superiority; just clarity and reflection.

When consent breaks down, the group becomes a liability to itself.

Lines of Legality, Morality, and Risk

Ethical clarity comes from separating what is legal, what is moral, and what is sustainable. This framework has roots in nonviolent resistance literature, especially civil disobedience models developed by Sharp and others (Sharp, 2010; Martin, 2007).

Use the following format to apply the "Three Lens Test":

Is graffiti illegal?
• Legal: Yes

- Moral: Maybe not
- Strategic: Possibly yes

Is physical self-defense legal?
- Legal: Sometimes
- Moral: Often yes
- Strategic: Context-dependent

Is drone surveillance of police legal?
- Legal: In many cases
- Moral: Yes
- Strategic: Likely yes

Is leaking internal documents legal?
- Legal: No
- Moral: Depends
- Strategic: High risk, high reward

Implementation:

- Use a "Three Lens Test" before action: *Is this legal? Is this right? Is this smart?*
- If two of three are "no," reconsider.
- If all three are "yes," prepare thoroughly and communicate with others.

Self-Assessment: Know Before You Go

Before participating in or planning direct action, assess yourself honestly:

- What risks can I afford? (Arrest? Public exposure? Online doxxing?)
- What resources can I offer? (Tech skills? Bail funds? Street medic training?)
- What consequences can I bear, for myself and for others?
- What values will I not compromise, no matter the cause?

Self-assessment tools are used in protest training, activist defense preparation, and even movement building workshops to align ethics with capability (Ruckus Society, 2015; National Lawyers Guild, 2019).

Implementation:

Use a written checklist before each action. Journaling or verbal processing helps define non-negotiables. Some movements use consent cards: small, prefilled forms indicating what each member consents to do, carry, or risk.

Your personal ethics are part of the gear you carry. Don't leave them behind.

When Lines Move

Conviction doesn't mean rigidity. People evolve. What you believe today may shift tomorrow, especially after trauma, betrayal, or moral breakthrough.

Give yourself room to adapt, but don't let your lines vanish. When they move, it should be intentional, not reactionary. Reflection practices borrowed from liberation pedagogy and movement learning models are essential here (Freire, 1970; hooks, 1994).

Implementation:

- Create a "values log" after actions: track what changed and why.
- Debrief with others: *Was your line respected? Did you cross it? Was it worth it?*

The strongest mavericks are not the most extreme. They are the most clear.

Practical Tools & Techniques for Defining and Holding Your Lines

Consent Cards
Small, prefilled forms or durable laminated cards carried by participants in an action, indicating what they consent to do, carry, or risk (e.g., arrest, medical support, media presence). Consent cards help organizers assign roles quickly and ethically while honoring personal boundaries (Spade, 2020; INCITE!, 2007).
When to use: At the start of an action, training, or meeting where participants may be assigned varying levels of risk or visibility.
Risks/limits: Cards can be lost or intercepted, revealing operational details. Keep physical cards minimal in detail and avoid carrying them if security risks are high.
Learn more:
https://www.mutualaidhub.org
https://www.incite-national.org

Risk Tier Systems
A pre-agreed classification of action roles by risk level, such as *support*, *presence*, and *frontline*. These tiers can be color-coded (e.g., green for legal observer, red for marshals, black for direct action participants) or labeled for clarity. This makes it easier to maintain consent and avoid accidental escalation (CrimethInc., 2020; Ruckus Society, 2015).
When to use: For actions with multiple simultaneous roles or varying levels of legal and physical risk.

Risks/limits: Publicly visible coding can make it easier for adversaries to target high-risk roles. Consider private role designation where possible.

Learn more:

https://crimethinc.com

https://ruckus.org

The Three Lens Test Template

A printed or digital decision-making aid that asks: *Is this legal? Is this moral? Is this strategic?* Participants complete the test before an action to clarify alignment with personal and group ethics (Sharp, 2010; Martin, 2007).

When to use: During planning sessions or last-minute decision points before engaging in direct action.

Risks/limits: Over-reliance on this tool may slow urgent decision-making. Not all scenarios will allow perfect alignment on all three questions.

Learn more:

https://www.aeinstein.org

https://www.bmartin.cc

Values Logs

Post-action journals or group debrief forms where participants record whether their ethical lines were crossed, respected, or shifted — and why. Helps maintain long-term moral clarity and track personal evolution over time (Freire, 1970; hooks, 1994).

When to use: Immediately after an action or during a scheduled debrief session.

Risks/limits: Written records can be subpoenaed or seized; anonymize entries or keep logs in secure, encrypted storage.

Learn more:

https://www.freire.org

https://www.routledge.com/Teaching-to-Transgress/hooks/p/book/9780415908085

Decision Trees for Rapid Ethics

Flowchart-style tools that map possible outcomes of an action, helping participants decide quickly under stress while still honoring personal and group ethics (National Lawyers Guild, 2019).

When to use: In actions with fast-moving developments, such as protest marches that may encounter sudden police presence.

Risks/limits: May oversimplify complex decisions; should be paired with deeper pre-action discussion.

Learn more:

https://www.nlg.org

End Note: *For guidance on building collective trust and avoiding internal sabotage, see Chapter 10. For burnout and long-term moral sustainability, see Chapter 12. For civil disobedience scenarios and digital tools that require prior risk assessments, see Disruption Module E and Disruption Module G.*

Selected References

CrimethInc. (2020). *From Democracy to Freedom*. CrimethInc Ex-Workers Collective.

Freire, P. (1970). *Pedagogy of the Oppressed*. Herder and Herder.

hooks, b. (1994). *Teaching to Transgress: Education as the Practice of Freedom*. Routledge.

INCITE! Women of Color Against Violence. (2007). *The Revolution Will Not Be Funded: Beyond the Non-Profit Industrial Complex*. South End Press.

Martin, B. (2007). *Justice Ignited: The Dynamics of Backfire*. Rowman & Littlefield.

National Lawyers Guild. (2019). *Know Your Rights: Legal Observing & Activist Defense Manual*.

Ruckus Society. (2015). *Action Strategy Guide*.

Sharp, G. (2010). *From Dictatorship to Democracy: A Conceptual Framework for Liberation*. Albert Einstein Institution.

Spade, D. (2020). *Mutual Aid: Building Solidarity During This Crisis (and the Next)*. Verso Books.

Wiesel, E. (1956). *Night*. Hill and Wang.

Zinn, H. (2002). *You Can't Be Neutral on a Moving Train: A Personal History of Our Times*. Beacon Press.

Chapter Twelve

Resilience Without Burnout

Health & Well-Being Disclaimer (read first)

This chapter addresses strategies for sustaining activism without burnout. It is not medical or psychological advice. If you are experiencing mental health challenges, stress disorders, or health risks, seek help from a qualified professional. The techniques described here are educational and supportive in nature but may not be suitable for everyone. Use judgment, prioritize your well-being, and consult medical or psychological resources where appropriate.

Burnout is not failure. It is a message.

Movements don't just collapse under pressure, they unravel when people exhaust themselves believing their value lies only in their output. Resistance demands stamina, but it also requires sustainability. You cannot outlast a system you imitate. And if your activism replicates the grind, guilt, and martyrdom culture of dominant institutions, it will break you (Freeman, 1973; Maslach & Leiter, 2016).

Resilience is not mere endurance. It's the capacity to bend and restore, individually and collectively. And in resistance, rest is a tactic, not a luxury.

> "Caring for myself is not self-indulgence, it is self-preservation—and that is an act of political warfare."
> — Audre Lorde, *A Burst of Light* (1988)

Revolution Without Martyrdom

The archetype of the burned-out revolutionary, the sleepless organizer, the always-on messenger, the exhausted healer, is not heroic. It's a trap. Burnout is often romanticized in activist spaces, mistaken for dedication. But chronic depletion leads to mistakes, violence, mistrust, and collapse (Pignarre & Stengers, 2005; Freeman, 1973).

Implementation:

- Name the signs early: resentment, detachment, hypervigilance, despair
- Reject guilt-based motivation structures ("If you really cared, you'd never rest")
- Build normalized rest into your calendar, not just emergency breaks

If a tactic requires your collapse, it's not a tactic. It's a sacrifice.

Burnout as Structural, Not Personal

Too often, burnout is framed as a personal failure to "cope." In reality, burnout is a collective systems issue—a predictable consequence of under-resourced labor, boundary erosion, and lack of communal care structures (Maslach & Leiter, 2016; Spade, 2020).

Implementation:

- In meetings, ask: *What would make this work sustainable for you?*
- Identify and redistribute invisible labor (logistics, emotional support, cleanup)
- Conduct regular "energy audits" of group members; not to police them, but to adapt together

Blaming individuals for their exhaustion reinforces the very systems we're trying to dismantle.

Sustainable Roles: The Resistance Ecosystem

You don't have to do everything. Movements survive because people occupy different roles at different times. Direct action isn't the only form of courage: logistics, legal prep, comms, digital safety, and community care are equally vital.

Use the "ecosystem" model:

- Pollinators – spread messages, build morale
- Root builders – anchor the community and ensure continuity
- Firekeepers – maintain emotional and spiritual health

- Frontline defenders – take physical or public risk

Implementation:

- Let people self-identify their capacity and preferred role
- Offer "low-burn" engagement options (e.g., zine design, signal boosting, post-action cleanup)
- Create offramps and reentry points; let people step back without shame, and return when ready

Refer to disability justice models for additional insight on pacing, flexibility, and consent (Mingus, 2011; brown, 2017).

Healing as Strategy

Movement healing is not a side project. It is the soil in which everything grows.

Collective trauma, from repression, betrayal, loss, or burnout, will haunt a group if it is not acknowledged. And in traumatized groups, decisions warp, trust erodes, and retaliation often masquerades as strategy (brown, 2017; hooks, 2000).

Implementation:

- Normalize decompression circles, especially after high-stakes actions
- Bring in outside facilitators for group healing and conflict navigation
- Use creative restoration tools: group meals, music, storytelling, silence

Your wounds are valid. But so is your right to heal without permission.

Self-Care Without Individualism

True self-care isn't about bubble baths and "grindset" breaks. It's about knowing yourself well enough to preserve your integrity under pressure, and about ensuring others don't collapse while you recharge.

This is mutual care, not lifestyle branding.

Implementation:

- Pair up in "care pods" or buddy systems for mutual check-ins
- Share medical, housing, and emotional needs in trusted spaces
- Rotate access to retreat spaces, meal trains, mental health care, or emergency funding pools

Activism that doesn't care for its people becomes cruelty dressed in purpose.

Practical Strategies for Resilience

Energy Audits

Regular check-ins—individually or as a group—to assess emotional, physical, and logistical capacity. Use prompts like "What can I give right now?" and "What do I need to recover?" This technique originates in occupational burnout research and has been adapted in activist circles as a preventive measure (Maslach & Leiter, 2016; Spade, 2020).

When to use: At the start of long campaigns, during debriefs, or whenever conflict emerges.

Risks/limits: Requires honest communication and a non-punitive culture; otherwise, people may hide depletion to avoid stigma.

Learn more:

https://www.maslachburnoutinventory.com

https://www.mutualaidhub.org

Role Rotation Systems

A planned schedule for shifting responsibilities—frontline to logistics, logistics to communications—so no one person bears the same pressure indefinitely. This concept is rooted in both labor organizing and disability justice principles, recognizing that sustained high-intensity roles accelerate burnout (Mingus, 2011; brown, 2017). Effective systems document each role's requirements so any member can step in with minimal confusion.

When to use: In ongoing campaigns or multi-day actions with repetitive, high-stress roles.

Risks/limits: Poor handoffs can cause confusion; ensure transitions include clear briefings and documentation.

Learn more:

https://leavingevidence.wordpress.com

https://www.akpress.org/emergentstrategy.html

Care Pods

Small, trust-based circles for mutual support, where members commit to checking in on each other's well-being, sharing resources, and flagging burnout signs early. The concept emerged from queer and disability justice organizing and is built on consent, reciprocity, and individualized support plans rather than generic "self-care" (Spade, 2020; Lorde, 1988). A pod may share contacts for emergency childcare, access to safe housing, or pooled mental health resources.

When to use: In any sustained organizing effort, especially those with high emotional or physical stakes.

Risks/limits: Can become emotionally draining if boundaries aren't maintained; pods work best with clear expectations of reciprocity.

Learn more:

https://www.mutualaidhub.org
https://www.audrelordeproject.org

Decompression Circles

Structured post-action gatherings focused on emotional processing, storytelling, and reducing stress hormone levels. Common in trauma-informed community organizing, these circles use listening rounds and grounding techniques to help members transition from crisis mode to recovery (hooks, 2000; brown, 2017).

When to use: Immediately after high-stakes actions, arrests, or traumatic events.

Risks/limits: Re-traumatization can occur if facilitation is poor; consider trained mediators for sensitive debriefs.

Learn more:

https://www.akpress.org/emergentstrategy.html
https://www.routledge.com/All-About-Love/hooks/p/book/9780060959470

Sustainable Engagement Calendars

A shared planning tool—digital or physical—that maps not only actions and meetings but also intentional rest days, low-burn tasks, and wellness events. Inspired by union strike calendars and permaculture cycles, this approach ensures energy peaks align with strategic needs (Freeman, 1973; Maslach & Leiter, 2016).

When to use: For long-term campaigns where overextension is a known risk.

Risks/limits: Can create complacency if rest is over-prioritized without maintaining momentum.

Learn more:

https://www.malor.com/burnout-the-cost-of-caring
https://www.akpress.org

Low-Burn Contribution Lists

A living document of tasks that require minimal energy but still contribute to the movement—such as editing flyers, moderating online chats, or archiving press clippings. The list serves as a lifeline for members in recovery, allowing them to remain engaged without overtaxing themselves (Mingus, 2011; Spade, 2020). In some movements, these lists are integrated into shared project management boards so "low-burn" work is visible and valued.

When to use: For members in recovery from burnout, illness, or personal crisis.

Risks/limits: May unintentionally sideline members if low-burn tasks are treated as less valuable.

Learn more:

https://leavingevidence.wordpress.com
https://www.mutualaidhub.org

Buddy Downtime Protocols

Pairing members specifically for off-duty hours, ensuring each person has an accountability partner to rest, hydrate, eat, and detach from work for set periods. Adapted from safety buddy systems in hazardous work environments, this tactic reframes "checking in" as a shared responsibility for rest (Lorde, 1988; brown, 2017).

When to use: During extended actions, travel, or organizing retreats.

Risks/limits: Works only when both parties respect boundaries; otherwise, the pairing can become another form of obligation.

Learn more:

https://www.audrelordeproject.org

https://www.akpress.org/emergentstrategy.html

Restorative Task Swaps

Temporary exchange of duties between members to match tasks with current capacity and interest. This method not only prevents monotony but also builds resilience by cross-training members (Freeman, 1973; Mingus, 2011). Examples include having a media coordinator take on cooking shifts or a street medic rotate into a legal observing role.

When to use: In campaigns with predictable, repetitive workloads.

Risks/limits: Can disrupt workflow if swaps aren't coordinated well; best done with consent and clear timelines.

Learn more:

https://leavingevidence.wordpress.com

https://www.akpress.org

Micro-Restorations

Short, low-effort breaks embedded into actions—such as breathwork, quiet corners, hydration points, or quick grounding exercises. These are especially useful in high-adrenaline events, where stress hormones can stay elevated for hours (hooks, 2000; brown, 2017).

When to use: During long marches, sit-ins, or all-day assemblies.

Risks/limits: May seem trivial to those unused to pacing, so leaders should model participation.

Learn more:

https://www.routledge.com/All-About-Love/hooks/p/book/9780060959470

https://www.akpress.org/emergentstrategy.html

Exit and Reentry Plans

Pre-agreed strategies for how members can step away from the movement without severing ties, and how they can reintegrate when ready. This tool draws from volunteer retention programs in disaster relief work, where the need for sustainable pacing is critical (Spade, 2020; Mingus, 2011). A well-designed plan includes clear communication channels, a no-blame policy for stepping back, and a structured re-onboarding process.

When to use: Before major campaigns or when recruiting new members.

Risks/limits: If poorly communicated, can lead to misunderstandings about commitment levels.

Learn more:

https://www.mutualaidhub.org

https://leavingevidence.wordpress.com

Parting Reflections: From Becoming to Breaking

Resistance begins within, but it cannot remain there.

In Part II, you examined the self not as a static identity, but as a weapon to be sharpened. You mapped your ethics, accepted uncertainty, and learned how to endure without disappearing. These lessons do not make you invincible. They make you ready.

To dissent is no longer enough. Systems don't just exploit labor or ideas, they exploit fatigue. They count on burnout. They reward caution. The path forward is not just moral clarity, but strategic disobedience.

Part III is not a metaphor. It is a manual.

You'll encounter controversial methods, unorthodox tools, and blueprints that blur the line between innovation and sabotage. Some will inspire. Some may unsettle. That tension is by design.

The next pages aren't about whether you believe change is necessary.

They're about whether you're ready to build it by hand.

End Note: *For guidance on personal boundaries and ethical alignment, see Chapter 11. For trauma-informed digital and legal safety tools, see Chapter 13. For mutual aid wellness models and physical recovery guides, see Disruption Module F.*

Selected References

brown, a. m. (2017). *Emergent Strategy: Shaping Change, Changing Worlds*. AK Press.

Freeman, J. (1973). *The Tyranny of Structurelessness*. Berkeley Journal of Sociology, 17, 151–164.

hooks, b. (2000). *All About Love: New Visions*. William Morrow.

Lorde, A. (1988). *A Burst of Light: And Other Essays*. Firebrand Books.

Maslach, C., & Leiter, M. P. (2016). *Burnout: The Cost of Caring*. Malor Books.

Mingus, M. (2011). "Access Intimacy: The Missing Link." *Leaving Evidence Blog*.

National Lawyers Guild (NLG). (2019). *Legal observer training manual*. National Lawyers Guild Foundation. https://www.nlg.org/legalobservers

Permaculture Association. (2018). *Designing for resilience: Principles and practices*. Permaculture Association. https://www.permaculture.org.uk

Pignarre, P., & Stengers, I. (2005). *Capitalist Sorcery: Breaking the Spell*. Palgrave Macmillan.

Ruckus Society. (2015). *Action strategy guide*. The Ruckus Society. https://ruckus.org

Spade, D. (2020). *Mutual Aid: Building Solidarity During This Crisis (and the Next)*. Verso Books.

Part III

The How: Disruption Modules

"Tools are never entirely neutral. What matters most is who dares to wield them...and for what cause."
— Unknown

DISRUPTION MODULE A

MESH NETWORKING FOR OFF-GRID COORDINATION

Legal Notice (read first)

This module discusses the use of mesh networking devices for communication outside traditional infrastructure. Radio frequency use, encryption, and device modification may be regulated or restricted under national or international law. The material is provided for educational purposes only and does not constitute legal advice. Readers are responsible for compliance with communications and technology laws in their jurisdiction. Neither the author nor publisher assumes liability for misuse.

Mesh networking is a transformative method of peer-to-peer communication that allows communities, protest groups, and mutual aid networks to operate independently of centralized infrastructure (Mekky et al., 2019; goTenna, n.d.). Unlike traditional cellular or Wi-Fi networks, mesh networks route messages device-to-device, forming a self-healing, decentralized web of communication (Mekky et al., 2019).

A goTenna device acts as a personal radio transceiver, pairing via Bluetooth with a smartphone to send and receive messages across a designated radio frequency band (goTenna, 2022). When two or more goTenna units are active in range of one another, they automatically form a mesh network by relaying encrypted messages from one device to the next, hopping across the network until they reach the intended recipient, even if the sender and recipient are not directly connected.

Whether you're facing surveillance blackouts, internet shutdowns, disaster zones, or simply organizing where towers don't reach, mesh networking is a resilient, legally accessible tool that should be part of every disobedient toolkit.

Overview: How It Works

A mesh network uses multiple devices ("nodes") that communicate directly with one another via radio frequencies.

Messages are sent from node to node, hopping across the network until they reach the intended recipient. Each node strengthens the network; more nodes = more coverage and more reliability.

- No internet, SIM card, or centralized access point is required
- Nodes can be mobile (attached to people) or stationary (rooftop relays)
- Works even when the internet is censored or physically unavailable

Most activist mesh networks rely on lightweight, battery-powered devices paired with smartphones via Bluetooth and controlled through a dedicated app.

Essential Hardware and Software

Primary Device: goTenna Mesh

- Frequency: 902–928 MHz ISM band (unlicensed in North America)
- Range: Typically 0.5–1.5 miles per hop, up to 4+ miles with elevation
- Battery: Rechargeable via USB-C (24+ hour battery life per charge)
- Cost: ~$179 per pair (as of 2025)

Alternative: goTenna Pro X2m

- Designed for professional or emergency response use
- Offers AES-256 encryption and wider RF compatibility
- Requires special approval or licensing for civilian use in some countries

Mobile App: goTenna App (iOS/Android)

- Free download from App Store / Google Play
- Features: Direct messaging, GPS sharing, group chat, public broadcast mode
- Can operate in full offline mode once paired with device

Recommended Accessories

- Waterproof cases (Pelican 1020 or similar)
- USB battery packs (10,000 mAh minimum)

- Carabiners or shoulder-mount clips
- Telescoping poles or tripods for elevated relay nodes

Official Resource & Manual

https://gotenna.com/pages/gotenna-mesh-user-manual

Step-by-Step Setup

1. Fully charge all goTenna Mesh devices
2. Install the goTenna App on each smartphone
3. Pair each phone with its goTenna device via Bluetooth
4. Assign unique goTenna IDs (GIDs) to each user
5. Test message delivery between devices at short and mid-range
6. Distribute nodes evenly across participants (ideal 0.5–1.5 mile spacing)
7. Place at least one node at a high elevation (e.g., rooftop, balcony, pole mount) to act as a relay beacon for wider coverage
8. Note: Obstructions such as concrete walls, dense foliage, and metal structures can significantly reduce mesh hop distance. Where possible, maintain line-of-sight between nodes or use elevation to bypass obstacles. Weather conditions, especially heavy rain, can also impact range — test during different conditions to understand your network's performance envelope.

Tip: You don't need a person to "wear" every node. Use stationary mesh units as permanent relays.

Deployment Scenarios

Mesh networking has been used successfully in diverse real-world applications:

- Hong Kong Protests (2014–2019): FireChat and goTenna allowed communication amid shutdowns (Chen, 2014)
- Burning Man / Black Rock City: Offline ad-hoc mesh used for first aid and logistics
- Puerto Rico Hurricane Recovery: goTenna Pro used by emergency responders after Hurricane Maria (Vincent, 2017)

- Mutual Aid in Rural Appalachia: Rooftop mesh relays helped support internet-poor communities during COVID-19 lockdowns (NYU Tandon, 2020)

Legal and Ethical Notes

Mesh networking is fully legal in the United States and most other jurisdictions, provided devices operate within approved unlicensed frequency bands (FCC, 2021). However:

- Avoid relaying or intercepting messages that aren't yours
- Use strong passphrases or private groups to reduce spoofing risk
- Do not deploy mesh in restricted frequency bands without proper licensing
- Be aware of local telecommunications laws outside of North America

In repressive or high-surveillance environments, encrypted overlays such as Briar or Bridgefy may offer better stealth, though mesh tools like goTenna are often less detectable due to their non-internet transmission (EFF, 2020). To further reduce risk, consider "stealth mounting" techniques for permanent or semi-permanent relays—using camouflage cases, natural concealment (tree lines, rooftop HVAC covers), or low-profile brackets—to minimize visual detection. This approach aligns with secure infrastructure practices detailed in Disruption Module E.

Adaptability and Expansion Ideas

Mesh networking isn't just a protest tool, it can support long-term resilience.

- Set up rooftop or tower-mounted permanent relays in underserved neighborhoods (Mesh++ Whitepaper, 2021)
- Integrate with Pi-hole or Tor routers for hybrid mesh-internet privacy (Fitzgerald, 2019)
- Combine with apps like Briar (for end-to-end encrypted P2P messaging) or Bridgefy for added redundancy
- Bundle mesh tools with first aid kits or disaster readiness gear
- Coordinate "quiet drills" where communities practice message relays without cell service

Mesh is strongest where the state is weakest or most hostile. For integration with privacy routers, see Disruption Module B for Raspberry Pi–based mesh-Internet hybrids. For rapid protest deployment or blackout scenarios, see Disruption Module E for complementary broadcast messaging strategies.

Field	Details / Notes
Node ID / GID	Unique identifier for each node
Assigned Role	(e.g., wearable, rooftop relay)
Location / Zone	Neighborhood quadrant or sector
Assigned Owner	Person responsible for node
Battery Pack	Is a spare backup attached? Y/N
Signal Tested	✓ = confirmed coverage
Relay Status	Elevated or edge node (Y/N)
Last Test Date	MM/DD/YYYY
Issues / Notes	E.g., low signal, obstructions

goTenna Mesh Deployment Checklist

End Note: *For advanced privacy routing integrations, see Disruption Module B (Raspberry Pi privacy routers). For blackout-ready broadcast strategies, see Disruption Module E (anonymous messaging under infrastructure denial). Mesh networking reduces reliance on centralized systems but does not guarantee security; readers are responsible for lawful use and ethical deployment in their jurisdictions.*

Selected References

Chen, A. (2014). *FireChat in Hong Kong: How protesters use a chat app without internet*. Wired. https://www.wired.com/2014/10/firechat-hong-kong-usage/

EFF (Electronic Frontier Foundation). (2020). *Choosing secure messaging apps*. https://www.eff.org/pages/secure-messaging-scorecard

FCC (Federal Communications Commission). (2021). *Unlicensed operations in the 902–928 MHz band*. https://www.fcc.gov

Fitzgerald, M. (2019). *Combining Tor with Pi-hole for maximum privacy*. Medium. https://medium.com/@mfitz

goTenna. (2022). *goTenna Mesh user manual*. https://gotenna.com/pages/gotenna-mesh-user-manual

goTenna. (n.d.). *What is mesh networking?* https://gotenna.com/pages/mesh-networking

Mesh++ Whitepaper. (2021). *Solar mesh for community connectivity*. https://meshplusplus.com

Mekky, H., Li, X., Ruan, Y., & Qiu, L. (2019). Characterizing and improving WiFi latency in large-scale mesh networks. *Proceedings of the ACM on Measurement and Analysis of Computing Systems, 3*(1), 1–26.

NYU Tandon School of Engineering. (2020). *Disaster resilience through mesh networking in rural communities*. https://engineering.nyu.edu/news

Vincent, J. (2017). *goTenna's mesh network helped reconnect Puerto Rico after Hurricane Maria*. The Verge. https://www.theverge.com/2017/10/10/gotenna-puerto-rico-hurricane-maria

Disruption Module B

Privacy & Routing with Raspberry Pi

Legal Notice (read first)

This module explores how to configure Raspberry Pi devices for privacy routing, filtering, and censorship circumvention. Such use may violate telecommunications or cybercrime laws depending on jurisdiction. The information is intended solely for educational purposes. Readers must assess risks independently and consult legal guidance before implementing these practices. Neither the author nor the publisher accepts liability for improper use.

Online Privacy

In an era where surveillance has become routine—whether by corporations harvesting user data or governments monitoring dissent—ordinary internet users face a profound challenge: how to reclaim privacy without needing advanced technical skills.

A Raspberry Pi–based privacy router offers one of the most accessible answers. The Raspberry Pi is a small, affordable computer board (starting at about $35). By combining Pi-hole, which blocks trackers and advertising at the network level, with Tor, which anonymizes outbound traffic by routing it through a global volunteer relay network, you can create a pocket-sized device that broadcasts an encrypted Wi-Fi hotspot. This tool is equally useful at home, in a co-working space, or at a protest camp.

Think of Pi-hole as an app (a piece of software) that runs on your Raspberry Pi mini-computer. When installed, it turns your Pi into a little server that filters internet traffic. Specifically, it acts like a "gatekeeper" for websites: every time a device on your Wi-Fi asks to visit a site, the Pi-hole app checks the request. If the request is for a known ad, tracker, or malicious site, Pi-hole blocks it. If it's safe, the request goes through normally. Unlike browser add-ons (which only protect one device at a time), Pi-hole works at the network level—so every phone, laptop, smart TV, or game console connected to your Raspberry Pi is protected automatically.

Why a Raspberry Pi Privacy Router?

Your regular home router (the box from your internet company) doesn't give you much control. It mostly just passes your internet connection along. A Raspberry Pi can sit next to it—like adding a helper computer—and run privacy software on your behalf. You don't replace your router; you plug the Pi into it, and then connect your devices through the Pi.

Think of it this way:

- The router is like your house's front door. Normally, it just lets anyone in and out.

- The Raspberry Pi becomes the doorman standing at that door, checking who's allowed through.

- The Pi-hole app running on the Pi is the doorman's list of "bad guys" (ad servers, trackers, malware sites) that get turned away.

- The Tor software is the cloak your visitors put on so no one knows where they came from or where they're going.

You're not cracking open your router. You're just adding a tiny, $35 helper computer that plugs into it with a cable or connects by Wi-Fi.

Key Advantages

- Protects all devices on the network, not just a single browser.

- Portable—small enough to carry in a backpack.

- Adaptable—can run from wall power or a USB battery pack.

- Transparent—you control the logs, the filters, and the setup.

Core Components

- **Pi-hole** – Free, DNS-based ad and tracker blocker. Documentation: https://pi-hole.net

- **Tor (The Onion Router)** – An anonymizing network. Project: https://www.torproject.org

- **DNS (Domain Name System)** – The "phonebook" of the internet. Overview: https://www.cloudflare.com/learning/dns/what-is-dns/

Digital Disobedience in Practice

Rather than depending on corporate promises of privacy, this setup embodies digital disobedience: reclaiming autonomy through tangible, user-controlled tools. With modest effort, users can create their own firewall and anonymizing router, strengthening security for households, affinity groups, or mutual aid hubs.

This is not about paranoia; it is about agency. In the same way activists use banners to reclaim physical space, this device reclaims digital space from surveillance capitalism and network-level monitoring.

Overview: What It Does

1. Ad and tracker blocking at the network level

Pi-hole sits between your devices and the internet. If a device requests a known advertising or tracking server, Pi-hole blocks it before the connection happens.

Result:

- Web pages load faster without ads.

- Smart TVs, consoles, and mobile apps are covered.

- You can see which apps are "phoning home."

2. Tor anonymization of outbound traffic

Instead of traffic going straight to a destination, Tor routes it through a chain of volunteer-run relays. Each relay only knows the next hop, never the full path.

For an outside observer—your ISP, campus IT, or coffee shop Wi-Fi—you appear to be speaking only to the Tor network. They cannot easily profile your browsing.

3. Portable Wi-Fi hub

The Pi can act as an access point, broadcasting its own Wi-Fi. Devices connect to it, and all traffic flows through Pi-hole and Tor.

Deployment options:

- At home as a permanent upgrade.

- In co-working or activist hubs.

- In protest camps or pop-up sites, powered by a battery pack.

Taken together, Pi-hole's blocking + Tor's anonymization + the Pi's portability form a compact privacy system for households, groups, or nomadic use.

Hardware and Software Requirements

Required:

- Raspberry Pi 3 or 4 – Mainboard. Pi 4 is better for multiple users.
- MicroSD Card (32 GB or larger) – Stores OS and software.
- Reliable Power Source – Wall adapter or USB battery pack (10,000–20,000 mAh).
- Raspberry Pi OS (Raspbian) – Base operating system.
- Pi-hole – Download: https://pi-hole.net
- Tor – Download: https://www.torproject.org

Optional Add-ons:

- USB Wi-Fi Adapter – If acting as both client and hotspot.
- OLED/LCD Display – To show stats such as blocked domains or Tor status.
- Case and Cooling – To protect the Pi and prevent overheating.

Step-by-Step Build Instructions

Install the Operating System
Download Raspberry Pi OS and flash it to your microSD card using Raspberry PiImager or BalenaEtcher.

Connect the Pi to Your Network
Plug into your router with Ethernet, or use Wi-Fi with a USB adapter. Configure a static IP so devices always know where to find it.

Install Pi-hole
Run the Pi-hole installer. It will filter DNS requests and block known ad and tracking domains.

Install Tor
Install Tor from repositories or the Tor Project. It routes outbound traffic through the anonymizing network.

Combine the Two

Configure the system so that DNS requests and outbound traffic flow through Pi-hole, then Tor.

Test and Verify

Use Pi-hole's dashboard to view blocked domains.

Use Tor's check page to confirm anonymization.

Secure the System

Keep the Pi updated, set strong passwords, and limit access.

Deployment Scenarios

    1. Home Networks – Protect all household devices at once.

    2. Shared Living or Co-working Spaces – Provide collective protection.

    3. Protest Camps – Deploy with a battery pack for trusted hotspots.

    4. Hacktivist Cafés or Community Spaces – Public demonstration of privacy tools.

    5. Nomadic or Field Journalism – Create secure Wi-Fi bubbles in hostile networks.

Legal and Ethical Considerations

1. Varying Legal Environments

- U.S.: FCC rules on consumer internet: https://www.fcc.gov/consumers
- UK: Ofcom telecoms guidance: https://www.ofcom.org.uk/
- India: Department of Telecommunications – check official site.
- Tor Project censorship wiki: https://community.torproject.org/censorship/
- Civil liberties guides: https://privacyinternational.org and https://ssd.eff.org

2. How Networks Respond to Encrypted Traffic

ISPs may flag Tor traffic as suspicious or throttle it. Institutions may block or monitor it.

3. Ethical Boundaries

Do not use for illegal marketplaces or harmful activity. Be transparent with users who connect.

4. Limitations

- Endpoint devices may still leak data.
- Browser fingerprinting can track users.
- Misconfigured apps may bypass Tor.

5. Collective Responsibility

If deployed in a group space, get consent and explain what the device does.

Adaptability and Expansion Ideas

1. Layer with a VPN (Onion-to-Tunnel) – Run a VPN upstream of Tor for added privacy.

2. Mesh Networking Integration – Use cjdns or Yggdrasil to link multiple Pis into a peer-to-peer network.

3. Multi-Node Clusters – Deploy Pis in multiple locations with aggregated oversight.

4. Visual Feedback with Displays – Attach OLED/LCD screens to show blocked domains or Tor status.

5. Expanded Filtering – Import blocklists for phishing or disinformation domains.

6. Field-Ready Ruggedization – Use rugged cases, waterproofing, and solar panels for long-term outdoor use.

Closing Note: A Tool for Agency, Not Escapism

The Raspberry Pi privacy router is more than a gadget. It is a way to take control of your own connection with a $35 board, a memory card, and a bit of learning.

It reduces risks but does not erase them. Tools must be paired with education, trust, and habits such as keeping devices updated. What matters most is the shift in agency: you decide what flows through your network.

End Note: *For further technical guidance, see Disruption Module B (Pi-hole) and Disruption Module E (offline communications). While these tools can reduce surveillance risks, they do not eliminate them. Readers are responsible for ensuring compliance with local laws and for using the technology ethically.*

Selected References

Cloudflare. (2022). *What is DNS?* https://www.cloudflare.com/learning/dns/what-is-dns/

EFF (Electronic Frontier Foundation). (2020). *Choosing secure messaging apps.* https://www.eff.org/pages/secure-messaging-scorecard

Fitzgerald, M. (2019). *Combining Tor with Pi-hole for maximum privacy.* Medium. https://medium.com/@mfitz

Pi-hole Documentation. (2024). *Using Tor with Pi-hole.* https://docs.pi-hole.net/guides/misc/tor/using-tor/

Privacy International. (2022). *Raspberry Pi: Set up and run Pi-hole.* https://privacyinternational.org/guide-step/4341/raspberry-pi-setup-and-run-pi-hole

Opensource.com. (2020). *Build a Tor proxy with Raspberry Pi.* https://opensource.com/article/20/4/tor-proxy-raspberry-pi

Tor Project. (2023). *Overview of Tor and how it works.* https://support.torproject.org/about/overview/

Disruption Module C

Guerrilla Projection and Light Tactics

Legal Notice (read first)

This module covers projection, light graffiti, and illumination tactics for activism. Unauthorized projection or alteration of private or public property may be unlawful and carry penalties. The examples here are historical and educational. They are not operational instructions. Readers bear full responsibility for the risks and legality of their actions. The author and publisher disclaim liability for misuse.

In a world where billboards are controlled by corporations and public spaces are saturated with commercial messaging, projection activism reclaims the visual landscape. Using light instead of paint, it delivers bold, temporary statements without permanent alteration, sidestepping vandalism charges while confronting power with visibility.

This module outlines how to execute light-based protest tactics using projectors, stencils, and mobile rigs. Whether you're amplifying a rally or projecting dissent across the side of a courthouse, these techniques empower direct, decentralized expression.

What Is Projection Activism?

Projection activism involves displaying messages, images, or symbols onto buildings or surfaces using portable projectors or focused light devices. Unlike graffiti or flyposting, projections do not physically alter property, making them a legally safer tool for high-impact visual protest (Chatzichristos, 2022).

This tactic has been used globally, from The Illuminator Collective's "99%" beam on Wall Street buildings, to Greenpeace activists projecting anti-pollution slogans on fossil fuel offices (Klein, 2020; Greenpeace, 2017).

Core Advantages

- **Non-destructive:** No paint, glue, or paste, just light.

- **Mobile and Fast:** Set up and pack down quickly; project from vehicles or backpacks.

- **Legally Gray:** Projections are harder to prosecute than physical defacement (EFF, 2020).

- **Visually Striking:** Instantly draws attention, especially when paired with sound or performance (Zettl, 2011).

Projection Types

1. **Digital Projections**
   Use portable digital projectors to display videos, slogans, or logos. Controlled by laptops or phones, these allow dynamic visuals and animation.

2. **Gobo Light Projections**
   Use a high-powered flashlight or stage light with a laser-cut stencil (gobo) to cast crisp monochrome images. Ideal for symbol-based messaging (like logos, fists, chains, etc.).

3. **Slide Projectors**
   An older but budget-friendly option: create physical slides with transparent sheets and permanent markers or laser printing.

Item	Purpose
Portable Projector (Digital)	Projects full-motion visuals or high-resolution images
Gobo Projector or Flashlight	Projects single-color images or symbols with a stencil
Laptop or Smartphone	Controls projection content or brightness remotely
External Battery or Power Bank	Enables field use without a power outlet
Tripod or Car Mount	Stabilizes projection from a fixed point or vehicle
Weatherproof Case or Bag	Protects gear from rain or dust during transport
Light Shield or Hood	Prevents beam from being visible from behind

Essential Equipment Table

Quick Reference Recap: Hardware, Software, and Build Overview

Projection bombing is the act of projecting activist or artistic messages onto public surfaces like buildings or monuments. It is a non-destructive, high-visibility tactic with strong visual and emotional impact. This section outlines key equipment, tools, and steps for quick deployment.

Hardware / Software Checklist

- 2,000–5,000 lumen projector (short-throw preferred)
- Deep-cycle battery, inverter, or portable generator
- Tripod, backpack, or vehicle roof-mount
- Laptop, HDMI stick, or Raspberry Pi media device
- Pre-rendered media: video loops, slideshows (PowerPoint, Keynote, After Effects)
- Link: https://www.instructables.com/PROJECTION-BOMBING/

Step-by-Step Deployment

1. Select a short-throw projector with high lumens (≥2,000)
2. Load media files onto your laptop or HDMI stick
3. Secure projector with tripod, backpack frame, or vehicle mount
4. Power the projector using a battery pack or inverter
5. Project visuals onto a flat surface—wall, monument, high-rise, or banner
6. Document or stream the projection using a smartphone or livestream feed

Build Your Rig: A Step-by-Step Walkthrough

Digital Projector Rig

1. Choose a short-throw or mini projector with high lumens (≥ 2,000 recommended).
2. Connect to a laptop, Raspberry Pi, or smartphone using HDMI or wireless.
3. Preload slideshows, video loops, or custom messages.
4. Mount to a vehicle dashboard or tripod.
5. Power via portable AC battery (e.g., Goal Zero or Anker PowerHouse).

6. Use a collapsible screen or direct surface (building, statue, or sheet).

Gobo Light Rig

1. Use a high-lumen LED flashlight or spotlight.

2. Laser-cut your message/logo into a metal disc or stencil film.

3. Mount the gobo in front of the light lens.

4. Focus the beam at the target surface from a short distance.

5. Optional: conceal the rig in a backpack with a cutout hole for stealth projection.

Situational Use Cases

- **Rallies & Demonstrations**
  Project slogans or visuals onto nearby buildings to expand the reach of a protest. This creates compelling imagery for livestreams, media coverage, and documentation (Lievrouw, 2011).

- **Pre-Action Signaling or "Psychological Seeding"**
  Project cryptic or symbolic images ahead of direct actions to create intrigue or unsettle adversaries. Used tactically, this can influence perception without confrontation (Juris, 2008).

- **Pop-Up Teach-Ins or Public Film Nights**
  Use projections to transform urban surfaces into temporary learning spaces. Ideal for documentaries, speaker feeds, or digital zines (Castells, 2015).

- **Urban Guerrilla Messaging**
  Target high-traffic zones, corporate HQs, or civic buildings with counter-narratives. Projection becomes weaponized public discourse (Demos, 2016).

Legal and Tactical Considerations

Although projection is non-invasive, municipalities may cite activists under ordinances for loitering, disorderly conduct, or unauthorized use of public property. The Electronic Frontier Foundation (2020) emphasizes maintaining mobility, limiting duration, and avoiding projection into private residences or roadways.

<u>Best Practices:</u>

- Keep projection moving or change surfaces often.

- Avoid projecting into residential windows or roadways.

- Have an observer document the projection for media/share-out.
- Know your local ordinances around assembly, signage, and property use.
- Deploy in pairs: one operator, one lookout or media recorder.

Safety and Ethics

Tactical light messaging must align with broader movement ethics. Avoid provoking panic (e.g., projecting threatening symbols) and respect boundaries that safeguard marginalized communities.

Ask:

- *Who benefits from this message?*
- *Who might be endangered by this visibility?*
- *Does this tactic support or distract from the goal?*

Adaptability and Expansion Ideas

- Use Raspberry Pi or mini PCs for automation and remote control.
- Integrate audio via portable speakers synced to video projections.
- Coordinate with drones for aerial beam stunts or nighttime displays.
- Pair projection with livestreams to broadcast in real-time.
- Use motion sensors to trigger projections only when people pass by.

End Note: *For instructions on how to combine this projection rig with portable mesh networks or privacy routers, see Disruption Module A and Disruption Module B. These integrations allow teams to communicate securely while executing mobile light actions, ensuring coordination without digital exposure.*

Selected References

Castells, M. (2015). *Networks of Outrage and Hope: Social Movements in the Internet Age.* Polity Press.

Chatzichristos, G. (2022). Protest by projection: Light graffiti and digital occupation. *Media, Culture & Society,* 44(6), 1123–1139.

Demos, T. J. (2016). *Decolonizing Nature: Contemporary Art and the Politics of Ecology.* Sternberg Press.

Electronic Frontier Foundation. (2020). *Legal basics for protest tools.* https://www.eff.org/issues/legal

Greenpeace International. (2017). Light projection protests: A safe form of civil disobedience. https://www.greenpeace.org/

Juris, J. S. (2008). *Networking Futures: The Movements against Corporate Globalization.* Duke University Press.

Klein, N. (2020). *On Fire: The (Burning) Case for a Green New Deal.* Simon & Schuster.

Lievrouw, L. A. (2011). *Alternative and Activist New Media.* Polity Press.

Opensource.com. (2021). *How to build a portable projection rig.* https://opensource.com/article/21/6/projection-activism

Privacy International. (2022). *Activist Toolkits.* https://privacyinternational.org

The Illuminator Collective. (2018). https://theilluminator.org/

Zettl, H. (2011). *Sight, Sound, Motion: Applied Media Aesthetics*.Cengage Learning.

Disruption Module D

AR Activism – Augmented Reality for Social Justice

Legal Notice (read first)

This module examines augmented reality overlays as activist tools. While creative, AR installations in public or private spaces may trigger legal, safety, or privacy concerns. The content is educational and illustrative only. It does not substitute for legal or technical guidance. Readers must ensure compliance with applicable laws. Neither the author nor publisher accepts liability for consequences of application.

Augmented reality offers a new frontier for symbolic protest and educational campaigns. AR allows activists to overlay digital information or art onto physical spaces, turning phones into portals for alternative histories and urgent messages.

Augmented Reality (AR) allows activists to superimpose digital images, symbols, or messages onto the physical world using smartphones, tablets, or AR glasses. In contrast to physical protest methods, AR actions leave no permanent trace but can still disrupt narratives, claim space, and deliver truth to power (Azuma, 1997; Azuma et al., 2001).

AR bypasses traditional censorship by turning any phone camera into a lens for civil resistance. From reclaiming colonized statues with Indigenous messages to overlaying eviction notices on bank logos, AR enables precise, powerful, and often anonymous interventions in both public and private spaces (McGonigal, 2011; Nugent, 2021).

AR activism reimagines public space, not as a fixed, corporate-controlled medium, but as a dynamic, contested layer of meaning open to those with vision and tools (Tactical Tech Collective, 2021).

Overview

AR allows activists to digitally augment real-world locations with messages, art, or memorials. It can reclaim space symbolically without risking legal action, making it ideal for highlighting erased histories or injustices.

Hardware/Software List

- Smartphone or tablet with camera

- AR platforms (Platform Details Below): *Adobe Aero, Spark AR, Unity + ARKit/ARCore, 8th WallZapWorks (Unity Technologies, 2020; OpenXR Tutorial 2024; Adobe Aero Docs, 2023)*

- 3D content or geotagged visuals

- <u>Optional</u>: GPS marker app or QR code generator
  Recommended: Map Marker Pro: GPS waypoint app for Android
  Print link: https://play.google.com/store/apps/details?id=com.mictale.gpsessentials

"GPS marker apps allow activists to log precise geographic coordinates for physical locations. These waypoints can be used to anchor location-based AR content such as protest overlays, digital memorials, or narrative AR trails. When paired with platforms like Unity or 8th Wall, these coordinates enable geofenced experiences visible only in defined areas, ideal for targeting statues, buildings, or protest zones while minimizing risk and maximizing relevance."
— (Azuma et al., 2001; Opensource XR Handbook, 2022)

- <u>Optional</u>: AR use in challenges to Power
  Title: "Nancy Baker Cahill on Using AR to Challenge Power"
  Podcast: *Clever Podcast*, Episode 175
  Print link: https://www.cleverpodcast.com/blog/ep-175-nancy-baker-cahill

Understanding AR Platforms

An AR platform is a software tool that allows users to build, position, and publish augmented reality scenes. These platforms vary in complexity—from simple drag-and-drop apps to full developer environments—and choosing the right one depends on your goals, technical skills, and audience.

- **Adobe Aero**
  A no-code tool designed for ease of use. Ideal for beginners, Aero allows users to place 2D or 3D elements into the real world using just a phone or tablet. Scenes can be exported for viewing through mobile devices with minimal setup.
  (Adobe Aero Documentation, 2023)

- **Spark AR**
  Developed by Meta, Spark AR enables the creation of face- and world-tracking effects for Instagram and

Facebook. It's slightly more technical than Aero but still beginner-accessible. Scenes are deployed via social media platforms.
(Meta Spark AR Studio Docs, 2023)

- **Unity + ARKit/ARCore**
This is the industry standard for complex, interactive AR applications. It requires programming knowledge and is best for developers building standalone apps or intricate, interactive scenes. ARKit is Apple's framework; ARCore is Google's.
(Unity Technologies, 2020)

- **8th Wall**
A WebAR platform that enables users to create AR experiences viewable directly in mobile browsers—no app installation required. Ideal for fast outreach and broad compatibility.
(8th Wall WebAR Documentation, 2023)

- **ZapWorks**
A flexible platform supporting both marker-based and WebAR development. ZapWorks supports a range of user levels, from designers using ZapWorks Studio to developers using ZapWorks Universal AR SDKs.
(ZapWorks Product Suite, 2022)

Step-by-Step Build

1. Choose AR platform (e.g., Adobe Aero for drag-and-drop design)

2. Create 3D object, image, or animation linked to social issue

3. Assign GPS coordinates or marker image

4. Export and publish via app or WebAR

5. Place markers in public (QR codes, posters)

6. Promote with campaign hashtag or story-based walkthrough

Core Capabilities

- **Geolocation Tagging**: Target locations with digital graffiti, educational pop-ups, or campaign messages (Azuma et al., 2001).

- **Marker-Based Overlays**: Use posters, murals, or even QR codes to anchor custom AR scenes (Unity Technologies, 2020).

- **Live AR Streaming**: Broadcast overlaid content in real-time via social platforms.
- **Multi-User Syncing**: Share a coordinated AR protest experience among dozens or hundreds of viewers simultaneously.

Example Campaigns

- In 2020, the artist collective MoMAR used AR to "hijack" gallery spaces inside the Museum of Modern Art, replacing curated exhibits with commentary on institutional bias (MoMAR Gallery, 2020).
- In 2019, the app *4th Wall* allowed users to project anti-surveillance messages onto major tech campuses (The Verge, 2019).
- Indigenous communities have used AR to tell ancestral stories or label stolen land digitally, visible only through an app, reclaiming space in the colonial landscape (Nugent, 2021).

Tool / Platform	Use Case	Skill Level	Cost
ZapWorks	Drag-and-drop AR web editor	Beginner	Free/$
8th Wall	WebAR campaigns via browser	Intermediate	$/$$
Unity + Vuforia	Custom AR apps, scalable overlays	Advanced	Free
Adobe Aero	Mobile-first AR scene builder	Beginner	Free
Lens Studio	Snapchat AR filter creation	Intermediate	Free
Spark AR	Instagram/Facebook filter creation	Intermediate	Free

Basic Tools for AR Disruption

AR Tactic Types

- **WebAR Drop Points**
  Host interactive messages viewable via phone browsers; no app install needed. Ideal for low-friction outreach.

- **Geo-Fenced Messages**
  Deploy virtual content visible only within a defined GPS radius (e.g., a police station or corporate HQ).

- **Art Layer Infiltration**
  Override public art or monuments using AR triggers. For example, users viewing a Confederate statue may see it crumbling digitally with a message about systemic racism.

- **Participatory AR Trails**
  Turn a protest route into an AR path with digital artifacts that tell a story or issue calls to action at physical checkpoints.

- **Invisible Flyers**
  Post a blank image in real space (wall, pole, window). Through an AR lens, it becomes a radical statement.

Build Your First AR Overlay: Step-by-Step

1. **Choose Your Method**: WebAR for simple links, marker-based if you're using posters, Unity if you're custom coding.

2. **Design the Message**: Keep visual messaging clear. Include call-to-action links, activist hashtags, or voiceover if using video.

3. **Host the Content**: For WebAR, you'll need a URL with the AR scene. Use platforms like 8th Wall or ZapWorks.

4. **Deploy the Trigger**: Posters, flyers, QR codes, or specific GPS locations can serve as activation triggers.

5. **Test and Launch**: Run multiple tests on Android and iOS. Share clear instructions with your community on how to access it.

Situational Use Cases

- **Protest Augmentation**: Overlay demands or visuals atop buildings, police lines, or monuments.

- **Street-to-AR Galleries**: Transform boarded-up storefronts into galleries for marginalized voices.

- **Digital Occupations**: Geofenced AR overlays on corporate buildings symbolically occupy space.

- **Surveillance Counter-Tagging**: Identify facial recognition zones and display counter-surveillance info.

Legal and Ethical Considerations

While AR does not mark property, some laws may apply if your AR experience incites action, defames individuals, or creates hazards (Electronic Frontier Foundation, 2021). Platforms like Meta (Facebook) may also remove activist AR filters. Keep backups and understand takedown policies (Privacy International, 2022).

Best Practices:

- Provide clear opt-ins for multi-user experiences.

- Avoid content that might trigger panic, confusion, or re-traumatization.
- Ensure accessibility—use alt-text, audio, and contrast-aware design.
- Include disclaimers and fallback links if platforms remove content.

Security

- Host scenes on secure servers.
- Use VPNs when uploading content.
- Anonymize account ownership where needed.
- Encrypt links shared across organizing spaces.

Adaptability & Expansion Ideas

- Combine with Disruption Module A (Mesh Networks) to host AR offline via peer-to-peer connections.
- Sync AR with projection rigs (Disruption Module C) for hybrid experiences.
- Use Bluetooth beacons to trigger AR in areas without strong GPS.
- Integrate AR with street theater or flash mobs.
- Develop cross-border AR protests that appear in real time across cities.

End Note: *For privacy routing integration see Disruption Module B. For projection layering tactics see Disruption Module C. For offline peer-to-peer hosting see Disruption Module A.*

Selected References

Adobe. (2023). *Adobe Aero: Create interactive AR experiences.* https://www.adobe.com/products/aero.html

Azuma, R. T. (1997). A survey of augmented reality. *Presence: Teleoperators & Virtual Environments*, 6(4), 355–385. https://doi.org/10.1162/pres.1997.6.4.355

Azuma, R., Baillot, Y., Behringer, R., Feiner, S., Julier, S., & MacIntyre, B. (2001). Recent advances in augmented reality. *IEEE Computer Graphics and Applications*, 21(6), 34–47. https://doi.org/10.1109/38.963459

Electronic Frontier Foundation. (2021). *Augmented Reality and the Law.* https://www.eff.org/pages/ar-legal-rights

McGonigal, J. (2011). *Reality is Broken: Why Games Make Us Better and How They Can Change the World.* Penguin Press.

Meta Spark AR Studio. (2023). *Spark AR documentation.* https://sparkar.facebook.com/ar-studio/learn/

MoMAR Gallery. (2020). https://momar.gallery/

Nugent, C. (2021). AR and Indigenous Space Reclamation. *Journal of Media Activism*, 12(3).

OpenXR Tutorial. (2024). *OpenXR tutorial v1.0.11.* Retrieved from https://openxr-tutorial.com/

Privacy International. (2022). *Digital Tools for Resistance.* https://privacyinternational.org

Tactical Tech Collective. (2021). *Data and Activism Toolkit.* https://tacticaltech.org/projects/data-activism

The Verge. (2019). *How 4th Wall used augmented reality to challenge surveillance culture.* https://www.theverge.com/2019/08/12/ar-activism-4th-wall

Unity Technologies. (2020). *Introduction to AR development with Unity and AR Foundation.* https://unity.com/features/arfoundation

ZapWorks. (2022). *ZapWorks Product Suite Overview.* https://zap.works/

8th Wall. (2023). *WebAR Development Platform Overview.* https://www.8thwall.com/

Disruption Module E

Anonymous Broadcast Messaging in Blackouts

Legal Notice (read first)

This module explains anonymous broadcast systems and blackout-ready communication. Use of such tools may be restricted by telecommunications or national security laws. This material is for educational purposes only. Readers are solely responsible for evaluating legal risks before deployment. The author and publisher disclaim liability for misuse.

In events where traditional communications are suppressed, authoritarian blackouts, natural disasters, digital censorship, activists require tools that are both resilient and anonymous (Khanna et al., 2016; Tufekci, 2017). While traditional broadcast methods are surveilled or outright blocked, anonymous peer-to-peer mesh networking offers a viable and legal fallback. These systems bypass internet and cellular infrastructure entirely, relying instead on the silent spread of encrypted signals between devices.

Mesh broadcast tools like Rangzen and Briar allow protest organizers and community defenders to distribute real-time alerts, safety bulletins, and even multimedia content without requiring SIM cards, data plans, or centralized control. This makes them ideal for coordinating resistance during internet shutdowns or when physical safety depends on digital invisibility (Briar Project, 2023; Privacy International, 2022).

> "The most powerful messages often travel in silence, passed hand to hand, unseen by those who would silence them."
> —Unknown

Core Capabilities

Peer-to-Peer Relay

Messages are passed anonymously between nearby devices via Bluetooth or Wi-Fi Direct, no internet or cell towers required.

No Traceable Accounts

Most mesh tools use no logins or server-side accounts, helping prevent traceable metadata or identity exposure (Anwar et al., 2017).

Proximity-Based Spread

Messages spread organically via human movement, ideal for dense crowds, protest marches, or curfews (Khanna et al., 2016).

Hardware / Software List

- Android smartphones with Bluetooth + Wi-Fi Direct

- Rangzen or Briar mesh-messaging apps (no login needed) (Briar Project, 2023; Khanna et al., 2016)

- QR Resource: Rangzen Research Whitepaper

    - https://arxiv.org/abs/1612.03371

- GPS Essentials (See Disruption Module D)

    - https://play.google.com/store/apps/details?id=com.mictale.gpsessentials

Why GPS tools matter: Offline mapping tools like GPS Essentials enhance strategic coordination by letting users mark drop zones, navigate to rally points, or geotag where content was received, without internet or central servers. When paired with mesh broadcasting, this enables geospatial situational awareness in blackout zones.
—(Privacy International, 2022)

Build Your Broadcast Mesh: Step-by-Step

1. Install a Rangzen-compatible app (e.g., Briar) on multiple Android phones.

2. Preload key protest messages or alerts.

3. Enable Bluetooth and Wi-Fi Direct (Airplane Mode ON is recommended)(FCC, 2021).

4. Walk the phones through crowds, messages hop device to device.

5. Repeat and rotate phones to saturate high-risk zones (Khanna et al., 2016).

Use Case Scenarios

- **Authoritarian Blackouts**: Spread messages when internet/cellular services are shut down by the state (EFF, 2021).

- **Natural Disasters**: Share routes, aid locations, or emergency alerts when infrastructure fails (Privacy International, 2022).

- **Activist Drills**: Test these tools in simulated blackouts or communication drills (Tufekci, 2017).

Legal and Ethical Considerations

- **No Internet, No Intercept**: Messages never leave local devices, immune to takedowns or server seizure (EFF, 2021).

- **FCC-Compliant**: U.S. law permits use of short-range peer wireless (FCC, 2021).

- **Use Responsibly**: Avoid panic, misinformation, or risky content. Accuracy saves lives (EFF, 2021; Tufekci, 2017).

Adaptability & Expansion Ideas

- Pair with Briar to share encrypted PDFs, alerts, or multimedia files via peer-to-peer mesh (Briar Project, 2023).

- Use GPS Essentials to coordinate safe houses, rally points, or navigable paths offline (OsmAnd Project, 2023).

- Build a local zine library for transfer between phones using tools like SHAREit or Files by Google (Privacy International, 2022).

- Link to Disruption Module A (Mesh Networks) for offline host deployment infrastructure (Tactical Tech Collective, 2021).

- Integrate with Disruption Module D (AR Activism) to trigger location-based overlays during network outages or alerts during network blackouts (McGonigal, 2011; Tufekci, 2017).

Expanded Hardware / Software Toolkit for Anonymous Broadcast Messaging

Many of the tools listed above extend the functionality of mesh and offline communications but may be unfamiliar to newcomers. For instance, OsmAnd~ provides detailed offline maps using OpenStreetMap data, ideal for movement without cell signal. RetroShare is a decentralized platform that enables encrypted chat, forums, and file sharing even in closed systems. LoRa modules, such as those running Meshtastic, offer long-range, low-bandwidth broadcasting of text-based signals over radio waves, often used in wilderness or urban blackout scenarios. RTL-SDR dongles can receive a wide array of broadcast signals, from weather alerts to unauthorized transmissions. Apps like SimpleX Chat and Zeno Radio offer serverless communication or local audio rebroadcast, preserving operational security during crisis conditions (Briar Project, 2023; Meshtastic Docs, 2023; OsmAnd, 2023; Open Research Institute, 2022; Privacy International, 2022).

Core Communication Tools

- **Android smartphone** (required for mesh messaging)

- **Rangzen** – Anonymous text broadcasting (research-stage)

- **Briar** – Fully encrypted, peer-to-peer chat over Bluetooth/Wi-Fi

    - https://briarproject.org

Infrastructure & Navigation

- **GPS Essentials** – Offline navigation and waypoint coordination

    - Google Play

- **OsmAnd~** – OpenStreetMap-based offline maps

    - https://osmand.net

Offline Media Distribution

- **RetroShare** – Decentralized forums, files, encrypted chat

    - https://retroshare.cc

- **SHAREit** or **Files by Google** – Offline file transfer

- **USB OTG drives** – Load and distribute zines, manifests, etc.

Tactical Visual Layers (See Disruption Module D)

- **AR Tools** – Unity, Adobe Aero, Spark AR, 8th Wall

- **GPS Marker Apps** – Geotag digital overlays in physical space

Secure Broadcast & Radios

- **LoRa modules (Meshtastic)** – Encrypted, long-range packet radio
    - https://meshtastic.org
- **RTL-SDR dongles** – Listen to emergency or unauthorized signals

Encryption & Obfuscation

- **Orbot** – Access the Tor network on Android
- **OpenKeychain** – Encrypt messages with GPG
- **SimpleX Chat** – Newer serverless messenger

Other Offline-First Tools

- **Zeno Radio** – Record + distribute protest messages offline
- **Serval Mesh** (archived) – Earlier inspiration for Rangzen/Briar

On Blackouts, Authoritarian or Otherwise

"The first thing any regime does when it feels threatened is pull the plug—on speech, on signal, on solidarity."
—Unknown

Intentional communication blackouts are a defining feature of authoritarian control. Whether during mass protests, elections, or perceived threats to power, governments in countries like Iran (2022), Myanmar (2021), and Egypt (2011) have repeatedly cut internet or cellular networks to obstruct resistance. Even in democratic nations, blackouts have occurred in disaster zones, like during Hurricane Maria in Puerto Rico, or amid civil unrest, either through technical failure or tactical denial. In all cases, the effect is the same: disconnection as control.

Blackouts exploit a dangerous asymmetry. While state actors retain secure channels, the public is cast into communicative darkness. Protesters, organizers, journalists, and medics lose the ability to coordinate, warn, or verify. Truth becomes delayable, if not fully deniable. Social trust frays when signals vanish.

Blackouts as a Tool of Control

Modern authoritarian regimes have developed playbooks for suppressing dissent via connectivity throttling. Methods include:

- **Total shutdowns** (complete disconnection of mobile/internet services)

- **Platform-specific blocks** (e.g., WhatsApp, Twitter, Signal)

- **Bandwidth shaping** to simulate "technical failure"

- **Kill switch infrastructure** at the ISP or telco level (Marczak et al., 2020)

These disruptions are often paired with curfews, disinformation campaigns, or police actions, making traditional organization nearly impossible. In many cases, the aim is not just to stop communication—but to sow fear and break momentum.

Legal and Technical Realities

In the U.S. and most democracies, intentional communication blackouts by the government are legally murky and often unconstitutional, yet they've occurred. In 2011, BART (Bay Area Rapid Transit) temporarily disabled mobile service in San Francisco stations to preempt protest coordination, a move condemned by civil liberties groups (ACLU, 2011). Similarly, shutdowns in India have increased in frequency and duration, often justified on grounds of "public safety," despite violating international norms (Access Now, 2022).

Technically, most blackouts rely on centralized network chokepoints. Peer-to-peer, Bluetooth-based tools like Briar or Rangzen bypass this by skipping the internet entirely. Tools like LoRa, offline GPS apps, and USB transfers become not just fallback options, but essential pathways for free expression.

Survival Communications in the Digital Age (See the link below)

https://tacticaltech.org/news/survival-communications/
– by Tactical Tech

Tactical Tech Survival Guide
https://survival.tacticaltech.org/sites/survival.tacticaltech.org/files/Digital_survival_book.pdf

Psychological Impact and Strategic Response

The goal of blackouts is not only to block protest logistics but to isolate individuals from solidarity. Silence breeds uncertainty: *Has the movement collapsed? Are others still acting? Are we alone?* This uncertainty can lead to apathy or surrender.

Mesh-based systems counter this by restoring visible movement. When a single encrypted message jumps from phone to phone—"You are not alone. The protest is on. Meet here."—it rekindles resistance.

Blackouts don't have to mean darkness.

End Note: *For router-based defenses and decentralized backhaul, see Disruption Module B. For visual protest layers deployable even in blackouts, see Disruption Module D.*

Selected References

Access Now. (2022). *The state of internet shutdowns around the world: Annual report.* https://www.access-now.org/internet-shutdowns-2022/

American Civil Liberties Union (ACLU). (2011). *BART Pulls the Plug on Free Speech.* https://www.aclu.org/blog/bart-pulls-plug-free-speech

Anwar, M., Hossain, M. A., Hassan, M. M., & Alzahrani, A. (2017). Privacy-preserving friend discovery in mobile social networks. *Proceedings on Privacy Enhancing Technologies*, 2017(3), 1–16. https://doi.org/10.1515/popets-2017-0001

Briar Project. (2023). *Briar secure messaging.* https://briarproject.org

Electronic Frontier Foundation. (2021). *Emergency communications security.* https://www.eff.org

Federal Communications Commission. (2021). *Personal device broadcast regulations.* https://www.fcc.gov

Khanna, G., Sherr, M., Slabe, R., & Levitt, K. (2016). *Rangzen: Anonymously broadcasting messages during blackouts.* arXiv. https://arxiv.org/abs/1612.03371

Marczak, B., Scott-Railton, J., Razzak, B. A., Anstis, S., & Deibert, R. (2020). *Routing around censorship: Circumvention of censorship in Iran and Kazakhstan*. Citizen Lab. https://citizenlab.ca/2020/10/routing-around-censorship-circumvention-iran-kazakhstan/

McGonigal, J. (2011). *Reality is broken: Why games make us better and how they can change the world*. Penguin Press.

Meshtastic. (2023). *LoRa mesh communication platform*. https://meshtastic.org

Open Research Institute. (2022). *Understanding RTL-SDR and low-band radio scanning*. https://openresearch.institute

OsmAnd. (2023). *Offline navigation with open maps*. https://osmand.net

Privacy International. (2022). *Resilient communication in crisis zones*. https://privacyinternational.org

RetroShare. (2023). *Decentralized communication platform*. https://retroshare.cc

SimpleX. (2023). *Anonymous messaging without servers*. https://simplex.chat

Tactical Tech Collective. (2021). *Data and activism toolkit*. https://tacticaltech.org/projects/data-activism

Tufekci, Z. (2017). *Twitter and tear gas: The power and fragility of networked protest*. Yale University Press.

Zeno Radio. (2022). *Offline audio broadcast tools for crisis*. https://zenoradio.com

Disruption Module F

Zine Warfare – Physical and Digital Subversion

Legal Notice (read first)

This module discusses the creation and distribution of activist zines and subversive publications. Unauthorized distribution on private property, copyright infringement, or digital replication may violate local laws. The content is educational and historical, not legal advice. Readers bear full responsibility for compliance. Neither the author nor publisher assumes liability for misuse.

Zines are the insurgent pulse of resistance media. Born from underground music scenes, feminist collectives, and radical bookstores, zines offer a decentralized and DIY (do-it-yourself) alternative to corporate or censored channels. In modern dissent, they persist as potent tools for spreading uncensored ideas, mobilizing people, and preserving memory. Whether photocopied by hand or shared as encrypted PDFs over mesh networks, zines are fast, personal, and hard to silence.

This module provides a tactical breakdown for producing, distributing, and defending zines in both physical and digital forms. From street corners to encrypted folders, from handmade protest art to QR-linked manifestos, zine warfare remains a cornerstone of nonviolent rebellion.

Tactical Overview

Zines bypass traditional publishing barriers and surveillance. They are ideal for:

- Circulating banned or controversial content
- Amplifying marginalized voices
- Teaching tactics for resistance or mutual aid

- Archiving eyewitness narratives or counter-histories

Unlike digital-only tools, printed zines cannot be firewalled, censored, or easily deleted. And unlike traditional books, zines can be produced overnight and distributed anonymously.

Hardware / Software Toolkit

- Laptop or smartphone with document editing software (LibreOffice, Google Docs, Canva)
- PDF editor or printer driver (CutePDF, Print to PDF)
- Access to printers (personal, public library, office supply stores)
- Long-arm stapler or thread for binding
- Scanners or smartphone scan apps for analog-to-digital conversion (e.g., Adobe Scan, Microsoft Lens)
- Mesh network file-sharing apps (e.g., Briar, RetroShare, SHAREit)
- File encryption tools (e.g., OpenKeychain, VeraCrypt)
- CryptPad or Lufi for privacy-respecting collaborative writing and file drop
- Optional: Risograph machine for high-volume, textured zine printing
- QR code generators (e.g., goQR or open-source alternatives) to link digital content anonymously
- Use PDF/A for long-term offline readability; .epub for screen-friendly layouts

A Risograph is a stencil duplicator that blends the speed of photocopying with the texture of screen printing. Favored for its low cost and unique aesthetic, it is a staple in zine and activist publishing (Creative Independent, 2019).

CryptPad and Lufi are open-source, privacy-first platforms that allow collaborative document editing and anonymous file sharing without login or surveillance (PrivacyTools.io, 2023).

PDF/A is an archival format designed for offline longevity. .epub is reflowable, ideal for smaller screens and adaptable presentation.

Step-by-Step: Build a Zine Resistance Pipeline

1. **Content Creation:** Draft articles, poems, comics, photos, or protest guides. Focus on relevance, clarity, and impact. Use pseudonyms or collective bylines for safety.

2. **Design:** Use simple layouts (half-fold or quarter-fold) for easy assembly. Avoid metadata-heavy templates.

3. **Print:** Print black-and-white to keep a low profile. Use community print shops or libraries if personal printers are not secure.

4. **Bind:** Staple, fold, or stitch. Keep it small and portable. Pocket-sized zines are ideal for hand-to-hand or stealthy drops.

5. **Distribute:**
    - Leave at cafes, bookstores, restrooms, bus stops
    - Hand out at protests, vigils, or teach-ins
    - Hide within magazines, textbooks, or packages
    - Upload digitally using encrypted file shares

6. **Protect:**
    - Strip metadata from PDF files
    - Use pseudonyms and encrypted tools
    - Never include contact details unless you choose to organize openly

Adaptability and Expansion Ideas

- Pair with mesh-based distribution (see Disruption Module A and E)
- Translate and redistribute across language groups
- Integrate scannable codes for music, videos, or real-time updates
- Create issue-based zine series for long-term campaigns
- Print zines onto unconventional materials (fabric, tape, adhesive stock)

Legal & Ethical Notes

- Zine distribution is protected under free speech laws in many countries but check local ordinances for public posting.
- Do not plagiarize. Cite sources or create original content.
- Respect safety and privacy of contributors.

- Avoid hate speech or content that puts others at risk.

Additional Legal Considerations:

- **Public Posting Laws Vary:** Unauthorized posting of zines on public infrastructure (e.g., light poles, bus shelters, fences) may be considered vandalism, littering, or trespassing depending on local regulations. Always verify city ordinances before widespread distribution.

- **Sedition and Censorship Laws:** In countries with authoritarian governments or restrictive regimes, publishing materials that criticize state actors, policies, or security forces—regardless of accuracy—may fall under sedition, incitement, or "fake news" laws. Dissenters should research relevant legal risks before distributing material in such contexts.

- **Encryption Tool Restrictions:** While tools like OpenKeychain, VeraCrypt, CryptPad, and Lufi are legal in many jurisdictions, their use may be monitored or even criminalized in others. In regions where encrypted communications are restricted or surveilled, possession of such tools may carry additional scrutiny or legal consequences.

- **Metadata & Anonymity:** Even after PDF export or conversion, documents may retain metadata (e.g., usernames, timestamps, device serials) unless properly scrubbed. Use trusted anonymization tools and avoid using personally linked accounts or hardware if anonymity is crucial.

- **Copyrighted Media in Zines:** Incorporating copyrighted images, logos, or lyrics without permission can lead to takedown notices or legal claims, especially when distributing digitally. When in doubt, use public domain resources or those clearly licensed under Creative Commons or equivalent open licenses.

Mini Glossary

LibreOffice
A free and open-source office suite with robust offline document editing tools. Suitable for zine drafting on privacy-respecting operating systems. No citation needed.

Canva
A web-based design platform offering drag-and-drop layout tools. While convenient, its online nature may compromise anonymity unless precautions are taken. No citation needed.

CutePDF / Print to PDF
Printer drivers that convert documents into PDF format. Simple but useful for generating print-ready or distributable zine files. No citation needed.

Adobe Scan / Microsoft Lens
Mobile applications that convert images of paper documents into searchable PDFs. Useful for digitizing handwritten or analog zine content. No citation needed.

Briar
A peer-to-peer encrypted messaging app that uses Bluetooth or Wi-Fi rather than internet access, enabling offline communication ideal for resistance work.
Source: Briar Project (2023)

RetroShare
An open-source platform for encrypted friend-to-friend (F2F) file sharing and chat, often used in mesh-based communications.
Source: RetroShare (2023); PrivacyTools.io (2023)

SHAREit
A fast file-transfer tool often used in regions with limited internet access. Though efficient, its privacy policies vary across versions and may require scrutiny.

OpenKeychain
An Android-based tool for OpenPGP encryption, allowing users to encrypt messages and files using public-key infrastructure.
Source: OpenKeychain (2022)

VeraCrypt
A free, open-source encryption utility used to create secure containers for files or whole drives.
Source: VeraCrypt (2023)

CryptPad / Lufi
CryptPad is a zero-knowledge collaborative editing suite. Lufi allows anonymous file hosting and sharing with expiration dates. Both respect user privacy and leave no metadata trails.
Source: PrivacyTools.io (2023)

goQR / QR code generators
Online and offline tools to encode URLs or messages into quick-scan codes. Open-source options or privacy-respecting platforms like goQR are preferred.
Source: goQR (2023); Privacy International (2022)

Risograph
A stencil duplicator that combines speed with low-ink cost and screen-print-like output, favored by zine-makers

and art collectives.
Source: Creative Independent (2019)

MAT2 (Metadata Anonymization Toolkit 2)
A command-line tool that strips metadata from various file types, crucial for maintaining anonymity in digital zine distribution.
Source: GNOME (2023)

ExifTool
A metadata inspection and removal utility supporting a wide range of file formats. Helpful for ensuring PDFs or images don't leak personal data.
Source: ExifTool by Phil Harvey (2023)

PDF/A
An ISO-standardized version of the PDF format used for archiving. Ensures consistent rendering across systems and time.
Source: PDF Association (2022)

.epub
A reflowable digital book format ideal for phones and e-readers. Allows easier distribution and readability than fixed-layout PDFs. No citation needed.

End Note: *For secure messaging methods to share zines during blackouts or authoritarian crackdowns, see Disruption Module E. For visual overlays that pair well with zine QR codes, see Disruption Module D.*

Selected References

Briar Project. (2023). *Briar Secure Messaging.* https://briarproject.org

Creative Independent. (2019). *How to Risograph*. https://thecreativeindependent.com

Duncombe, S. (1997). *Notes from Underground: Zines and the Politics of Alternative Culture*. Verso.

Electronic Frontier Foundation. (2021). *Surveillance Self-Defense*. https://ssd.eff.org

ExifTool by Phil Harvey. (2023). *Metadata Removal Tool*. https://exiftool.org

GNOME. (2023). *Metadata Anonymization Toolkit 2 (MAT2)*. https://0xacab.org/jvoisin/mat2

goQR. (2023). *Free QR Code Generator*. https://goqr.me

OpenKeychain. (2022). *OpenPGP for Android*. https://www.openkeychain.org

PDF Association. (2022). *What is PDF/A?* https://www.pdfa.org/resource/what-is-pdfa

Privacy International. (2022). *Digital Tools for Resistance*. https://privacyinternational.org

PrivacyTools.io. (2023). *Encrypted Collaboration Platforms*. https://www.privacytools.io/

Red Scholezine Collective. (2020). *The Radical Zine Primer*. https://redscholezines.net

RetroShare. (2023). *Secure Friend-to-Friend Communication*. https://retroshare.cc

Tufekci, Z. (2017). *Twitter and Tear Gas: The Power and Fragility of Networked Protest*. Yale University Press.

VeraCrypt. (2023). *VeraCrypt Official Documentation*. https://www.veracrypt.fr

Disruption Module G

Drone-Based Messaging and Aerial Tactics

Legal Notice (read first)

This module explores drone deployment for messaging, leafleting, and visual disruption. Drone use is heavily regulated worldwide. Unauthorized flights may violate aviation, privacy, or safety laws and result in penalties. This module is provided for educational purposes only and does not constitute legal or flight training advice. Readers are responsible for full compliance with local aviation regulations. Neither the author nor publisher accepts liability for misuse.

When the ground is watched and the net is censored, the sky remains.

Civilian drones have become powerful tools for tactical messaging: they can drop printed flyers over fences, flash LED statements in the night, or carry symbolic payloads into spaces otherwise unreachable. This module outlines how to use drones for peaceful disruption; legally, precisely, and effectively.

It assumes no prior expertise, but it does not shy away from complexity. Each section offers plain-language explanations of the tools and tactics used, including terminology, hardware specs, and legal boundaries. If you're new to drones, flight planning, or payload design, treat this module as both a primer and a toolkit. If you're experienced, treat it as refinement. Either way, the goal is the same: to make the sky speak.

> "The engine is the heart of an airplane, but the pilot is its soul."
> —Walter Raleigh, *The Story of Aviation* (1929)

Tactical Overview

Drone messaging allows for:

- Bypassing ground barriers (police lines, fences, checkpoints)

- Messaging in high-visibility zones (corporate rooftops, government buildings)

- Distraction or redirection during coordinated protest events

- Symbolic intervention (e.g., flying protest banners or lights above monuments)

Compared to projections or zines, drone drops are ephemeral, but visible. Their spectacle can magnify the message when timed well.

Hardware / Software Toolkit

- **Consumer Drone with Payload Capability**
  DJI Mini, Parrot Anafi, Autel EVO, or similar models with camera and payload mods (DroneDJ, 2022; Consumer Reports, 2023).

- **Payload Mechanism Options**

  - **Servo-drop rig**:
    Controlled release using drone's auxiliary port or flight app scripting (DIY Drones, 2021).

  - **Timed drop**:
    Lightweight drop systems using servo motors or basic mechanical triggers can be assembled with hobbyist components or microcontroller timers (Instructables, n.d.).

  - **Manual release**:
    Fly low and tilt until object falls (least accurate).

- **Onboard Messaging Tools**

  - LED banner modules (programmable via mobile apps)

  - Flag poles / banner clips for micro-signage

  - Lightweight speakers (for chime alerts or slogans)

- **Flight Planning Software**

  - DJI Fly, Litchi, or open-source equivalents (e.g., QGroundControl) for waypoints (QGroundControl, 2023; Litchi, 2023).

  - Offline maps and pre-programmed routes reduce error and limit app dependency.

Step-by-Step: Drone Leaflet or Message Drop

1. **Prepare the Message**:
   - Design flyers, QR codes, or visual tags.
   - Use biodegradable paper or seed paper to reduce environmental impact.
   - QR codes can lead to encrypted zines or activist toolkits (see Disruption Module F) (EFF, 2021) – for operational security and privacy.

2. **Configure the Payload**:
   - Attach with lightweight tape, string, or drop hook.
   - Balance the load to prevent unstable flight.
   - Test the release from low height to ensure function.

3. **Pre-Program the Flight Path**:
   - Target open areas like rooftops, intersections, or parade routes.
   - Use offline planning tools to reduce location tracking.

4. **Fly and Drop**:
   - Fly during calm wind, preferably at dusk or night.
   - Monitor via FPV or from a hidden vantage point.

5. **Disengage and Exit**:
   - Land at a pre-planned site.
   - Power down, scrub flight logs, and secure equipment.

Legal & Ethical Considerations

<u>Know Your Airspace:</u>

- U.S. FAA rules (14 CFR Part 107) prohibit drones from flying over people, at night (without waivers), or in controlled airspace without permission (FAA, 2023a).

- Use B4UFLY (U.S.) or Drone Assist (UK) to check no-fly zones and Temporary Flight Restrictions (TFRs) (FAA, 2023b; UK Civil Aviation Authority, 2022).

- Altitude limit: 400 feet above ground level.

- Visual line of sight (VLOS) is required unless operating under special conditions.

Avoid Weaponization:

- Never attach hazardous materials, even symbolic ones (e.g., glitter, paint, red powder). These can violate anti-terror statutes or provoke dangerous reactions.

- Example: In the U.S., unauthorized drone use near power plants or "critical infrastructure" is a federal offense under the FAA Reauthorization Act (2018) (FAA Reauthorization Act, 2018).

Anonymity & Logs:

- Delete telemetry and app logs after the flight. Many drone apps upload data to cloud accounts unless disabled (EFF, 2021; Wired Staff, 2023).

- Avoid account-linked flight apps.

- Consider using burner phones and local storage modes.

Privacy & Trespass:

- Do not fly close to windows or homes.

- Focus on public landmarks or symbolic targets visible from the ground.

Environmental Ethics:

- Do not disrupt bird nests, roosting sites, or wildlife preserves.

- Avoid areas with endangered species or high ecological sensitivity.

Core Capabilities

- **High-Visibility Leaflet Drops**: Short aerial dispersals over marches, plazas, or public gatherings.

- **Symbolic Flyovers**: Banner flights over high-profile buildings or monuments.

- **LED Sky Messages**: Pre-programmed scrolling messages at night for visibility from ground.

- **QR-Tagged Payloads**: Zines or cards linking to offline activist toolkits (see Disruption Module A, E) (Privacy International, 2022; see also Disruption Module E)(Privacy International, 2022).

- **Emergency Drop Points**: Deliver flash-drives, encrypted messages, or first aid in disrupted zones.

Situational Use Cases

- **During Protests**: Release flyers above closed-off squares to inform or redirect crowds.

- **Silent Demos**: Fly symbolic items (e.g., child shoes, flowers) over war memorials or corporate buildings.

- **Counter-Messaging**: Deploy QR-embedded tags or zines on rooftops near propaganda displays.

- **Blackout Communication**: Drop USB keys with mesh software or emergency media during network outages (goTenna, 2023; NYU Tandon School of Engineering, 2021).

Adaptability & Expansion

- Pair with projection tools (Disruption Module C) for coordinated light-and-sky campaigns

- Use with mesh networking (Disruption Module A) to share real-time drone location and content

- Integrate with AR overlays (Disruption Module D) by pre-mapping drop zones with visual markers

- Train drone flight in VR or flight sims to reduce practice risk

Technical Explainers (Drone Messaging Terms)

DJI Mini / Parrot Anafi / Autel EVO

These are compact, consumer-grade drones with different capabilities:

- **DJI Mini**: Weighs under 250g, often avoids registration in the U.S. and other jurisdictions. Reliable for silent drops with moderate range.

- **Parrot Anafi**: Foldable and lightweight, noted for quiet operation and high vertical tilt.

- **Autel EVO**: Heavier but offers 4K cameras and modular upgrades for extended tasks.
  Reference: FAA (2023); Consumer Drone Guide by Wired, 2022.

Servo-Drop Rig

A mechanical payload release system operated by a small servo motor, wired into the drone's auxiliary port. The servo activates mid-flight via controller button or app command, allowing precise delivery of items such as zines,

USBs, or symbolic artifacts.
Reference: DroneU (2021), Servo Mechanisms in Tactical UAV Deployment.

Timed Drop
An alternative to servo mechanisms, these use a delay circuit (simple timer board or fuse-based mechanism) to trigger a release a few seconds after liftoff. Less precise but useful when signal access is limited.
Reference: Practical Electronics Journal (2020).

Manual Tilt Drop
Payloads are taped or clipped lightly under the drone, and the drone is flown at a sharp angle to cause the object to fall. Crude but requires no hardware.
Note: Best used for low-weight paper leaflets only.

LED Banner Modules
Strip-style programmable LED screens mounted on the drone body or a suspended frame, displaying scrolling text. Controlled via apps like Marquee LED, often linked to Android devices. Visibility varies by altitude and night conditions.
Reference: TechDIY (2023), Mobile LED Messaging Devices.

Litchi / QGroundControl

- **Litchi** is a commercial app for DJI drones that enables pre-set waypoint programming, autonomous path execution, and camera control. https://flylitchi.com/

- **QGroundControl** is open-source and supports non-DJI drones using PX4 or ArduPilot firmware. http://qgroundcontrol.com/
  These apps allow precise routing, critical for flyovers or targeted drops.
  Reference: IEEE Drone Systems 2021 Conference.

FPV (First-Person View)
A real-time video feed from the drone's camera streamed to a phone, tablet, or FPV goggles, enabling remote piloting even when the drone is out of sight. Essential for situational awareness in dynamic or sensitive drop zones.
https://oscarliang.com/fpv/
Reference: FAA Remote ID Report, 2023.

B4UFLY / Drone Assist

- **B4UFLY**: FAA's U.S.-based mobile app that informs users about airspace restrictions, no-fly zones, and local regulations. https://www.faa.gov/uas/getting_started/b4ufly

- **Drone Assist**: UK Civil Aviation Authority's app with similar features. Both ensure legal, safe, and

conflict-free operations. https://dronesafe.uk/drone-assist/
Reference: FAA (2023), UK Civil Aviation Authority (2022).

VLOS (Visual Line of Sight)

Most aviation authorities require drone pilots to maintain direct visual contact with their aircraft throughout the flight unless granted a **BVLOS** (Beyond Visual Line of Sight) waiver. Violations can result in legal penalties or confiscation.
Reference: FAA Part 107 Regulations; European UAS Rules, 2021.

QR-Tagged Payloads

Attaching printed QR codes to zines or cards allows drones to deliver access to digital content, such as encrypted PDFs, activist toolkits, or coordination messages. These can be scanned by recipients to download materials offline.
Reference: EFF Secure Comms Guide (2022).

USB Drop

Drones can carry flash drives containing emergency media (e.g., offline mesh network apps, protest footage, signal toolkits) to be dropped at predetermined locations.
Drives should be encrypted using tools like VeraCrypt.
Reference: Privacy International (2023); see also Disruption Module E.

Burner Phone

A low-cost, disposable phone used for controlling the drone and flight software, without linking it to personal accounts or identifiers. Prevents digital tracing if the drone is recovered or apps log usage.
Reference: EFF Surveillance Self-Defense, 2021.

Telemetry Logs

Drones automatically log flight paths, camera feeds, and environmental data. These logs may be stored locally or in the cloud via linked apps (e.g., DJI Fly). Delete or scrub these logs post-mission to avoid retrospective tracking.
Reference: Wired (2022), *"How Drones Store Your Data."*

Preloaded Maps & Airspace Overlays

To support safe and legal deployment, activists can use preloaded KML/KMZ map overlays for visualizing:

- No-Fly Zones (NFZs) near critical infrastructure

- Temporary Flight Restrictions (TFRs) during protests or events

- Safe launch/recovery corridors in urban terrain

- Pre-mapped protest routes or assembly zones
- Rooftop target zones for message drops or LED visibility

Map Overlays & Downloadable Example Pack

These overlays are provided in .kml (Keyhole Markup Language) and .kmz (compressed KML) file formats, standard for mapping tools such as Google Earth, QGroundControl, and Litchi (Google Earth Outreach, 2021; OpenStreetMap Foundation, 2022). They allow planners to visualize no-fly zones, ideal drop zones, symbolic targets, or landing paths on real-world maps. These files are especially useful in offline or network-denied environments, where mobile signal is weak or intentionally blocked.

Example Overlay Pack (For Demonstration Only)

To illustrate how overlays can assist drone-based messaging and protest planning, this module refers to sample files used by many mapping tools. These are not live links but represent typical file types for offline use.

Note: You do not need internet access to use these files once saved locally. They can be transferred via USB, Bluetooth, microSD, or shared over mesh networks (see Disruption Module A).

Contents include:

- NoFlyZones_2025.kml – Sample overlay of FAA-restricted airspace and key infrastructure
- MarchRoute_DowntownXYZ.kml – Demonstration path through symbolic public zones
- LandingCorridors_HighRisk.kmz – Compressed map of tight drone flight paths for obstacle-heavy areas
- DropTargets_PublicSquares.kml – Common symbolic targets such as courtyards, statues, or intersections

How to Use:
These files are readable in apps like Google Earth, QGroundControl, and Litchi. Users can import them on mobile or desktop devices and view them in 3D map layers. This simulates tactical flight paths or message drop zones.

Important:
If used during real operations, overlays should be customized to match local geography. Do not rely on sample files in active zones. Note: .kml files are readable by most GPS-capable mapping apps and can be imported directly into planning software. .kmz files contain the same info but are compressed for size and speed. Always verify route safety manually before deployment.

Use discretion when deploying in real-time. Ensure overlays are locally saved and not automatically synced to cloud accounts or tracking services.

End Note: *For digital content to pair with leaflet drops, see Disruption Module F. For anti-surveillance routing during drone prep or recovery, see Disruption Module B.*

Selected References

B4UFLY. (2023). *Mobile app and airspace education tools.* Federal Aviation Administration. https://www.faa.gov/uas/getting_started/b4ufly

Civil Aviation Authority. (2022). *Drone Assist user guidance.* https://www.caa.co.uk

Consumer Reports. (2022). *Best drones for beginners and hobbyists.* https://www.consumerreports.org

DJI. (2023). *DJI Mini 2 SE specifications.* https://www.dji.com/mini-2-se

DIY Drones. (2021). *Servo-drop rig mods and release mechanisms.* https://diydrones.com

DroneDJ. (2022). *Best drones for payload and mods.* https://dronedj.com

Electronic Frontier Foundation. (2021). *Surveillance self-defense.* https://ssd.eff.org

FAA. (2023). *Summary of Part 107 drone regulations.* Federal Aviation Administration. https://www.faa.gov/uas

Federal Aviation Administration. (2018). *FAA Reauthorization Act of 2018.* https://www.congress.gov/bill/115th-congress/house-bill/302

Google Earth Outreach. (2021). *KML reference guide.* https://developers.google.com/kml/documentation

goTenna. (2023). *Off-grid communications and mesh device ecosystem.* https://gotenna.com

Instructables. (n.d.). *Drone payload drop system: 7 steps.* Retrieved July 28, 2025, from https://www.instructables.com/Drone-Payload-Drop-System/

Litchi. (2023). *Waypoint mission software for drones.* https://flylitchi.com

NYU Tandon School of Engineering. (2021). *Mesh networks and disaster recovery.* https://engineering.nyu.edu

OpenStreetMap Foundation. (2022). *Using map overlays for civic planning.* https://wiki.openstreetmap.org

Privacy International. (2022). *Digital tools for resistance.* https://privacyinternational.org

QGroundControl. (2023). *Waypoint-based flight planning.* https://docs.qgroundcontrol.com

Raleigh, W. (1929). *The story of aviation.* Garden City Publishing.

Wired Staff. (2022). *The best drones for every budget. Wired Magazine.* https://www.wired.com/story/best-drones/

Disruption Module H

Bonus Tools and References

Legal Notice (read first)

This module lists supplementary tools for privacy, communication, and resistance. Some may be restricted or unlawful depending on jurisdiction. The information is provided for educational purposes only and does not constitute legal, security, or professional advice. Readers must ensure lawful and ethical use. The author and publisher disclaim liability for misuse.

For every disobedient campaign, there are tools that don't neatly fit into just one category. This module gathers diverse but essential instruments that complement the tactics covered elsewhere in this book. These include encryption apps, analog backups, visual range planning tools, and quick-reference templates to support offline readiness. Whether you're in a blackout, a surveillance zone, or simply working without a smartphone, these bonus tools help ensure your signal, *or your silence*, is intentional.

Encryption & Communication Tools

OpenKeychain
OpenKeychain uses OpenPGP public-key cryptography to encrypt, decrypt, and sign messages, files, or emails on Android devices. It's especially useful for distributing zines, route maps, or credentials without relying on cloud services. It integrates with apps like K-9 Mail and works offline, enabling peer-to-peer key sharing via QR code or NFC. Because it uses standard PGP keys, it's compatible with desktop tools like GPG, making it ideal for hybrid mobile-desktop workflows (Friedrich, 2022; OpenKeychain Project, 2023).

SimpleX Chat
SimpleX is a privacy-first, metadata-free messaging platform. Unlike Signal or WhatsApp, it does not require phone numbers or usernames. Each conversation is an ephemeral session tied to a temporary ID, ideal for protest comms

or short-term operations. Messages are routed through relay servers without revealing who is communicating, and all data is end-to-end encrypted. SimpleX supports group chats, file attachments, and asynchronous delivery, even over Tor (Petrov, 2023; Privacy International, 2023).

GNU Privacy Guard (GPG)

GPG is the gold standard for desktop encryption. It's command-line based but widely used for securing file shares, signing activist petitions, and protecting protester lists from interception. GPG works with email clients and can be layered with Tor or offline USB transport. It supports both symmetric and asymmetric encryption and offers advanced features like key expiration, revocation certificates, and trust signatures, making it a flexible tool for long-term operational security (Koch & GNU Project, 2022; EFF, 2021).

Mesh Messaging Integration

These encryption tools can be paired with goTenna Mesh, Briar, or other apps detailed in Disruption Modules A and E to create hybrid systems: encrypted, decentralized, and operational in offline or hostile environments.

Range and Visual Distance Tables

Legal Protest Distance Reference Table

A quick guide for understanding the legal boundaries of protesting near embassies, corporate HQs, or government sites. Always verify local laws. Sample values:

Location Type	Suggested Minimum Distance (U.S.)	Visual Planning Range
Government Buildings	100–300 ft (First Amendment zones)	~500 ft visibility
Private Residences	300 ft (varies by city)	~200–500 ft
Airports / Infrastructure	500 ft+ (Restricted by FAA)	>1000 ft (optics only)

(ACLU, 2022; FAA, 2023)

Visual Planning with Laser Rangefinders

Laser rangefinders help determine whether your projected light, drone drop, or physical presence will be visible from a distance. This assists in both legal compliance and message clarity. Some tactical units use DIY range charts based on Google Earth or KML overlays (Google Earth Outreach, 2021; Tactical Tech, 2020).

QR-Based Checklists & Emergency Templates

A QR code (Quick Response code) is a square-shaped, scannable barcode that stores information, most commonly links to websites, PDFs, images, or encrypted data. When printed or displayed, it can be scanned by most phone cameras or offline QR reader apps to instantly open preloaded content. In protest environments, QR codes serve as fast, stealthy delivery tools, often when speech, networks, or direct contact is risky (Electronic Frontier Foundation, 2021; Privacy International, 2022).

Use in Civil Resistance

QR codes are compact delivery mechanisms for PDFs, images, offline mesh links, encrypted zines, or zipped activist toolkits. They're especially useful when deployed via:

- Posters or zines (see Disruption Module F)

- Flash drives dropped by drone (Disruption Module G)

- Visual overlays in AR or shared signs (Disruption Module D)

Printable QR Checklists

- Bug-out bag contents for protest prep

- Medical response flowcharts for first responders or street medics

- Surveillance awareness checklists (e.g., spotting drones, detecting tailing)
  Embed QR codes in zines, posters, handouts, or even armbands for instant access. Scannable from low-resolution prints or even screens, these checklists enable rapid mobilization without verbal instructions (EFF, 2021; goTenna, 2023).

Emergency Broadcast Templates

- Pre-filled SMS alerts for dispersal or regrouping

- Offline webpages with mesh network setup guides

- Encrypted PDFs with legal contact info, digital safety protocols, or site instructions

- Flash-drive payloads with scannable labels linking to secure local files (e.g., encrypted zines, offline maps, or audio instructions)
  Flash drives can be air-dropped (see Disruption Module G) or handed off quietly. QR labels enable fast retrieval on any offline laptop or mobile device (DroneDJ, 2022; NYU Tandon School of Engineering, 2021).

Optional Expansion Tools

Tool	Use Case	Notes
goTenna Mesh	Off-grid texting and GPS pings	See Appendix A
Signal backup via QR	Manual QR handoff for verified contacts	No SIM or network needed
Paper key backups	Write down GPG keys in analog format	Laminate and store securely
QR-coded USB keys	Encrypted activist kits + offline guides	Use low-profile drives with basic .txt guide

These redundantly distributed QR tools ensure tactical reach even under blackout or surveillance conditions (Privacy International, 2022; OpenStreetMap Foundation, 2022).

Note on QR Code Generation

Use offline and FOSS (Free and Open Source Software) QR code generators such as:

- QR Code Generator (Offline, FOSS)

- QRTool on F-Droid
  Avoid personal or traceable URLs. Instead, use anonymous pastebin services or expiring cloud links. Always scan test your QR codes before printing or distributing (EFF, 2021; Legal Aid Society, 2022).

Hacktivist Operating Frameworks

Digital resistance can be more than messaging. Groups like Hacking//Hustling offer strategies for sex workers, queer dissidents, and marginalized communities targeted by surveillance capitalism. These networks develop:

- Operational security (OpSec) guidance specific to trans/queer activists

- Guides for resisting biometric surveillance and facial recognition

- Digital literacy for navigating platforms while evading algorithmic profiling

Learn more:
https://hackinghustling.org
https://hackblossom.org (for feminist cybersecurity guides)
https://github.com/hacktivist-fm/manual (Hacktivist Field Manual project archive)

Analog Fallback Systems

In blackout conditions, whether caused by state shutdowns, natural disasters, or targeted infrastructure sabotage, fallback tools become critical for preserving communication, organizing resistance, and documenting abuse. These tools are resilient, low-profile, and often legally ambiguous but vital.

CB Radios (Citizens Band)

CB radios allow unlicensed two-way communication across short distances—typically 1–5 miles depending on terrain and weather. They operate on 40 shared channels in the 27 MHz band, with Channel 9 reserved for emergencies and Channel 19 popular for general use and trucker chatter. CB radios require no infrastructure or cell towers, making them reliable in shutdowns or rural convoys. Handheld models are cheap and easy to use, though they offer no encryption or privacy (FCC, 2021; ARRL, 2023).

Learn more: https://www.fcc.gov/general/citizens-band-cb-service

HAM Radios (Amateur Radio)

HAM radio operators must pass a licensing test, but once certified, they can use high-powered radios to communicate locally, nationally, or even globally. HAM setups use a broad frequency range, including VHF, UHF, and HF bands. Voice, Morse code, and packet data are all supported, and many protest tech collectives use encrypted overlays or analog fallbacks with HAM infrastructure. Repeaters extend range, and solar or battery packs can keep systems running during blackouts (ARRL, 2023; Hackaday, 2022).

Learn more: https://www.arrl.org/getting-licensed

Shortwave Receivers

Shortwave radios passively receive global broadcasts on frequencies between 1.6 and 30 MHz. They don't transmit, so no license is needed. Listeners can access independent news, uncensored global radio, and encrypted activist updates outside censorship firewalls. Compact models work off AA batteries or solar, and many include NOAA weather bands or emergency alerts (Eibispace.de, 2023; SWLing Post, 2022).

Learn more: https://swling.com

Learn more: https://www.eibispace.de

Signal Mirrors

Signal mirrors are small, polished devices used to reflect sunlight and flash coded signals across long distances. Ideal for line-of-sight signaling during marches, border actions, or wilderness movement. Basic models include sighting holes for accuracy and can be seen from several miles away in sunlight. No electronics, batteries, or training required (Military Survival Manual FM 21-76, 2002).

Learn more: LoRa modules transmit data over kilometers using ultra-low-power signals. Projects like Meshtastic and Disaster.Radio build mesh networks with LoRa to send location data, short encrypted messages, and alerts. These devices are ideal for blackouts, border zones, and remote regions. No cell or Wi-Fi needed, just power and line-of-sight (for optimal performance)https://www.practicalsurvivor.com/signalmirror

LoRa (Long Range Radio Modules)
LoRa is a low-power digital radio protocol for transmitting encrypted packets over several kilometers. Paired with tools like Meshtastic or Disaster. Radio, it forms off-grid mesh networks for sending GPS, alerts, or messages, perfect for blackouts or remote actions (Meshtastic Project, 2022).
Learn more: https://meshtastic.org
Learn more: https://disaster.radio

OnionShare
OnionShare is a secure file-sharing app that works entirely over the Tor network. It creates a temporary, anonymous onion service to let users send files, host static websites, or receive messages without logging in or using cloud storage. Metadata is stripped, and content disappears after use. OnionShare runs on desktop and mobile, including Linux-based protest OSes (OnionShare Project, 2023).
Learn more: https://onionshare.org

Portable Solar Battery Packs
Solar USB battery packs charge phones, radios, mesh devices, and headlamps using sunlight. Useful in long-term occupations or remote actions, many models also include hand cranks, water resistance, and built-in flashlights. Choose high mAh capacity (10,000+) and test charging speed in advance. Some models can power LoRa, goTenna, or even HAM rigs (Wired, 2022).
Learn more: https://www.wired.com/story/best-portable-solar-chargers/

Emergency USBs with "Dead Man" TimersJust
These special flash drives auto-delete or publish their contents if not accessed within a set time. This protects critical files—like testimony, encrypted plans, or photos—if someone is detained or disappears. Some activist versions include hardware triggers, while others use open-source **Learn more**: https://securityinabox.org/en/guide/encrypted-usb/
Learn more: https://ssd.eff.orgscripts for Linux (EFF, 2021; Privacy International, 2022).

End Note: *For mesh networking protocols to support QR-distributed files and emergency broadcasts, see Disruption Module A and Disruption Module E. For projection-compatible overlays that pair with scannable visuals, consult Disruption Module C and D.*

Selected References

American Radio Relay League (ARRL). (2023). *What is HAM Radio?* https://www.arrl.org/what-is-ham-radio

Electronic Frontier Foundation (EFF). (2021). *Surveillance Self-Defense.* https://ssd.eff.org

Eibispace.de. (2023). *Shortwave Broadcast Schedules.* https://eibispace.de/

Federal Aviation Administration (FAA). (2023). *B4UFLY app and airspace rules for drone operators* https://www.faa.gov/uas/getting_started/b4ufly

Federal Communications Commission (FCC). (2021). *Citizens Band Radio Service.* https://www.fcc.gov/general/citizens-band-cb-service

Friedrich, V. (2022). *OpenKeychain: OpenPGP for Android.* OpenKeychain Project. https://www.openkeychain.org

Google Earth Outreach. (2021). *KML Reference Guide.* https://developers.google.com/kml/documentation

Hackaday. (2022). *Getting Started with Amateur Radio.* https://hackaday.com/tag/ham-radio/

HackBlossom. (n.d.). *DIY Guide to Feminist Cybersecurity.* Retrieved from https://hackblossom.org

Hacktivist Field Manual. (2020). *Mutual aid and disruption in digital space.* Retrieved from https://github.com/hacktivist-fm/manual

Hacking//Hustling. (n.d.). *Digital justice for sex workers and marginalized communities.* Retrieved from https://hackinghustling.org

Koch, W., & GNU Project. (2022). *GNU Privacy Guard.* https://gnupg.org

Legal Aid Society. (2022). *Know Your Rights Guide for Protesters.* https://legalaidnyc.org

Meshtastic Project. (2022). *LoRa-based mesh communication toolkit*. https://meshtastic.org

Military Survival Manual FM 21-76. (2002). *U.S. Army Survival Manual*. Department of the Army. https://archive.org/details/FM21-76

OnionShare Project. (2023). *Anonymous file sharing with OnionShare*. https://onionshare.org

OpenKeychain Project. (2023). *Security and Implementation Details*. https://github.com/open-keychain/open-keychain

Petrov, A. (2023). *SimpleX Chat Whitepaper*. https://github.com/simplex-chat/simplex-chat

Practical Survivor. (n.d.). *Signal Mirror Use and Techniques*. https://www.practicalsurvivor.com/signalmirror

Privacy International. (2022). *Digital Tools for Resistance*. https://privacyinternational.org

SWLing Post. (2022). *Field Guide to Shortwave Listening*. https://swling.com/

Tactical Tech. (2020). *Exposing the Invisible: Visibility and Distance in Civic Tech*. https://tacticaltech.org

Wired. (2022). *Best Solar Power Banks of the Year*. https://www.wired.com

Part IV

Staying Smart, Staying Safe

"Courage without caution is a trap. Smart dissenters live to fight again."
— Unknown

Chapter Thirteen

Real-Time Rescue: Emergency Legal Tactics and Contacts

Legal Notice (read first)

The information provided in this chapter is for educational purposes only. It does not constitute formal legal advice and should not be relied upon as a substitute for consultation with a licensed attorney. Laws vary by state and may change over time. If you are arrested, charged, or otherwise facing legal action, seek immediate assistance from a qualified lawyer or trusted legal aid organization in your jurisdiction.

Part III focused on the tactical arsenal: the tools and methods that make disruption possible. Part IV shifts the lens to survival: how dissenters stay smart and stay safe under pressure. This chapter begins with legal literacy, the foundation of all resilient action.

Field Note: The First Ten Minutes

The most dangerous time is the first ten minutes of detention. Words spoken in fear can be used against you; hesitation can leave you isolated. Rescue begins not with lawyers in courtrooms but with the choices you make in those moments: silence, preparation, and connection to those already waiting on the outside.

Context: Arrest Is a Tactic

Authoritarian systems use arrest as disruption. It is meant to separate leaders from groups, create fear, and generate confusion. Yet communities have survived—and resisted—by turning rescue into a tactic of its own. From Freedom Riders in the 1960s to Standing Rock water protectors in the 2010s, rapid-response jail support and preplanned legal networks have transformed individual detention into a collective defense strategy.

This chapter focuses on the **real-time phase of rescue**: what to do if you are seized, how to trigger support systems, and how to preserve your rights when the state attempts to take them away.

Tools of Real-Time Rescue

- **Jail Support Structure**: Jail support means that when one person is taken, others are ready outside. Having allies who can track arrestees, bring food, post bail, or wait outside detention centers prevents isolation and sends a signal of solidarity. Without this, a protester risks vanishing into the system unnoticed. Movements from Black Lives Matter to anti–pipeline blockades have shown that jail support pods transform detention from a silencing tactic into a shared moment of resilience.
  Learn more: *National Lawyers Guild Jail Support* – https://www.nlg.org/massdefense

- **Emergency Contacts**: Phones are often confiscated or disabled in custody. Writing emergency numbers (lawyer, family, bail fund) on your body with permanent marker ensures access when digital tools fail. This simple tactic prevents critical delays in notifying allies or arranging release.
  Learn more: *ACLU Protest Tips* – https://www.aclu.org/know-your-rights

- **Legal Rights Statements**: Stress and intimidation cause people to speak too much. A prepared, concise rights statement keeps you from self-incrimination. Carrying or memorizing a card with phrases like *"I am invoking my right to remain silent. I want a lawyer."* ensures consistency under pressure and protects against coercive questioning.
  Download: *NLG Bust Card Templates* – https://www.nlg.org/bustcards

- **Prepared Verbal Responses**: Police rely on fear to elicit information. Practicing specific verbal responses in advance; short, calm, repetitive, shields you from accidental disclosures. These mantras also communicate to others nearby how to assert their rights. Think of them as muscle memory for the mind.
  Learn more: *Miranda Rights Basics (US Courts)* – https://www.uscourts.gov/about-federal-courts/educational-resources/constitutional-highlights/bill-rights

- **Community Legal Networks**: Few individuals can navigate the legal system alone. Community legal networks—lawyer collectives, bail funds, immigrant support groups—exist precisely to prevent isolation. By plugging into them before you act, you ensure immediate backup when the state moves against you.
  Directory: *Community Justice Exchange Bail Funds* – https://www.communityjusticeexchange.org/nbfn-directory

Know the Signs

Recognizing when rights are violated is the first defense. Free speech is curtailed when chants are labeled "incitement." Unlawful searches occur when bags are rifled without cause. Excessive force escalates from dispersal tactics to beatings. Denial of counsel begins the moment you are interrogated without a lawyer.

If you can identify these moments, you can document them, resist them lawfully, and trigger accountability processes. Ignorance leaves you defenseless.

Resource: *ACLU Know Your Rights Guides* – https://www.aclu.org/know-your-rights

Recording is evidence—but evidence can be seized or turned against you. Many cases of police brutality only reached courts because someone filmed. But open filming can invite retaliation or confiscation. Apps like **ACLU Mobile Justice** send video directly to secure servers, while **ObscuraCam** blurs bystanders to prevent later targeting. Safe recording balances the need for accountability with protection for yourself and others.

- **ACLU Mobile Justice** – https://www.aclu.org/issues/criminal-law-reform/reforming-police/mobile-justice
- **ObscuraCam** – https://guardianproject.info/apps/obscuracam

Legal Resource Networks

When you are detained, the support you've arranged dictates how quickly you return.

- **National Lawyers Guild (NLG)** – Provides trained legal observers at protests and coordinates jail support. (https://www.nlg.org/massdefense)
- **ACLU State Chapters** – Offers legal challenge and litigation support. (https://www.aclu.org/about/affiliates)
- **First Amendment Lawyers** – Independent attorneys with expertise in protest defense. (https://firstamendment.law/)
- **National Immigration Law Center (NILC)** – Critical for immigrant and undocumented protesters facing detention risk. (https://www.nilc.org/)
- **Bail Fund Collectives** – Pools of money that free people quickly, keeping communities intact. (https://www.communityjusticeexchange.org/nbfn-directory)

State-Specific Tools

Every jurisdiction is different. Some states have strong protections, others criminalize assembly aggressively. Knowing local tools means faster action:

- Call "Know Your Rights" hotlines where available (https://www.nlg.org/bustcards).

- Contact law school clinics that offer emergency advocacy.
- Identify civil rights attorneys with protest defense experience via ACLU affiliate directories (https://www.aclu.org/about/affiliates).

Local knowledge turns a national movement into a community-specific shield.

Digital Escalation

Evidence is worthless if lost. Uploading to encrypted cloud services (like *Proton Drive* – https://proton.me/drive) ensures survival beyond device seizure. Platforms like *SecureDrop* (https://securedrop.org/) allow whistleblowers to submit material safely. Timed release functions mean even if you are detained, information spreads. Digital escalation is the modern equivalent of smuggling letters out of prison—an act of survival and of defiance.

Organize Locally

Real-time rescue cannot be outsourced. Local rapid response groups—mutual aid pods, watchdog organizations, bail collectives—act immediately, while national organizations mobilize more slowly. At Standing Rock, local rapid response was the difference between release within hours and disappearance into federal custody.

- **Mutual Aid Hub** – https://www.mutualaidhub.org/
- **Mapping Police Violence** – https://mappingpoliceviolence.org/

Templates and Scripts

Stress makes speech unreliable. Scripts are anchors:

- **Asserting Rights**: *"I am invoking my right to remain silent. I want a lawyer."*
- **Contacting Legal Aid**: *"I was arrested at [location]. Please notify my legal contact."*
- **Reporting Abuse**: Complaint templates from the *National Police Accountability Project* (https://www.nlg-npap.org/) guide victims in documenting misconduct.

These prepared words prevent panic from becoming self-incrimination.

End Note: *For broader legal context, including constitutional precedents and long-term legal risks, see Chapter 14: Legal Considerations and Risks. For communication strategies during blackouts and raids, consult Disruption Module E: Anonymous Broadcast Messaging.*

Selected References

American Civil Liberties Union. (n.d.). *Know your rights: Demonstrations and protests.* https://www.aclu.org/know-your-rights

Community Justice Exchange. (n.d.). *National bail fund directory.* https://www.communityjusticeexchange.org/nbfn-directory

Guardian Project. (n.d.). *ObscuraCam.* https://guardianproject.info/apps/obscuracam/

Mutual Aid Hub. (n.d.). *Directory of local mutual aid networks.* https://www.mutualaidhub.org/

National Lawyers Guild. (n.d.). *Mass defense program.* https://www.nlg.org/massdefense

National Police Accountability Project. (n.d.). *Resources and complaint templates.* https://www.nlg-npap.org/

Proton AG. (n.d.). *Proton Drive: Encrypted cloud storage.* https://proton.me/drive

SecureDrop. (n.d.). *Whistleblower submission platform.* https://securedrop.org/

U.S. Courts. (n.d.). *Bill of Rights.* https://www.uscourts.gov/about-federal-courts/educational-resources/constitutional-highlights/bill-rights

Chapter Fourteen

Legal Considerations and Risks

Legal Disclaimer

The information provided in this chapter is for educational purposes only. It does not constitute formal legal advice and should not be relied upon as a substitute for consultation with a licensed attorney. Laws vary by state and may change over time. If you are arrested, charged, or otherwise facing legal action, seek immediate assistance from a qualified lawyer or trusted legal aid organization in your jurisdiction.

Field Note: Emergencies Pass, Records Remain
The handcuffs may come off, but the system rarely lets go so quickly. Charges, surveillance files, and immigration risks linger long after the sirens fade. Surviving detention is only the first test. The second is living with what the state tries to make permanent.

Context: Why After Matters

Chapter 13 focused on **real-time rescue**: how to protect yourself in the crucial first minutes of arrest. This chapter addresses what comes next — the long tail of legal risk. Arrests do not end when you leave a cell. Court hearings, immigration proceedings, surveillance records, and public narratives all continue. Preparing for these consequences ensures that one bad night does not destroy a life, a family, or a movement.

Understanding the Legal Terrain

Constitutional protections still exist in the United States — but they are selectively enforced. After protest arrests, prosecutors and police often stretch the law to set examples, chilling dissent. Understanding your rights helps you anticipate charges and defend against overreach.

- **First Amendment**: Protects speech, press, and assembly, but not incitement, credible threats, or property

destruction.
See full text: https://www.archives.gov/founding-docs/bill-of-rights-transcript (see also *Tinker v. Des Moines*, 1969).

- **Fourth Amendment**: Guards against unreasonable searches and seizures. In practice, phones and digital devices are frequently targeted (see *Riley v. California*, 2014).
See full text: https://www.archives.gov/founding-docs/bill-of-rights-transcript

- **Fifth Amendment**: Grants the right to remain silent and not self-incriminate — crucial once interrogations begin after an arrest (see *Miranda v. Arizona*, 1966).
See full text: https://www.archives.gov/founding-docs/bill-of-rights-transcript

Case Law Examples:

- *Tinker v. Des Moines* (1969) — Protected student protest rights unless substantially disruptive.

- *Riley v. California* (2014) — Required a warrant to search digital contents of a cellphone.

- *Carpenter v. United States* (2018) — Warrant required for historical cell site location data.

Why this matters after an arrest:
Emergencies end, but legal exposure unfolds in stages: citation or booking → arraignment → discovery → motions → plea/trial → sentencing → record consequences. Knowing where your case sits on this timeline helps you decide what to say (usually nothing), what to gather (documents, witnesses), and when to push (motions to suppress based on unlawful search/seizure, or to dismiss vague/overbroad charges). Guidance from civil liberties groups can also orient your choices at each stage (American Civil Liberties Union [ACLU], n.d.).

Immigration and Citizenship Risks

For immigrants and even legal residents, the aftermath of arrest is far riskier. ICE detainers can turn minor infractions into deportation proceedings.

- **Birthright Citizenship** (14th Amendment) protects those born on U.S. soil, but undocumented individuals face removal even for low-level charges (*United States v. Wong Kim Ark*, 1898).
Full text: https://www.archives.gov/founding-docs/amendments-11-27

- **DACA and TPS recipients** are especially vulnerable to status revocation (National Immigration Law Center [NILC], n.d.).

- **Naturalized citizens** can face rare but serious denaturalization if fraud is alleged (American Immigration Lawyers Association [AILA], n.d.).

Case Law Examples:

- *United States v. Wong Kim Ark* (1898) — Confirmed birthright citizenship.

- *Zadvydas v. Davis* (2001) — Limited indefinite detention of non-citizens.

- *Arizona v. United States* (2012) — Affirmed federal supremacy over immigration enforcement.

Why the "after" is different for non-citizens:

Post-arrest, even dismissed charges can trigger **ICE detainers**, immigration court dates, or bond hearings. Outcomes hinge on paperwork and timing: ensure counsel immediately requests **immigration-safe dispositions**, and that you have a **family preparedness plan** (emergency caregivers for children, powers of attorney, medical consent forms). Practical, multilingual materials from advocacy groups can help you prepare (NILC, n.d.; Immigrant Legal Resource Center [ILRC], n.d.; Immigrant Defense Project [IDP], n.d.; AILA, n.d.).

QR Resources and Key Tools:

- National Immigration Law Center (NILC): https://www.nilc.org/ (NILC, n.d.)

- Immigrant Defense Project – ICE Encounter Card: https://www.immigrantdefenseproject.org/icewatch (IDP, n.d.)

- Immigrant Defense Project – ICE Encounter Card (Spanish): https://www.immigrantdefenseproject.org/icewatch-spanish (IDP, n.d.)

- ACLU Immigration Rights Resources: https://www.aclu.org/issues/immigrants-rights (ACLU, n.d.)

Additional Immigration Support Resources:

- Local ACLU Affiliate Locator: https://www.aclu.org/about/affiliates (ACLU, n.d.)

- National Immigration Law Center – Community Education Resources: https://www.nilc.org/get-involved/community-education-resources/know-your-rights/ (NILC, n.d.)

- Toolkit for Responding to Worksite Immigration Raids (ILRC): https://www.ilrc.org/worksite-enforcement-toolkit (ILRC, n.d.)

- Immigrant Legal Resource Center: https://www.ilrc.org/ (ILRC, n.d.)

- American Immigration Lawyers Association: https://www.aila.org/ (AILA, n.d.)

Civil Disobedience vs. Criminal Activity

Acts of **civil disobedience** — sit-ins, road blockades, refusing dispersal orders — are intentional, nonviolent lawbreaking. Courts may still impose fines, probation, or records. Prosecutors, however, often escalate charges toward conspiracy or riot, reframing protest as crime.

Case Reference:

- *Brandenburg v. Ohio* (1969) — Speech cannot be punished unless it incites imminent lawless action.

Why this matters:
Understanding the line between civil disobedience and criminal activity allows movements to calibrate risk. Defense strategies can invoke historical precedents of civil disobedience to contextualize actions as legitimate dissent, not criminal mischief (ACLU, n.d.).

High-Risk Identities and Marginalized Vulnerabilities

After arrest, the system is not neutral. Some groups face harsher outcomes:

- **BIPOC protesters** — disproportionately charged and brutalized.

- **Trans and queer activists** — risk misgendering and unsafe jail placements.

- **Disabled activists** — may be denied medication or mobility aids in custody.

- **Undocumented people** — risk ICE notification.

- **Journalists, medics, and observers** — increasingly swept up despite supposed protections.

Why this matters:
Post-arrest treatment reflects systemic bias. Allyship means anticipating these vulnerabilities and structuring support networks accordingly (ACLU, n.d.; National Lawyers Guild [NLG], n.d.).

Digital Surveillance in the Aftermath

Even if you walk free, your devices and digital trail may remain in the system. Metadata and app use can be subpoenaed. Encryption tools are legal, but prosecutors often frame them as evidence of secrecy.

- **Metadata is not protected** — your communication patterns can be used (*United States v. Graham*, 2016).

- **Biometric unlocks** (face/fingerprint) are less protected than PINs (see *Riley v. California*, 2014).

- **Faraday bags, burner phones, and VPNs** can reduce exposure but are not foolproof (Electronic

Frontier Foundation [EFF], n.d.; Digital Defense Fund [DDF], n.d.).

Case Law Examples:

- *United States v. Graham* (2016) — Metadata collection upheld under the third-party doctrine.

- *Carpenter v. United States* (2018) — Warrants required for cell site data.

After the Protest: Damage Control & Repair

Emergencies end, but the paperwork begins. Long-term resistance requires damage repair:

- **Seek movement lawyers** — public defenders are overburdened (NLG, n.d.; ACLU, n.d.).

- **Document everything** — badge numbers, times, witnesses (ACLU, n.d.).

- **Stay offline about charges** — prosecutors scour social media (ACLU, n.d.; EFF, n.d.).

- **Pursue record sealing/expungement** where possible (National Association of Criminal Defense Lawyers [NACDL], n.d.).

If bail or fines create barriers to release or court compliance, look for mutual-aid bail networks and directories that can assist with rapid financial support (Community Justice Exchange, n.d.).

Tools:

- NACDL Record Clearing Guide: https://www.nacdl.org/Legal-Resources/Record-Sealing-Expungement (NACDL, n.d.)

Why this matters:
Damage control prevents one arrest from defining a lifetime of vulnerability. Criminal records can affect employment, housing, immigration, and custody battles. Expungement or record sealing is not guaranteed but is often underutilized; proactive legal repair can restore mobility and reduce long-term surveillance (NACDL, n.d.; ACLU, n.d.).

Organizations to Know

- National Lawyers Guild — protest defense, jail support: https://www.nlg.org/massdefense (NLG, n.d.)

- ACLU — civil liberties litigation and guidance: https://www.aclu.org/ (ACLU, n.d.)

- Electronic Frontier Foundation (EFF) — digital rights: https://www.eff.org/ (EFF, n.d.)

- Digital Defense Fund — encryption and abortion access security: https://digitaldefensefund.org/ (DDF, n.d.)

- Firestorm Coop and local mutual aid legal collectives: https://firestorm.coop/ (Firestorm Coop, n.d.)

Tactical Legal Literacy: Turning Law into Leverage

Even after facing charges, dissenters can weaponize the law itself:

- **Bureaucratic flooding** — overwhelm systems with FOIA requests or permit filings.

- **Rule literalism** — obey absurd laws so precisely they reveal their contradictions.

- **Legal mimicry** — use the language of courts and bureaucracy against itself.

- **Lawful absurdity** — satire through hyper-compliance.

These tactics are most effective when coupled with public education and movement legal support (NLG, n.d.; ACLU, n.d.).

End Note: *For immediate guidance on what to do in the moment of arrest, see Chapter 13: Real-Time Rescue. For technical countermeasures to surveillance and escalation tools, see Disruption Modules G and H.*

Selected References

American Civil Liberties Union. (n.d.). *Know your rights: Demonstrations and protests.* https://www.aclu.org/know-your-rights

American Immigration Lawyers Association. (n.d.). *Immigration law resources.* https://www.aila.org/

Arizona v. United States, 567 U.S. 387 (2012).

Brandenburg v. Ohio, 395 U.S. 444 (1969).

Carpenter v. United States, 585 U.S. ___ (2018).

Community Justice Exchange. (n.d.). *National bail fund directory.* https://www.communityjusticeexchange.org/nbfn-directory

Digital Defense Fund. (n.d.). *Security resources.* https://digitaldefensefund.org/

Electronic Frontier Foundation. (n.d.). *Digital rights resources.* https://www.eff.org/

Firestorm Coop. (n.d.). *Collective resources.* https://firestorm.coop/

Immigrant Defense Project. (n.d.). *ICE encounter cards.* https://www.immigrantdefenseproject.org/icewatch

Immigrant Legal Resource Center. (n.d.). *Worksite enforcement toolkit.* https://www.ilrc.org/worksite-enforcement-toolkit

Miranda v. Arizona, 384 U.S. 436 (1966).

National Association of Criminal Defense Lawyers. (n.d.). *Record clearing guide.* https://www.nacdl.org/Legal-Resources/Record-Sealing-Expungement

National Immigration Law Center. (n.d.). *Know your rights resources.* https://www.nilc.org/get-involved/community-education-resources/know-your-rights/

National Lawyers Guild. (n.d.). *Mass defense program.* https://www.nlg.org/massdefense

Riley v. California, 573 U.S. 373 (2014).

Tinker v. Des Moines Independent Community School District, 393 U.S. 503 (1969).

United States v. Graham, 824 F.3d 421 (4th Cir. 2016).

United States v. Wong Kim Ark, 169 U.S. 649 (1898).

Zadvydas v. Davis, 533 U.S. 678 (2001).

Chapter Fifteen

Funding the Fight: Economics of Resistance

Financial & Compliance Disclaimer

The information in this chapter is for educational purposes only. It is not legal, financial, tax, or compliance advice. Laws and platform policies vary by jurisdiction and change over time. Consult a qualified attorney, accountant, or compliance professional before implementing any strategy described here (IRS, 2024; FinCEN, 2019; OFAC, 2021).

Field Note: Money as a Weapon

Movements rise on passion, but they endure on resources. Every authoritarian regime understands this truth. That is why they target bank accounts, criminalize fundraising, and monitor donations. To resist effectively, dissenters must learn to treat economics as part of their strategy — a battlefield where power is won or lost.

Context: The Economics of Dissent

Repression is not just physical. It is financial. Bail amounts, legal fees, medical costs, surveillance technology, and even loss of employment are intended to drain movements dry. Funding resistance, therefore, is not charity — it is infrastructure.

History shows this clearly. Civil rights movements relied on church tithes and pooled community bail funds. Anti-apartheid struggles built global boycotts and solidarity funding networks. Contemporary protest movements have turned to mutual aid, crowdfunding, and cryptocurrency to evade blockades (Boykoff, 2011; McAlevey, 2016; Spade, 2020).

Why this matters: If funding collapses, legal defense fails, arrestees languish, organizing stalls, and the public narrative tilts toward "unsustainable chaos." If funding is resilient, resistance stabilizes, defendants return to the streets, and momentum continues (McAlevey, 2016; Spade, 2020).

Tools for Funding Resistance

Bail Funds and Legal Defense Pools

Collectives like the Community Justice Exchange maintain bail and bond networks so arrestees are not trapped by poverty (Community Justice Exchange, n.d.). These funds turn community care into immediate freedom and blunt the state's use of pre-trial detention as punishment.

Why it matters
Bail is not about guilt or innocence — it is about wealth. A wealthy person can leave jail the same night; a poor person may sit for months awaiting trial. Bail funds neutralize this inequality and keep organizers active.

How to implement
Set intake criteria, such as which charges are supported. Create a release follow-up system (for example, text reminders for court dates). Establish reimbursement rules for when bail is returned. Pair this with court support volunteers and "defendant navigators" — people who guide defendants through confusing legal steps like arraignments or plea hearings. Use a "revolving fund" model, meaning money returned from bail goes back into the pool to free someone else.

Governance and transparency
Adopt written rules on conflicts of interest, case selection, repayment handling, and privacy. Publish quarterly anonymized dashboards (how many supported, how much posted, outcomes) to prove accountability.

Risks and mitigations
Banks may freeze activist funds. Keep accounts at more than one bank and hold a portion of funds in non-bank reserves (Open Collective, n.d.). Donor fatigue is another risk. Rotate fundraising appeals, diversify donors, and demonstrate real results.

Key metrics
Percentage bailed within 24 hours; average bail size; rate of court appearances.

Mutual Aid and Community Chests

Mutual aid extends beyond food and housing; it sustains activism by covering transport, child care, medications, and emergency stipends (Spade, 2020). Small, local contributions add up to big resilience.

Why it matters
Repression isolates people. Mutual aid bridges that gap by ensuring no one has to abandon activism due to costs like rent, bus fare, or medicine.

How to implement
Map recurring needs. Build a micro-grant system (very small grants, often under a few hundred dollars, that can be distributed quickly). Aim for 48-hour turnaround. Sometimes provide non-cash support like gift cards or transit passes. Keep records visible but anonymized so donors know where money goes while recipients stay safe (EFF, n.d.; Open Collective, n.d.).

Risks and mitigations
If too much personal data is collected, participants can be exposed. Minimize data collection and restrict access (EFF, n.d.). If only a few people decide on disbursements, favoritism may creep in. Rotate reviewers and publish equitable criteria.

Key metrics
Requests met versus requests unmet; average time to disbursement; percent of aid reaching marginalized groups.

Crowdfunding and Digital Platforms

GoFundMe, Action Network, and Open Collective can raise money quickly but may freeze accounts if campaigns are deemed "political" or controversial (Open Collective, n.d.).

Why it matters
Crowdfunding can raise thousands in small donations and build solidarity. The downside is dependency on corporate platforms that can ban accounts without warning.

How to implement
Run "mirror campaigns," meaning the same fundraiser on at least two platforms at once. Withdraw funds every 48–72 hours to reduce exposure. Set up an off-platform fallback such as mailed checks or direct transfers. Prepare a "continuity kit" — a backup copy of your campaign text, graphics, and donor list — so you can relaunch quickly if de-platformed.

Governance and controls
Post budgets and receipts publicly. Require two people to approve withdrawals (dual-control). *Dual-control simply means two authorized people must approve any movement of funds, reducing error and fraud.* Publish monthly aggregate income and expense statements.

Risks and mitigations

Platforms may shut down campaigns unexpectedly. Maintain redundancy and keep archives. Fraud concerns can undermine trust; appoint independent treasurers, enforce dual logins, and do internal audits.

Key metrics

Total fees taken by platforms, donor churn, average gift size, percent of funds frozen or reversed. *Donor churn means the percentage of prior donors who do not give again in a later period.*

Cryptocurrencies and Alternative Finance

When banks or processors block activists, cryptocurrency can serve as a backup. Bitcoin is widely used but traceable. Privacy coins like **Monero** are designed to obscure sender and receiver. **Stablecoins** are tokens pegged to a fiat currency like the U.S. dollar, meant to reduce volatility (Coin Center, n.d.; FinCEN, 2019; OFAC, 2021; IRS, 2024).

Why include this tool

Governments often pressure banks to cut off movements. Cryptocurrency is harder to censor, can cross borders instantly, and supports anonymous giving when managed carefully.

Plain-language essentials

- **Wallets and keys:** A wallet is a program or device that stores your private key. That key is like a password: whoever controls it controls the money. Hardware wallets (small USB-like devices) keep keys offline, making them safer than laptops or phones.

- **Hot versus cold storage:** A "hot wallet" is connected to the internet and used for small, frequent transactions. A "cold wallet" is kept completely offline for large reserves. Think of a hot wallet like the cash in your pocket and cold storage like a safe in the basement.

- **Multisig (multi-signature):** Multisig requires more than one approval before money moves. For example, a 2-of-3 arrangement means three people each hold a key, and at least two must approve a withdrawal. This protects against theft, mistakes, or a lost key.

- **On- and off-ramps:** These are the services that let you buy crypto with cash (on-ramp) or sell it back to cash (off-ramp). Most regulated services require government ID for these steps.

- **Stablecoins:** Cryptocurrencies tied to stable assets such as the dollar. They reduce volatility but depend on issuers. Diversifying issuers (for example, USDC and DAI) reduces risk.

- **Privacy trade-offs:** Bitcoin is transparent; anyone can trace transactions. Privacy coins reduce linkability, but using illegal "mixers" can trigger compliance issues (OFAC, 2021).

How to implement

Design a treasury with multisig so no single person can move funds. Store most funds offline in cold storage; keep only small amounts online. Write paper-based runbooks with step-by-step guides for transactions and store them securely in more than one place. Log every transaction with date, purpose, and value; reconcile monthly (IRS, 2024). Publish simple donor guidance (for example, warning that funds from sanctioned addresses cannot be accepted). Train at least two people in setup and recovery drills.

Risks and mitigations

Key loss or theft can destroy access to funds. Mitigate with multisig, hardware wallets, and recovery practice. Legal risks include sanctions or reporting duties; screen transactions and keep a quarantine option (OFAC, 2021). Converting crypto to cash creates tax obligations; track all conversions (IRS, 2024). Volatility can be reduced by converting donations quickly into stablecoins or cash reserves.

Key metrics

Percent of funds in cold storage; days of operating runway covered; exposure to volatility.

Boycotts and Divestment Campaigns

Redirecting capital can be as powerful as raising it. Boycotts weaken corporate collaborators, and divestment forces institutions to withdraw funding from harmful industries (Boykoff, 2011).

Why it matters

Money is leverage. Boycotts and divestment deny resources to oppressive actors and pressure them to change.

How to implement

Pick narrow, winnable targets. Define demands and exit criteria. Build coalitions. Track results with petitions, corporate statements, divestment commitments, and press coverage.

Risks and mitigations

Broad or vague campaigns lose focus. Set specific goals, use timelines, and create visible milestones.

Key metrics

Number of divestment commitments, policy changes, media coverage.

Cooperative Economics

Worker cooperatives and community-run businesses — such as print shops, cafés, or farms — create sustainable funding and anchor local power. Properly structured, they are harder to seize than personal accounts (McAlevey, 2016; Spade, 2020).

Why it matters

Donations may dry up. Co-ops create renewable revenue streams and embed the movement in durable, lawful institutions.

How to implement

Choose the right structure (co-op, nonprofit, or social enterprise). Draft bylaws for democratic decision-making and rules for how profits are reinvested. Build conservative cash-flow projections and maintain reserves for legal emergencies. Add an "asset lock" clause — a rule in co-op bylaws that prevents members from selling off assets for personal profit.

Risks and mitigations

Mission drift is common. Codify values in bylaws to keep focus. Managerial overload can happen; train multiple treasurers and keep clear written procedures.

Key metrics

Percent of revenue reinvested in movement goals; number of months of reserves.

Additional Tools

- **Governance & Transparency Controls**
  Establish a finance committee; adopt a **two-signature** rule for disbursements; schedule **quarterly mini-audits**; publish **anonymized transparency reports**. These practices deter fraud and build donor confidence (Open Collective, n.d.).

- **Platform Risk & Redundancy**
  Map exposure to banks/processors (ACH, wires, Stripe/PayPal). Maintain **secondary bank accounts**, a **credit union** option, and at least one **non-platform donation method** (PO Box + checks/money orders). De-risk by distributing balances across institutions. ACH (Automated Clearing House) means bank-to-bank transfers processed in batches; they are slower than wires but cheaper and widely supported.

- **Donor Privacy & Data Security**
  Collect only what you need; encrypt donor spreadsheets; restrict access by role; set **90-day deletion** policies; rehearse breach response (EFF, n.d.; DDF, n.d.).

- **Budgeting & Scenario Planning**
  Track **burn rate**; maintain **3–6 months runway**; plan **best/base/worst case** scenarios; set **trigger points** for spending freezes or emergency appeals. *Track burn rate (average monthly spending) and maintain 3–6 months of runway (the number of months you can operate with current cash if income stopped).*

- **Compliance 101 (Nonprofit & Political)**

If operating through a 501(c)(3)/(c)(4), learn lobbying/campaign limits; document **restricted vs. unrestricted** gifts; consult counsel on **international donations**, currency controls, and reporting (IRS, 2024; FinCEN, 2019).

End Note: *Economics is not an afterthought. It is the bloodstream of resistance. For guidance on emergency bail strategies, see Chapter 13: Real-Time Rescue. For long-term legal repair and financial protection, see Chapter 14: Legal Considerations and Risks.*

Selected References

Boykoff, J. (2011). *The suppression of dissent: How the state and mass media squash protest.* Routledge.

Coin Center. (n.d.). *Policy resources on cryptocurrency and civil liberties.* https://coincenter.org/

Community Justice Exchange. (n.d.). *National bail fund directory.* https://www.communityjusticeexchange.org/nbfn-directory

Digital Defense Fund. (n.d.). *Security guidance for nonprofits and clinics.* https://digitaldefensefund.org/

Electronic Frontier Foundation. (n.d.). *Atlas of surveillance.* https://atlasofsurveillance.org/atlas

Electronic Frontier Foundation. (n.d.). *Security and privacy resources for organizers.* https://www.eff.org/

Financial Crimes Enforcement Network (FinCEN). (2019). *Application of FinCEN's regulations to certain business models involving convertible virtual currencies.* https://www.fincen.gov/

GoFundMe. (n.d.). *Crowdfunding campaigns.* https://www.gofundme.com/

Internal Revenue Service (IRS). (2024). *Virtual currency—FAQs on tax treatment.* https://www.irs.gov/

McAlevey, J. (2016). *No shortcuts: Organizing for power in the new gilded age.* Oxford University Press.

Mutual Aid Hub. (n.d.). *Directory of mutual aid groups.* https://www.mutualaidhub.org/

Office of Foreign Assets Control (OFAC). (2021). *Sanctions compliance guidance and virtual currency FAQs*. https://home.treasury.gov/policy-issues/financial-sanctions/faqs

Open Collective. (n.d.). *Transparent community finance and fiscal hosting*. https://opencollective.com/

Spade, D. (2020). *Mutual aid: Building solidarity during this crisis (and the next)*. Verso.

Chapter Sixteen

Knowing More, Risking Less: Tactical Intelligence for Resistance

Legal–Ethical Use Notice (read first)

This chapter focuses on *lawful* and *ethical* information practices that use publicly available sources and consent-based data. Nothing here authorizes or encourages harassment, hacking, stalking, trespass, doxxing (publishing someone's private information without consent), or evasion of law enforcement. Follow the law where you live, the terms of service of any platform or dataset, and your movement's code of conduct. When in doubt, get legal advice and choose the safer path.

Why intelligence matters

You cannot counter repression without awareness. Tactical intelligence — the process of gathering and validating information — allows activists to anticipate risks, recognize misinformation, and stay one step ahead of hostile forces. Here we explore the practical use of open sources, social media, counter-infiltration practices, legal trend monitoring, tactical mapping, and misinformation detection. All of these tools rely on careful use of public data, transparency, and safety culture.

OSINT for Activists: Search, Maps, and Metadata

Open-source intelligence (OSINT) refers to information available from public sources such as websites, social media, satellite imagery, news articles, and court records. Used correctly, OSINT helps activists verify claims, locate resources, and identify risks.

Practical applications:

- **Search verification.** Use "lateral searching" by opening new tabs to check who created a claim, whether reliable outlets corroborate it, and if original sources are accessible. The SIFT method (Stop, Investigate the source, Find better coverage, Trace to the original) is a simple workflow for this process.
  Resource: https://hapgood.us/2019/06/19/sift-the-four-moves/

- **Geolocation.** Geolocation means determining where a photo or video was taken using visible landmarks, signage, or natural features. Comparing these against maps like OpenStreetMap can confirm location.
  Resource: https://www.bellingcat.com/resources/how-tos/2014/07/09/a-beginners-guide-to-geolocation/

- **Chronolocation.** Chronolocation is the process of confirming *when* media was captured. Clues include weather conditions, sun angle, or event-specific context.

- **Metadata.** Metadata is "data about data." In photos, **EXIF** (Exchangeable Image File Format) may include timestamp, GPS location, camera type, and lens settings. It is useful for verification but can also reveal private details if not removed before sharing.
  Resources: https://en.wikipedia.org/wiki/Exif ; https://photographylife.com/what-is-exif-data

Risks:

Publishing unredacted EXIF may expose activists' personal locations. Always strip sensitive metadata before posting; preserve originals securely when evidence may be legally important.

Social Media Monitoring of Opposition Groups

Monitoring **public posts** and **open groups** can provide early warnings of counter-protests or organized campaigns. This must be done without harassment, impersonation, or deception.

Key patterns:

- **Coordinated inauthentic behavior (CIB).** CIB describes groups of accounts that pose as ordinary users but are centrally coordinated to push a message. Signs include identical posts, synchronized timing, or artificial amplification.
  Resources: https://graphika.com/bad-reputation ; https://cyber.fsi.stanford.edu/news/how-coordinated-inauthentic-behavior-continues-social-platforms

- **Provocateur accounts.** These are social media accounts that encourage activists to escalate into illegal or dangerous actions. They often appear suddenly, lack history, and push extreme rhetoric.

Verification practices:

Cross-check all posts before amplifying. Use tools like reverse image search, secondary coverage checks, and OSINT methods to validate claims.

Risks:

Amplifying false narratives gives them reach. Avoid reposting questionable material unless it is for analysis, and then only share within trusted circles.

Counter-Infiltration by Building a Culture of Safety

Infiltration occurs when outside actors join meetings or chats to gather intelligence or incite actions. The best defense is not paranoia or witch-hunts but cultivating a **security culture**: collective norms and practices that reduce risk.

Practical methods:

- Apply need-to-know access: only share sensitive details with those directly responsible.
- Use two-person integrity: require two trusted members to approve sensitive actions.
- Draft a short code of conduct stating that incitement, secrecy pressure, or pushing violence are unacceptable behaviors.
- Collect as little data as possible and securely delete unnecessary records after events.

Risks:

Paranoia and false accusations can fracture movements. Focus on safeguarding processes, not labeling individuals.

Resource: Security in-a-Box (Front Line Defenders and Tactical Tech) https://securityinabox.org/en/

Tracking Legal Trends

Laws shift quickly. Tracking legal changes keeps activists from being blindsided by protest restrictions, surveillance budgets, or new prosecution tactics.

Sources to monitor:

- **Court records:** PACER (paid) and CourtListener/RECAP (free archive).
  PACER: https://pacer.uscourts.gov/
  CourtListener RECAP: https://www.courtlistener.com/recap/
- **State legislation:** Open States provides search and alert functions.

https://open.pluralpolicy.com/

- **Local surveillance tech:** EFF's Atlas of Surveillance catalogs where police use drones, body cams, or facial recognition.
  https://atlasofsurveillance.org/atlas

- **FOIA and public records:** MuckRock provides guides and tools for filing requests.
  https://www.muckrock.com/about/foia-101/

Risks:
Legal texts are often technical and may be misinterpreted. Partner with lawyers or advocacy groups for clarity.

Tactical Mapping and Movement Pattern Analysis

Mapping is not only for city planners. Tactical mapping ensures protests are safe, accessible, and prepared for emergencies.

Applications:

- Use **OpenStreetMap** to mark paths, ramps, and dispersal routes.
  https://www.hotosm.org/

- Apply **QGIS** (open-source mapping software) to overlay elevation, transit, or first-aid locations.
  https://docs.qgis.org/latest/en/docs/user_manual/index.html

Best practices:

- Plan multiple dispersal routes.

- Place medics and water near density points.

- Always print physical maps; digital devices can fail.

Risks:
Avoid publishing sensitive routes or details. Keep public maps generic and circulate detailed versions only to trusted roles.

Strategic Misinformation Detection

Falsehoods can cripple movements. Distinguishing misinformation (false, not malicious), disinformation (false and malicious), and malinformation (true but weaponized) is critical.

Methods:

- Apply the **SIFT method** for every claim.
  https://hapgood.us/2019/06/19/sift-the-four-moves/

- Verify media with reverse image search and geolocation.
  Guide: https://www.bellingcat.com/resources/2021/11/01/a-beginners-guide-to-social-media-verification/

Provocateur accounts:

Recognize patterns: sudden creation, extreme rhetoric, and pushing violence. Document posts with timestamps but avoid amplifying.

Risks:

False alarms can erode trust. Always confirm with a second reviewer before issuing advisories.

End Note: *For emergency legal defense, see Chapter 13. For post-arrest recovery and long-term protections, see Chapter 14. For financial sustainability of movements, see Chapter 15. Together, these chapters complement Chapter 16, showing how lawful information gathering works as both shield and strategy when combined with defense, recovery, and sustainability practices.*

Selected References

Amnesty International. (n.d.). *Citizen Evidence Lab*. Retrieved from https://citizenevidence.org/

Bellingcat. (2014, July 9). *A beginner's guide to geolocation*. Retrieved from https://www.bellingcat.com/resources/how-tos/2014/07/09/a-beginners-guide-to-geolocation/

Bellingcat. (2021, November 1). *A beginner's guide to social media verification*. Retrieved from https://www.bellingcat.com/resources/2021/11/01/a-beginners-guide-to-social-media-verification/

Caulfield, M. (2019). *SIFT: The four moves.* Retrieved from https://hapgood.us/2019/06/19/sift-the-four-moves/

Electronic Frontier Foundation. (n.d.). *Atlas of surveillance.* Retrieved from https://atlasofsurveillance.org/atlas

Electronic Frontier Foundation. (n.d.). *Surveillance self-defense.* Retrieved from https://ssd.eff.org/

Exposing the Invisible. (n.d.). *Behind the data: Metadata investigations.* Tactical Tech. Retrieved from https://exposingtheinvisible.org/en/guides/behind-the-data-metadata-investigations/

Graphika. (n.d.). *Bad reputation: Research reports on inauthentic networks.* Retrieved from https://graphika.com/bad-reputation

MuckRock. (n.d.). *FOIA 101.* Retrieved from https://www.muckrock.com/about/foia-101/

Open States. (n.d.). *Legislative search and API.* Retrieved from https://open.pluralpolicy.com/

Stanford Internet Observatory. (2023). *How coordinated inauthentic behavior continues on social platforms.* Retrieved from https://cyber.fsi.stanford.edu/news/how-coordinated-inauthentic-behavior-continues-social-platforms

Wardle, C., & Derakhshan, H. (2017). *Information disorder: Toward an interdisciplinary framework for research and policymaking.* Council of Europe. Retrieved from https://edoc.coe.int/en/media/7495-information-disorder-toward-an-interdisciplinary-framework-for-research-and-policy-making.html

Wikipedia. (n.d.). *Exchangeable image file format (EXIF).* Retrieved from https://en.wikipedia.org/wiki/Exif

Chapter Seventeen

Security and Anonymity in Activism

Legal–Ethical Use Notice (read first)

This chapter addresses ways to strengthen anonymity and security in lawful activist practice. Nothing here authorizes or encourages harassment, hacking, impersonation, or unlawful concealment from legal obligations. Follow the law where you live, honor your movement's code of conduct, and seek independent legal counsel when in doubt.

Why Security and Anonymity Matter

Movements cannot endure without protecting their people. Surveillance, infiltration, and coercion thrive where security culture is weak. Conversely, when activists adopt disciplined practices, they sustain momentum even under heavy scrutiny. Security defends against unwanted access. Anonymity obscures personal identity. Together, they give a movement breathing room to persist.

Authoritarian states know this. From East Germany's Stasi to the FBI's COINTELPRO, repression has often succeeded not by overpowering ideas but by exploiting weak security practices. Movements that lasted, the samizdat underground in the Soviet bloc, the Zapatistas in Mexico, civil rights organizers in the U.S. South, endured because they created cultures of protection around their members.

> "Anonymity is a shield from the tyranny of the majority." — Justice John Paul Stevens, *McIntyre v. Ohio Elections Commission* (1995)

Anonymity and security are not luxuries. They are conditions of survival.

Digital Discipline: Shrinking Your Attack Surface

Every click, search, and message generates a digital exhaust: logs of time, location, and device that can be pieced together to identify a person. Most breaches are not caused by spectacular hacks but by small leaks in everyday behavior.

Applications:

- Minimize the number of devices/accounts tied to your identity.

- Use dedicated activist browsers (e.g., Firefox with privacy extensions) while keeping personal browsing elsewhere.

- Strip metadata from photos before sharing with https://exiftool.org/l or the Guardian Project's https://guardianproject.info/apps/obscuracam/.

Risks:

- Syncing calendars, fitness trackers, or smart assistants can betray movements.

- A VPN or Tor browser helps, but poor habits (reusing logins, linking accounts) erase any benefit.

Best practice: Start with behavior, not tools. Adopt a group norm that phones are off during sensitive planning and that accounts used for movement work never cross into personal life.

Burners and Compartmentalization

Disposable phones and laptops are not magical shields — they are only effective when combined with strict discipline. A burner phone used once to log into a personal email address is no longer a burner; it is simply a second phone. The principle is separation.

Applications:

- One device for research, one for communications, one for storage.

- SIM cards purchased with cash and rotated regularly.

- Apps installed only as needed; avoid personalization.

Risks:

- Crossing compartments even once (e.g., logging into social media on a burner) can collapse the wall.

- Repeated purchase patterns (same store, same payment method) can still link burners together.

Resources:

https://www.privacyguides.org/en/mobile-phones/

Physical OPSEC: Protecting Presence

Operational security in the physical world protects against observation and pattern recognition.

Applications:

- Vary routes and transportation methods.
- Meet in public, fluid spaces (libraries, community centers) rather than homes.
- Keep physical notes minimal; shred or burn when no longer needed.

Risks:

- Identifiable accessories (backpacks, hats, pins) can connect appearances across protests.
- Consistent routines make surveillance easy.

Behavioral Security: The Human Factor

The hardest leaks to patch are human. The Black Panthers collapsed under FBI infiltration less because their ideas were weak than because discipline around access was uneven.

Applications:

- Adopt "need-to-know" access rules.
- Draft a movement code of conduct rejecting secrecy pressure or incitement.
- Conduct periodic "red-team drills" simulating phishing, infiltration, or misinformation attempts.

Risks:

- Overzealous suspicion can fracture groups.
- Paranoia without structure leads to burnout.

Resource: https://tacticaltech.org/projects/security-in-a-box/ (Front Line Defenders & Tactical Tech).

Biometric Traces and the Expanding Net of Surveillance

Modern surveillance hunts not only names and numbers but bodies. Biometrics include fingerprints, facial recognition, iris scans, voiceprints, and gait.

Applications:

- Disable biometric unlock features (Face ID, Touch ID) before actions; rely on strong passcodes.

- Practice "panic shortcuts" (e.g., iPhone's side button press to require passcode).

- Alter predictable behaviors (stride, voice exposure).

Risks:

- Courts often compel fingerprints or facial unlocks but protect memorized passcodes (*Riley v. California*, 2014; EFF, 2021).

The Trap of Everyday Metadata

Fitness trackers, smart watches, and vehicles with telematics constantly emit metadata. Police now use automated license plate readers (ALPRs) across cities.

Applications:

- Power down devices during sensitive activity.

- Favor public transit or shared rides over personal cars with GPS logs.

- Use Faraday bags to block signals when carrying devices.

Resource: https://ssd.eff.org/.

Collective Anonymity and Its Double-Edged Sword

Movements throughout history have adopted collective identities to shield individuals — from Soviet-era samizdat writers to the modern Anonymous collective.

Applications:

- Shared accounts must have rotating custodianship and internal logging.

- Pseudonyms help separate speech from legal identity.

- Consensus required before posting under collective banners.

Risks:

- Collective anonymity without governance creates openings for provocateurs.
- Lack of accountability can erode trust.

Emergency Vanish Protocols

When risk spikes, survival depends on the ability to vanish quickly.

Applications:

- Maintain "go bags" with essentials for sudden relocation.
- Prepare digital vanish kits: encrypted partitions, prepaid SIMs, and hotkey-triggered data wipes.
- Rehearse protocols as drills, like fire alarms.

Resource: https://freedom.press/digisec/guides/.

Silent Signals and Low-Tech Anonymity

High-tech tools are not the only means of anonymous communication. Silent signals — chalk marks, ribbons, folded papers — have coordinated resistance for centuries.

Applications:

- Use symbols that blend into the environment.
- Maintain simple codes only insiders understand.

Risks:

- Over-complication reduces usability.
- Public discovery may compromise signals.

The Psychological Toll of Disappearing

Living under multiple identities creates paranoia and fatigue. Edward Snowden (2019) described it as "a prison without bars."

Applications:

- Peer support groups ("care pods").

- Affinity group debriefs that address emotional health.

- Rituals of decompression: meals, storytelling, walking together.

Risks:

- Over-securing beyond real risks can cause isolation.

- Neglecting mental health erodes long-term resilience.

End Note: *For legal consequences of exposure, see Chapter 13 (Legal Considerations and Risks). For technical countermeasures and secure setups, see Disruption Module A (Building a Mesh Network) and Disruption Module B (Raspberry Pi Protest Tools). Disruption Module H lists additional encryption tools. Together, these reinforce that security is not a single action but a culture: sustained, disciplined, and collective.*

Selected References

American Civil Liberties Union. (2020). *Know your rights: Digital privacy at protests*. ACLU. https://www.aclu.org/

Coleman, G. (2014). *Hacker, hoaxer, whistleblower, spy: The many faces of Anonymous*. Verso Books.

Dingledine, R., Mathewson, N., & Syverson, P. (2004). Tor: The second-generation onion router. *Proceedings of the 13th USENIX Security Symposium*, 303–320.

Electronic Frontier Foundation. (2021). *Face ID and fingerprints: Know the risks of biometrics*. Electronic Frontier Foundation. https://www.eff.org/deeplinks/2021/07/face-id-and-fingerprints-know-risks-biometrics

Electronic Frontier Foundation. (n.d.). *Surveillance self-defense*. Electronic Frontier Foundation. https://ssd.eff.org/

Exposing the Invisible. (n.d.). *Behind the data: Metadata investigations*. Tactical Tech. https://exposingtheinvisible.org/en/guides/behind-the-data-metadata-investigations/

Ferguson, A. (2019). *The rise of big data policing: Surveillance, race, and the future of law enforcement*. NYU Press.

Freedom of the Press Foundation. (n.d.). *Emergency security resources*. Freedom of the Press Foundation. https://freedom.press/training/

Greenberg, A. (2017). *This machine kills secrets*. Penguin.

Mitnick, K. D., & Simon, W. L. (2002). *The art of deception: Controlling the human element of security*. Wiley.

Narayanan, A., & Shmatikov, V. (2008). Robust de-anonymization of large sparse datasets. *IEEE Symposium on Security and Privacy*, 111–125.

Patel, V., Chellappa, R., Chandra, D., & Barbello, B. (2015). Continuous speaker verification using background noise modeling. *IEEE Transactions on Audio, Speech, and Language Processing, 23*(3), 401–412.

Scott, J. (2018). Against anonymity theater: Real security in protest movements. *Journal of Resistance Studies, 4*(1), 65–84.

Snowden, E. (2019). *Permanent record*. Metropolitan Books.

United States Supreme Court. (1995). *McIntyre v. Ohio Elections Commission*, 514 U.S. 334.

Wired. (2022, June). Why you should turn off Face ID at protests. *Wired Magazine*. https://www.wired.com/

Part V

For the Future: Sustaining the Spark

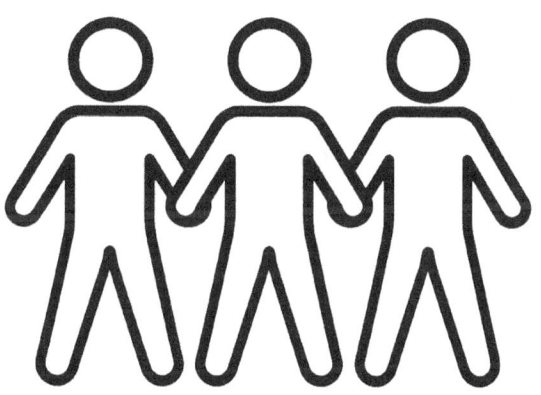

"The spark survives only when passed from one hand to the next."
— Unknown

Chapter Eighteen

Being Disappeared

Movements are not measured by a single march, protest, or moment of confrontation. Their endurance is tested in the long years that follow, when authorities grow subtler in their repression, and when fatigue threatens to hollow out resolve. To sustain the spark is to recognize that resistance is never a sprint but always a relay: knowledge and courage passed forward, adapted to changing terrain.

This section offers strategies for building longevity into movements. It asks how activists can endure, protect each other, and grow even under relentless pressure. If Part IV was about surviving the storm, Part V is about what happens when the storm never fully ends—how to live, organize, and fight in ways that remain viable into the future.

Legal–Ethical Use Notice (read first)

This chapter discusses lawful strategies for preventing, surviving, and responding to "disappearing" tactics—secretive arrests, transfers, or digital targeting that conceal a person's location or status. Nothing here encourages evasion of lawful process. Know your jurisdiction, assert your rights, and get independent legal advice when in doubt.

What It Means To "Be Disappeared"

In international human rights law, enforced disappearance is the deprivation of liberty by agents of a state (or by groups acting with its support), followed by refusal to acknowledge the detention or disclose the person's fate or whereabouts—placing the person "outside the protection of the law." It's condemned as a grave violation and, when widespread, a crime against humanity (United Nations, 2006). While the most notorious examples come from military dictatorships, the *logic* of disappearance also appears in democracies through opaque arrests, secret transfers, communication blackouts, and data-driven dragnets that sweep up innocents first and sort out legality later.

The Modern Disappearance Toolkit (and Why This Chapter Exists)

In the last few months alone, U.S. institutions have deployed tactics that, taken together, can simulate "disappearing" in practice: mass and selective campus arrests with poor notification; immigration detentions of student activists; and reverse digital warrants that start with a location or a keyword and then trawl for suspects—often snaring people with no individualized probable cause. These moves collide with bedrock rights: speech, assembly, due process, and freedom from unreasonable searches. Courts and civil liberties groups are actively contesting them right now (American Civil Liberties Union, Amnesty International, & Human Rights Watch, 2024; ACLU, 2024; TIME, 2025; The Washington Post, 2025).

Vocabulary for the Fight (defined where used)

- **Geofence warrant**: a demand (usually to Google) to search its *entire* location-history database and return a list of devices present within a geographic area and time window. Several appellate courts now split sharply on whether these are constitutional. In May 2025, the Fourth Circuit affirmed a conviction without deciding the big constitutional question, while the Fifth Circuit has said geofence warrants are inherently unconstitutional. Expect a Supreme Court reckoning (EPIC, 2024; Electronic Frontier Foundation, 2025; Harvard Law Review Blog, 2025; Congressional Research Service, 2025).

- **Reverse keyword warrant**: compels a provider to disclose who searched for certain terms—again, without naming a suspect first. Researchers and advocates argue these look like forbidden "general warrants." States are moving to ban them (Harvard Law Review Blog, 2025).

- **Kettling**: a crowd-control tactic where police encircle protesters, block exits, and then arrest or use force. New York City has paid out record settlements over kettling of 2020 protesters, and agreed to policy reforms limiting its use (AP News, 2023–2024).

Philosophy of Disappearance: Why Power Prefers the Dark

Disappearance is about narrative control. If no one can confirm where you are, the story of what happened to you can be rewritten by those holding you. If your group can't verify your status, momentum dies in uncertainty. Authoritarians understand this; so should movements. The counter-strategy is *visibility with precision*: pre-commitments, check-in rituals, verified witnesses, and data trails under the movement's control—not the state's.

Before the Storm: Build "Proof-of-Life" Culture

Proof-of-life means pre-arranged signals that verify someone is safe and at liberty. Think of it as a human heartbeat monitor for organizers.

- **Time-boxed check-ins**: Every high-risk participant has a check-in cadence.

- **Witnessing grid**: Assign trained **Legal Observers** (distinct, neutral documentarians of police behavior) to actions; they log arrests and handoff points in real time (National Lawyers Guild, n.d.). The National Lawyers Guild also provides training manuals and downloadable materials for observers, which can be accessed directly (https://www.nlg.org/legalobservers).

- **Consent-to-be-found**: Before an action, each person states what the group may disclose to locate them.

- **Data escrow**: Store essential info with counsel/POC.

If You Are Seized: Rights That Travel With You

- **Say little, ask clearly**.

- **No consent to searches**.

- **Name and basic ID**.

- **Call-out**.

These basics are well-known, but in "disappearance" scenarios, the priority is preserving process visibility: creating a record other people can follow.

If Someone Vanishes: A 4-Hour Locator Protocol

A disappearance window often lasts hours, not days. Treat the first four hours as decisive.

1. **Establish last knowns**.

2. **Check hospitals and local jails**.

3. **If immigration is possible**: Use ICE's Online Detainee Locator (**ODLS**) after 48 hours in custody; have legal name, country of birth, or A-Number ready. The ODLS can be searched online at ICE's official website, which provides instructions for detainee searches and updates (https://locator.ice.gov).

4. **Contact legal networks**: Local ACLU affiliates and the **National Lawyers Guild** track arrestees during protests and can coordinate counsel (National Lawyers Guild, n.d.).

5. **Document everything**.

Campus & Street: The New Flashpoints

Campus crackdowns since late 2024 and throughout spring 2025 brought mass arrests, less-lethal munitions, and aggressive clearing of encampments, raising serious First Amendment concerns. Civil-rights groups warned university leaders that calling in police to discipline peaceful protest risks unlawful force and chilled speech (American Civil Liberties Union, Amnesty International, & Human Rights Watch, 2024; ACLU, 2024).

Arrests & immigration consequences: International students engaged in protest have faced detention, visa cancellation, and fast-tracked removal proceedings—a powerful chilling effect even where no crime is alleged (TIME, 2025).

Kettling litigation: Settlements and reforms following 2020's kettling crackdowns confirm how quickly lawful assemblies can be turned into mass arrests without individualized cause (AP News, 2023–2024).

Data Dragnets: Reverse Warrants as Disappearance by Database

Geofence and **reverse-keyword** warrants invert the Fourth Amendment—start with a place or a word, then fish for people. The legal fight is live and unsettled: one circuit denounces geofences categorically; another sidesteps the core question; a third permits limited use. Meanwhile, companies are changing retention practices to curb the data supply (Electronic Frontier Foundation, 2025; EPIC, 2024; Forbes, 2024; Harvard Law Review Blog, 2025; Congressional Research Service, 2025). For current updates on law enforcement access to Google location data and industry changes, readers may consult Forbes' reporting (https://www.forbes.com/sites/thomasbrewster/2024/12/13/google-to-stop-sharing-location-data-with-law-enforcement).

When Power Hides the Paper Trail: Habeas as a Headlamp

Habeas corpus is the ancient right to challenge unlawful detention in court. In practice, movements activate habeas by getting counsel to file emergency petitions when a person is held incommunicado (unreachable, undisclosed location) or is being transferred to frustrate access to courts. Time is everything: document each attempted contact; note which officials refuse information; and push for judicial review.

Psychological Survival: Not Breaking in the Dark

Disappearance tactics aim to isolate. Counter with care engineered into the plan: care pods, decompression rituals, role rotation, proportional security. These are not niceties; they are countermeasures to a strategy designed to make targets feel alone.

Documentation Is Rescue

Your movement's records—arrest logs, time-stamped videos, radio/phone call sheets, observer notes—become the backbone of litigation and the map for families trying to find people. In New York's kettling cases—mass-arrest incidents where police trapped protesters in enclosed areas—settlements and reforms rested on meticulous, time-aligned footage and observer logs (AP News, 2023–2024). Treat documentation as mutual aid that travels through time.

Strategy for the Next Five Months (Because This Is Not Over)

- **Embed locator steps in every action plan**.

- **Publish a movement "Where To Find Us" guide**.

- **Train Legal Observers and marshals**: normalize the neon hats; normalize the clipboards. They are your anti-disappearance gear (National Lawyers Guild, n.d.). Resources for training new Legal Observers are provided directly by the NLG (https://www.nlg.org/legalobservers).

- **Track the courts**: the geofence/keyword fight is evolving fast; your policies should evolve with it (Electronic Frontier Foundation, 2025; EPIC, 2024; Harvard Law Review Blog, 2025; Congressional Research Service, 2025).

End Note: *For legal escalation and motion practice, see Chapter 13 (Legal Considerations and Risks). For operational device discipline and comms setup, see Disruption Module A (Building a Mesh Network) and Disruption Module B (Raspberry Pi Protest Tools). For psychological supports embedded in action planning, see Chapter 17 (Security & Anonymity) – The Psychological Toll.*

Selected References

American Civil Liberties Union, Amnesty International, & Human Rights Watch. (2024, October 31). *Joint letter urging universities to protect student protest rights.*

ACLU. (2024, October 31). *Universities should protect students' right to protest.*

AP News. (2023–2024). Reports on NYPD "kettling" settlements and reforms.

Congressional Research Service. (2025, May 9). *Geofence warrants and the Fourth Amendment.*

Electronic Frontier Foundation. (2025, May 7). *Appeals court sidesteps big questions on geofence warrants.*

EPIC. (2024, August 13). *Fifth Circuit rules geofence warrants inherently unconstitutional (U.S. v. Jamarr Smith).*

Forbes. (2024). *Google to stop sharing location data with law enforcement via geofence warrants.*

Harvard Law Review Blog. (2025, February 18). *Much ado about geofence warrants.*

National Lawyers Guild. (n.d.). *Legal Observer program.*

TIME. (2025, March–April). Reports on immigration enforcement targeting campus activists.

The Washington Post. (2025, May 7). *Arrests at Columbia University protest.*

Chapter Nineteen

Education as a Revolutionary Act

Legal–Ethical Use Notice (read first)

This chapter discusses lawful methods of learning, teaching, and sharing knowledge for activist purposes. It does not encourage indoctrination, harassment, or the spread of disinformation. Educational resistance must remain grounded in truth, accessibility, and care for the communities it serves.

Why Education Matters in Resistance

Authoritarians understand that education is not neutral. What people know—and how they learn it—shapes whether they accept or resist power. School curricula can normalize surveillance, glorify militarism, or erase histories of resistance. In turn, radical pedagogy has long been used to challenge these distortions, equipping communities with the tools to think critically and act collectively.

Education is a revolutionary act because it transforms students from passive recipients into active participants. Paulo Freire described this in *Pedagogy of the Oppressed*, calling for "problem-posing education" that invites learners to analyze their conditions rather than memorize official narratives (Freire, 1970/2018). Movements that teach their members to read power critically and share knowledge freely become harder to silence.

Pedagogy as Protest

When governments censor curricula, restrict library access, or criminalize certain topics, teaching those very subjects becomes a form of protest. Underground schools have appeared in refugee camps, banned books have circulated through zines and encrypted PDFs, and mutual-aid workshops have substituted for institutional learning.

History offers examples: the Freedom Schools of the U.S. Civil Rights Movement taught students both literacy and resistance strategies. More recently, protest encampments have hosted teach-ins on law, history, and media literacy. These moments demonstrate that pedagogy is not confined to classrooms—it is a frontline tactic.

Decolonizing Knowledge

Education as resistance also means examining *who controls knowledge.* Colonized communities have often been denied access to their languages, histories, and cultural practices. To reverse this, movements emphasize decolonizing pedagogy: restoring Indigenous teaching methods, privileging oral histories, and resisting imposed narratives.

For activists, this can include language revival workshops, community archives, or cultural storytelling circles. These methods not only transmit knowledge but also affirm identity against efforts to erase it. Resources on decolonial pedagogy are maintained by academic collectives and Indigenous organizations (Smith, 2012).

Tools for Radical Learning

Radical education thrives on creativity and adaptability. Several practical tools can embed revolutionary learning in movements:

- **Teach-ins**: Short, focused gatherings where participants break down complex issues into accessible lessons.

- **People's Libraries**: Movements often create informal lending libraries stocked with banned or neglected texts. In the digital age, this includes encrypted archives or QR code collections linked to open resources.

- **Skill-Sharing Circles**: Activists exchange practical skills—digital security, first aid, sustainable living—through structured peer teaching. These sessions treat every participant as both learner and teacher.

- **Popular Education Workshops**: Based on Freire's model, these use dialogue and problem-solving rather than lectures. A facilitator poses a shared problem, and the group collectively develops knowledge to address it. Resources and toolkits for designing such workshops are available from groups like Popular Education International (https://www.popedint.org).

Prison Education and Knowledge Behind Walls

Prisons are designed to isolate, but education often penetrates those walls. From the writings of political prisoners like Nelson Mandela to literacy programs organized inside U.S. penitentiaries, knowledge-sharing has historically functioned as an act of survival and defiance. Activists outside also support this effort through prison book programs and correspondence study.

Organizations such as Books to Prisoners (https://www.bookstoprisoners.net) and PEN America's Prison Writing Program (https://pen.org/prison-writing) provide resources for starting prison education initiatives, distributing literature, and amplifying incarcerated voices. These tools allow movements to resist the erasure of imprisoned members and to affirm that even in captivity, learning continues as resistance (Davis, 2003).

Guerrilla Syllabi

In recent years, activists and academics have created open-source "syllabi" to confront moments of crisis. Hashtags like #FergusonSyllabus, #AbolitionSyllabus, and #StandingRockSyllabus collected reading lists, essays, and teaching resources shared freely online. These syllabi operate as decentralized curricula: rapidly curated, collectively maintained, and open to anyone.

Guerrilla syllabi turn education into a living archive of resistance. They allow movements to shape discourse outside of official institutions and ensure that people confronting injustice have access to context and history. Resources on building community syllabi are available through networks such as the American Association of University Professors (AAUP, 2020, https://www.aaup.org).

Digital Samizdat

In the Soviet Union, dissidents circulated forbidden texts through *samizdat:* hand-copied manuscripts shared at great risk. Today's equivalent is digital samizdat: encrypted file sharing, offline mesh networks, and USB "sneakernets" used to distribute censored texts, zines, or media.

Activists have revived this practice in regions facing internet shutdowns or book bans. Instructions for building offline digital libraries are offered by collectives like Library Freedom Project (https://libraryfreedom.org), which also trains communities in privacy-centered digital infrastructure. Digital samizdat demonstrates that even in the age of surveillance, forbidden ideas will find ways to travel (Klinenberg, 2018).

Intergenerational Transmission

Resistance cannot rely on single generations. Movements endure when elders pass on hard-earned knowledge to younger activists—stories of past victories, failures, and tactics. Oral history circles, community archives, and "living library" events—where elders make themselves available as interactive resources—ensure continuity.

This transmission is not nostalgic; it is strategic. Movements that forget their histories risk repeating mistakes. Scholars of social movements argue that continuity is itself a form of power (Polletta, 2006). Activists can use low-cost tools—recordings, transcripts, archives—to preserve these stories. Groups like StoryCorps provide public resources for documenting oral histories (https://storycorps.org).

Education as Healing

Education is not only resistance against external repression; it is also recovery from internal wounds. Trauma can silence communities as effectively as censorship. Pedagogies that center healing, storytelling workshops, art-based learning, intergenerational dialogues, create space for resilience.

bell hooks emphasized this in *Teaching to Transgress*, framing education as both a practice of freedom and a practice of love (hooks, 1994). Movements that integrate healing into their teaching prevent burnout and remind participants that the purpose of resistance is not just to fight but to live fully.

Education Against Surveillance

Just as movements teach digital security, they must also teach media literacy to counter disinformation and manipulation. Protesters increasingly face waves of online propaganda, deepfakes, and false charges amplified on social media. Radical pedagogy equips people to recognize these tactics, fact-check claims, and resist narrative control.

This makes workshops on critical digital literacy as important as street protest training. Some activist organizations publish guides on spotting misinformation and teaching these skills in community settings (First Draft, 2020, https://firstdraftnews.org).

Barriers and Risks

Educational spaces are often surveilled. Teachers face professional retaliation, libraries are defunded, and student groups are targeted for their reading lists. Movements must prepare for these risks. Strategies include:

- Hosting decentralized or mobile workshops that leave little trace.
- Using encrypted file-sharing for sensitive texts.
- Training facilitators in legal rights around teaching contested material.

Education cannot be separated from security. Protecting spaces of learning is as vital as protecting protest marches.

Psychological Dimensions of Learning Together

Education also combats isolation. Shared study sessions, even informal ones, create solidarity. When people learn together, they rehearse the skills of cooperation and dialogue that sustain movements. Collective learning affirms that resistance is not only defensive but constructive: a community that teaches itself is already building the world it wants.

Sustaining the Spark Through Education

Education ensures movements do not fade when individuals are silenced. Every activist who learns and teaches extends the chain of continuity. By embedding radical learning practices into their core, movements resist erasure and ensure that knowledge outlives repression.

End Note: *For training in practical communications tools, see Disruption Module A (Building a Mesh Network) and Disruption Module B (Raspberry Pi Protest Tools). For counter-propaganda strategies, see Chapter 7 (Critical Thinking and Skepticism). For mental resilience in activist spaces, see Chapter 12 (Resilience without Burnout) Chapter 17 (Security & Anonymity in Activism).*

Selected References

AAUP. (2020). *Academic freedom and the creation of syllabi.* American Association of University Professors. Retrieved from https://www.aaup.org

Books to Prisoners. (n.d.). *About us.* Retrieved from https://www.bookstoprisoners.net

Davis, A. Y. (2003). *Are prisons obsolete?* Seven Stories Press.

First Draft. (2020). *Essential guides on misinformation and digital literacy.* Retrieved from https://firstdraftnews.org

Freire, P. (2018). *Pedagogy of the oppressed* (50th anniversary ed.). Bloomsbury Academic. (Original work published 1970)

hooks, b. (1994). *Teaching to transgress: Education as the practice of freedom.* Routledge.

Klinenberg, E. (2018). *Palaces for the people: How social infrastructure can help fight inequality, polarization, and the decline of civic life.* Crown.

Library Freedom Project. (n.d.). *About the project.* Retrieved from https://libraryfreedom.org

PEN America. (n.d.). *Prison writing program.* Retrieved from https://pen.org/prison-writing

Polletta, F. (2006). *It was like a fever: Storytelling in protest and politics.* University of Chicago Press.

Popular Education International. (n.d.). *Resources and toolkits for popular education.* Retrieved from https://www.popedint.org

Smith, L. T. (2012). *Decolonizing methodologies: Research and Indigenous peoples* (2nd ed.). Zed Books.

StoryCorps. (n.d.). *Recording and preserving oral histories.* Retrieved from https://storycorps.org

Chapter Twenty

Art as a Weapon

Legal–Ethical Use Notice (read first)

This chapter addresses how artistic practice can serve as lawful protest and political commentary. It does not authorize defacement, vandalism, or destruction of property. The focus is on public art, cultural expression, and creative intervention as forms of protected speech and movement-building.

Why Art Matters in Resistance

Art destabilizes the monopoly of official narratives. Where governments insist on one truth, murals, performances, and interventions create plural truths in public view. Protest art communicates beyond policy documents or speeches; it compresses emotion, critique, and identity into images and performances that anyone can understand.

As Susan Sontag argued, aesthetics can sharpen perception and awaken moral urgency (Sontag, 2003). In movements, art functions as both mirror and weapon: reflecting lived injustice while cutting through the fog of propaganda.

Murals, Banners, and Visual Occupation

Street murals, protest banners, and large-scale visuals transform public space into contested space. They operate as both symbolic disruption and cultural record. Examples include the massive "Black Lives Matter" street paintings in U.S. cities (2020) and long-standing murals in Northern Ireland documenting community struggles.

Tactical advantage: such visuals cannot be ignored. They scale protest to architectural proportions, forcing city officials and passersby to confront dissent. Activist manuals from groups like Beautiful Trouble (https://beautifultrouble.org) offer practical guides to designing impactful banners and murals.

XR Interventions and Aesthetic Disruption

Extinction Rebellion (XR) popularized the use of bold, theatrical aesthetics: red-robed "blood of the earth" processions, die-ins, and dramatic blockades. These interventions demonstrate how performance art magnifies political critique. XR's success shows that aesthetics are not decoration but central to disruption.

Resources for designing aesthetic interventions are maintained by art-activist collectives such as the Laboratory for Aesthetics and Politics (https://thelabla.org). These serve as toolkits for crafting interventions that blur art, theater, and protest.

Performance Art as Protest

Performance art situates the body itself as canvas and message. From ACT UP's die-ins during the AIDS crisis to Pussy Riot's guerrilla performances in Russia, embodied art can bypass censorship by turning the act of performance into confrontation.

Tactically, performance art thrives in ephemeral presence: harder to police than static murals, but equally resonant. Activist artists often publish guides to safe and effective protest performances (Boyd & Mitchell, 2012).

Digital Subversion and Memetic Art

The internet has expanded protest aesthetics into the realm of memes, viral graphics, and digital collage. Memetic warfare, humor, satire, and remix culture undermines propaganda by reframing it. During the Arab Spring and Hong Kong protests, memes spread faster than state messaging, carrying critique in shareable form.

Digital art interventions also include glitch aesthetics (manipulating images to distort official symbols) and augmented-reality overlays (see Chapter 17 and Disruption Module D for AR tactics). Groups like Tactical Tech publish toolkits on digital art interventions (https://tacticaltech.org).

Reclaiming Propaganda

Authoritarian regimes saturate public space with propaganda: statues, posters, slogans. One resistance strategy is culture jamming: subverting those symbols through parody, alteration, or context-shifting. The Billboard Liberation Front in the U.S. famously "edited" corporate billboards to critique consumer culture.

This practice reminds movements that propaganda is never neutral. Even a minor alteration destabilizes the authority of an image, revealing its fragility (Lasn, 1999).

Music and Sound as Resistance

Sound carries protest where visuals cannot. Chants, drumming, and protest songs galvanize participants while signaling presence. From South Africa's anti-apartheid freedom songs to contemporary hip-hop addressing systemic racism, music embeds memory into movements.

Sound can also disrupt. Chilean feminist collective Las Tesis staged the global performance "Un violador en tu camino" (2019), combining chant and choreography to indict state violence. Such actions exemplify how soundscapes weaponize emotion and solidarity.

Memorial Art and Collective Memory

Art also sustains resistance by memorializing injustice. Vigils with candles, ghost shoes laid out for victims of police violence, and quilt projects like the AIDS Memorial Quilt function as both art and archive. These works refuse erasure by placing collective grief into public space.

Memorial art reminds movements that resistance is not only confrontation but remembrance. It transforms mourning into a persistent accusation against power.

Barriers and Risks

Protest art often draws retaliation. Artists face defunding, censorship, or legal harassment. Public installations may be removed under the guise of "safety" or "cleanliness." Movements must anticipate these barriers by:

- Using ephemeral art (chalk, projections) that can be quickly deployed and redone.
- Documenting protest art with time-stamped images before removal.
- Training participants on legal rights around expressive conduct (see Chapter 13, Legal Considerations and Risks).

Psychological Dimensions of Creative Protest

Art is not only outward-facing; it strengthens participants internally. Creative acts relieve stress, build community, and transform fear into expression. bell hooks argued that aesthetic expression is itself a form of survival under oppression (hooks, 1995). By making beauty in struggle, movements affirm life against forces that seek to diminish it.

Sustaining the Spark Through Art

Art keeps movements visible across time. A mural can outlast a protest. A song can carry memory across generations. A performance can inspire beyond the moment. By embedding aesthetics into activism, movements ensure that their spark is not only sustained but amplified.

End Note: *For tactics on projection-based art, see Disruption Module C (Guerrilla Projection Tactics). For augmented-reality interventions, see Disruption Module D (AR Activism for Social Justice). For collective healing practices, see Chapter 19 (Education as a Revolutionary Act).*

Selected References

Beautiful Trouble. (n.d.). *Beautiful Trouble: Toolbox for revolution.* Retrieved from https://beautifultrouble.org

Boyd, A., & Mitchell, D. O. (2012). *Beautiful trouble: A toolbox for revolution.* OR Books.

hooks, b. (1995). *Art on my mind: Visual politics.* The New Press.

Lasn, K. (1999). *Culture jam: The uncooling of America.* HarperCollins.

Sontag, S. (2003). *Regarding the pain of others.* Farrar, Straus and Giroux.

Tactical Tech. (n.d.). *Art and activism resources.* Retrieved from https://tacticaltech.org

The Laboratory for Aesthetics and Politics. (n.d.). *Projects and publications.* Retrieved from https://thelabla.org

Chapter Twenty-One

Sustaining the Spark: A Call to Future Disobedients

Legal–Ethical Use Notice (read first)

This closing chapter affirms lawful methods of organizing, teaching, and resisting. It does not advocate violence, harassment, or unlawful acts. The reflections and calls offered here are for strengthening communities, protecting rights, and advancing democratic accountability.

Opening Reflection

You have moved through the architecture of modern repression and the counter-architecture of protection. You have met the practical grammar of resistance—security and anonymity, care and community, education, art, and documentation. You have also met the pressures that bend movements out of shape: surveillance, isolation, fatigue, fear. Feeling that weight is not failure; it is the baseline from which sustainable resistance must be built (hooks, 1994; Freire, 2018).

Hope is not an accident. It is a discipline learned in community and practiced under constraint. Movements endure when knowledge circulates, when roles rotate, when memory is preserved, and when people are trained to act with care as well as courage (Polletta, 2006; Tarrow, 2011; Tilly, 2004).

Principles of Sustainable Resistance

Protect people from burnout. Burnout is not a personal flaw but a structural signal that work and care are misaligned. Evidence shows that sustained overload, low control, and value conflicts predict exhaustion and withdrawal (Maslach & Leiter, 2016). Movements counter this by building cycles of rest, role rotation, and explicit debriefs; by normalizing step-backs; and by embedding care pods that distribute emotional labor (hooks, 1994).

Build resilience structures, not just moments. Spontaneity can spark uprisings, but endurance comes from organization—clear roles, decision rules, conflict resolution, training pipelines, and redundancy so one arrest or outage does not collapse capacity (Tarrow, 2011; Tufekci, 2017). Practical movements pair horizontal energy with enough structure to learn and adapt between actions (Ganz, 2009).

Institutionalize memory. Stories, archives, and oral histories are not ornament; they are operating systems. Movements that document their methods, codify lessons, and pass them forward avoid repeating preventable errors (Polletta, 2006; Tilly, 2004). See Chapter 19 and Chapter 20 on education and art as vehicles for storing and transmitting movement memory.

Adapt without losing mission focus. Repression evolves; so must tactics. But adaptation should be tethered to a clear purpose so that novelty does not become drift. The record of successful nonviolent campaigns shows that strategic discipline—shifts in repertoire that still serve the goal—correlates with success (Chenoweth & Stephan, 2011; Scott, 1985).

Lessons from Movement History

Polish Solidarity (1980s). A labor uprising that survived martial law by becoming a social network of mutual aid, underground press, and culture—linking workers, students, and clergy. It sustained itself through parallel institutions and narrative discipline until political openings emerged (Kenney, 2002; Tarrow, 2011).

Women of Liberia Mass Action for Peace (2003). A coalition that used churches, markets, and daily sit-ins to force negotiations in a civil war context, pairing moral authority with relentless persistence. Leadership rotation and shared caregiving protected stamina; public prayer and white-clothing symbolism unified message and crowd (Gbowee, 2011).

Indigenous Land and Water Defense (21st century). From Idle No More to Standing Rock, Indigenous movements have combined ceremony, legal strategy, and media to assert sovereignty and protect land—sustaining resistance through culture, intergenerational leadership, and global ally networks (Estes, 2019).

Chile's Arpilleras under Dictatorship (1970s–1980s). Hand-sewn textile scenes made by women documented disappearances and hunger, traveled clandestinely, and funded survival. Art became both archive and economy, allowing testimony to circulate when speech was criminalized (Adams, 2013).

Common patterns. Durable movements decentralize operational risk, centralize mission, embed training, and preserve narrative control. Movements that collapse often do so from leader-centrism, isolation from communities, failure to rotate roles, or strategic drift once repression intensifies (Chenoweth & Stephan, 2011; Ganz, 2009; Tarrow, 2011).

From You, Forward

You are a node in a wider network. Most nodes are not spectacular; they are reliable. Reliability compounds. A weekly study circle that never misses; a documentation team that timestamps and backs up; an art crew that keeps the visuals sharp; a care pod that checks in after every action—these ordinary practices create extraordinary endurance (Polletta, 2006; Tufekci, 2017).

Not all victories will be visible in your lifetime. The task is to reduce the distance between what is possible now and what must exist later. Plant knowledge where it can be found, teach what you have learned, pass on responsibility before you are forced to, and make your work legible enough that someone else can pick it up without you (Freire, 2018; hooks, 1994).

For training curricula that help groups operationalize rotation, facilitation, and debriefs, see Training for Change; their site offers free modules on meeting design, conflict navigation, and train-the-trainer methods that extend capacity across volunteers (Training for Change, n.d., https://www.trainingforchange.org). For open libraries of tactics, facilitation tools, and case studies, the Commons Social Change Library curates downloadable guides that movements can adapt locally (Commons Social Change Library, n.d., https://commonslibrary.org).

Toolkits for the Long Haul

Movements cannot rely on improvisation alone. They require practical resources that support resilience, continuity, and clarity of purpose. Several toolkits created by activist organizations and research centers provide blueprints for this work.

The *Solidarity Is* project of the Building Movement Project curates frameworks designed to help activists map capacity, distribute care, and integrate sustainability into everyday organizing. Their resources include the Movement Pantry, which helps groups assess what they already have and what they lack; the Movement Leadership Stool, a visual model for balancing skills, accountability, and vision; and the Ecosystem of Well-Being, which shows how self-care and community care function together as a structural necessity rather than an individual luxury. These frameworks are available as open resources at *Solidarity Is* (Building Movement Project, 2025, https://www.solidarityis.org/tools-resources).

Research from George Mason University expands this practice with the **Thriving Activist Toolkit**, a set of educational modules that address burnout, trauma, and resilience in social justice movements. This toolkit translates decades of research on well-being into practical exercises: mindfulness strategies that can be adapted for protest settings, facilitation techniques that reduce hierarchical strain, and community reflection practices that deepen trust. It is designed not just for individuals but for entire activist teams to embed resilience practices into their culture (Gorski & Chen, 2025, https://wellbeing.gmu.edu/research/thriving-activist-toolkit).

For everyday self-care in activist life, the *Activist Handbook* maintains a **Wellbeing Guide** written for grassroots organizers. Unlike research-heavy toolkits, this resource is field-oriented: it includes practical reminders for hydration, nutrition, and sleep during extended campaigns; simple methods for regulating stress before and after demonstrations; and techniques for supporting peers through trauma-informed approaches. It situates wellbeing as part of tactical planning rather than an afterthought (Activist Handbook, 2024, https://activisthandbook.org/wellbeing).

Youth movements, which often face both repression and adult dismissal, have their own specialized resources. The **Youth Activist Toolkit** created by Advocates for Youth offers a comprehensive curriculum on group dynamics, planning, and resilience. It trains young organizers in conflict resolution, emphasizes the importance of care practices within youth-led spaces, and provides practical lessons on building collective power while avoiding burnout. Because early habits become lifelong practices, this toolkit is particularly valuable for sustaining disobedience across generations (Advocates for Youth, 2019, https://www.advocatesforyouth.org/wp-content/uploads/2019/04/Youth-Activist-Toolkit.pdf).

Legal sustainability is addressed by the **Toolkit for the Movement** from the Center for Constitutional Rights. This collection provides legal resources on protest planning, government surveillance, and interaction with law enforcement. Guides like *If an Agent Knocks* and the *Protest Planner* distill decades of movement experience into practical checklists, ensuring activists can protect themselves from unnecessary legal exposure while preserving organizational capacity. These resources are freely available through the CCR website (CCR, 2020, https://ccrjustice.org/toolkit-for-the-movement).

Finally, for groups building long-term campaign momentum, the **Movement Power Zine** by Tipping Point UK provides a creative and accessible manual. It translates strategic planning into visual guides, case studies, and worksheets that can be adapted by grassroots organizers. The zine emphasizes collective power over individual leadership, offering lessons on scaling, coalition-building, and avoiding the fatigue of isolated campaigns. Its strength lies in accessibility: it is designed to be printed, shared, and circulated in activist spaces, continuing the tradition of zine-based education (Tipping Point UK, 2024, https://commonslibrary.org/movement-power-a-toolkit-for-building-people-power-in-a-time-of-crisis-zine).

These resources differ in form; some academic, some field-tested, some legal, some cultural, but together they embody the principle that sustainability is not an accident. It must be cultivated through knowledge, structure, and care. Incorporating these toolkits into organizing practice ensures that the spark of resistance is not only ignited but also sustained across time.

Call to Future Disobedients

Do not mistake exhaustion for the end of the story. Rest, rotate, return. Do not mistake confusion for lack of direction. Re-state the mission and cut away what does not serve it. Do not mistake isolation for reality. Rebuild the smallest circle and widen it again.

Refuse the seduction of cynicism. It flatters the intellect while it empties the heart. Choose instead the discipline of hope: to prepare when it would be easier to complain, to teach when it would be easier to perform, to share credit when it would be easier to hoard it.

Take what you have learned here—security to reduce harm; anonymity to buy time; education to grow capacity; art to hold attention; documentation to anchor truth—and put it to work. Hand it to others. Codify what you invent. Correct what fails. Keep your people safe. Keep your purpose clear.

You will be told to wait for permission. Do not. You will be told to simplify what is complex or complicate what is simple. Decline both. You will be told that nothing changes. Read history again.

To future disobedients: act with urgency and with care; with courage and with humility; with clarity and with imagination. You are not alone. You inherit a living archive. Add to it. Protect it. Pass it on.

The spark is yours to sustain.

End Note: *For practical methods that support sustainability, see Chapter 17 (Security and Anonymity in Activism) on behavioral discipline and psychological care; Chapter 18 (Being Disappeared) on documentation and locator protocols; Chapter 19 (Education as a Revolutionary Act) on knowledge transfer; and Chapter 20 (Art as a Weapon) on memorial art and public narrative. For blackout-resilient communications, see Disruption Module E (Anonymous Broadcast Messaging in Blackouts); for training aids and workshop scaffolds, see Disruption Module A and Disruption Module B.*

Selected References

Adams, J. (2013). *Art against dictatorship: Making the arpilleras of Chile*. University of Washington Press.

Chenoweth, E., & Stephan, M. J. (2011). *Why civil resistance works: The strategic logic of nonviolent conflict*. Columbia University Press.

Commons Social Change Library. (n.d.). *Resources for activists and campaigners*. Retrieved from https://commonslibrary.org

Estes, N. (2019). *Our history is the future: Standing Rock versus the Dakota Access Pipeline, and the long tradition of Indigenous resistance*. Verso.

Freire, P. (2018). *Pedagogy of the oppressed* (50th anniversary ed.). Bloomsbury Academic. (Original work published 1970)

Ganz, M. (2009). *Why David sometimes wins: Leadership, organization, and strategy in the California farm worker movement*. Oxford University Press.

Gbowee, L. (2011). *Mighty be our powers: How sisterhood, prayer, and sex changed a nation at war*. Beast Books.

hooks, b. (1994). *Teaching to transgress: Education as the practice of freedom*. Routledge.

Kenney, P. (2002). *A carnival of revolution: Central Europe, 1989*. Princeton University Press.

Maslach, C., & Leiter, M. P. (2016). Understanding the burnout experience: Recent research and its implications for psychiatry. *World Psychiatry, 15*(2), 103–111.

Polletta, F. (2006). *It was like a fever: Storytelling in protest and politics*. University of Chicago Press.

Scott, J. C. (1985). *Weapons of the weak: Everyday forms of peasant resistance*. Yale University Press.

Tarrow, S. (2011). *Power in movement: Social movements and contentious politics* (3rd ed.). Cambridge University Press.

Training for Change. (n.d.). *Free training tools for organizers*. Retrieved from https://www.trainingforchange.org

Tilly, C. (2004). *Social movements, 1768–2004*. Paradigm Publishers.

Tufekci, Z. (2017). *Twitter and tear gas: The power and fragility of networked protest*. Yale University Press.

GLOSSARY

AES (Advanced Encryption Standard): A widely used encryption algorithm that secures digital communications and stored files.

Anonymity Networks: Systems like Tor or I2P that reroute traffic through multiple relays to conceal the origin and destination of data.

Augmented Reality (AR): Technology that overlays digital images, sounds, or text onto the real world, often through smartphones or AR glasses.

Bandwidth: The maximum rate at which data can be transmitted over an internet connection in a given time, usually measured in **megabits per second (Mbps)**.

Biometrics: Unique physical traits such as fingerprints, facial structure, or iris scans used for digital identification and surveillance.

Burner Phone: A prepaid mobile phone purchased without a contract and used temporarily to avoid long-term tracking.

Cryptography: The science of encoding and decoding messages so that only intended recipients can read them.

DNS (Domain Name System): The system that translates human-readable website addresses into machine-readable IP addresses.

Drone Payload: An object (such as a leaflet container or small sensor) carried and released by a drone.

Encryption: The process of transforming information into unreadable form without the correct key or password.

Exchangeable Image File Format (EXIF) Metadata: Data stored in digital photos that includes time, date, camera model, and sometimes GPS coordinates.

GNU (a recursive acronym for "GNU's Not Unix") Privacy Guard (GPG): A free encryption tool for securing files and communications, often used for email and file signing.

IP Address: A unique number assigned to each device connected to the internet, used to identify and route communications.

Mesh Network: A decentralized communication system where devices connect directly to each other, creating resilient coverage without central towers.

Metadata: Background information automatically attached to files or communications (e.g., sender, time, device, location) that can reveal patterns even if the content is encrypted.

Open-Source Software: Software whose code is made freely available for anyone to inspect, modify, and distribute.

OPSEC (Operational Security): Practices that protect sensitive information from adversaries, including habits, behaviors, and digital hygiene.

QR (Quick Response) Code: A square barcode that stores digital information (like URLs) that can be scanned with a phone camera.

Raspberry Pi: A small, affordable computer used for experiments, privacy tools, and DIY hardware projects.

Tor (The Onion Router): A network that anonymizes internet traffic by routing it through multiple relays with layered encryption.

VPN (Virtual Private Network): A service that encrypts your internet traffic and routes it through remote servers to hide your location and protect data.

Zine: A small, self-published booklet, often made with low-cost printing, used for subcultural expression or political messaging.

INDEX

ACLU (American Civil Liberties Union): Ch. 1, 13, 14, 18
    Affiliate directories: Ch. 13, 14
    Know Your Rights: Ch. 1, 13, 14
    Mobile Justice: Ch. 13
    Protest tips: Ch. 13

Albert Einstein Institution: Ch. 11

Amnesty International: Ch. 18

Augmented Reality (AR): Glossary; Module D

Bandwidth: Glossary

Beautiful Trouble: Ch. 1, 12, 14, 20; Modules C, F, G
    Clown Army: Ch. 9
    Google bombing: Ch. 9
    Light Projection: Ch. 1; Module C
    Mock funerals: Ch. 9
    Pattern disruption: Ch. 9
    Rule following: Ch. 9
    Silent protest: Ch. 9
    Tactic Star: Ch. 12

Bellingcat: Ch. 16

Biometrics: Glossary

Books to Prisoners: Ch. 19

Bust cards (NLG): Ch. 13, 14

Burner Phone: Glossary

Citizen Lab: Ch. 9; Module E

Commons Library: Ch. 21

Community Justice Exchange: Ch. 13, 14, 15
    National Bail Fund Directory: Ch. 13, 14, 15

Confirmation bias: Ch. 7

CrimethInc: Ch. 9, 11; Modules F, G
    Clowning as resistance: Ch. 9
    System jamming: Ch. 9
    Zine Warfare: Module F

Cryptography: Glossary

Data & Society: Ch. 7

Digital Defense Fund (DDF): Ch. 14, 15

DNS (Domain Name System): Glossary; Module B

Drone DIY guides: Overlaps
    Payload drops: Module G

Drone Payload: Glossary

EFF (Electronic Frontier Foundation): Ch. 10, 11, 12, 13, 14, 15, 16, 17, 18; Modules A–H
    Atlas of Surveillance: Ch. 15, 16
    Surveillance Self-Defense: Ch. 10, 11, 12, 17

Encryption: Glossary

Exchangeable Image File Format (EXIF) Metadata: Glossary; Ch. 16

Exposing the Invisible: Ch. 16, 17

FactCheck.org: Ch. 7

Federal Communications Commission (FCC): Modules A, B, E

Firestorm Coop: Ch. 14, 15

First Draft: Ch. 19

First Amendment (legal): Ch. 13, 14

First Draft News: Ch. 19

GCHQ (Government Communications Headquarters, UK): Modules (if cited, check)

GitHub: Module 9 (PokemonGo Feeder, Maltrail, OpenKeychain, SimpleX Chat)

GNU (GNU's Not Unix) Privacy Guard (GPG): Glossary; Module F

GoFundMe: Ch. 15

goQR: Module F; Overlaps

goTenna: Modules A, G; Overlaps
    Mesh manual: Module A
    Mesh networking: Module A
    Puerto Rico hurricane response: Module A

Graphika: Ch. 16

Greater Good Science Center (Berkeley): Ch. 8

Greenpeace International: Module C

Hacking//Hustling: Module H

HackBlossom: Module H

Hacktivist Field Manual: Module H

Headspace: Ch. 12

HOTOSM (Humanitarian OpenStreetMap Team): Ch. 16

HowlRound: Module 9

Human Rights Connected: Ch. 8

Human Rights Watch: Ch. 18

ICE (Immigration and Customs Enforcement): Ch. 18
    Online Detainee Locator: Ch. 18

ILRC (Immigrant Legal Resource Center): Ch. 14, 15

Immigrant Defense Project: Ch. 14, 15
    ICE Encounter Cards (English/Spanish): Ch. 14

INCITE!: Ch. 11

Index on Censorship: Omit if not cited

Information Disorder (Wardle & Derakhshan): Ch. 16

Instructables: Modules C, G

Internet Protocol (IP) Address: Glossary

IPFS (InterPlanetary File System): Ch. 10

IRS (Internal Revenue Service): Ch. 15

Journalists' Guides (Freedom of the Press Foundation): Ch. 17

KeePassXC: Ch. 10

Kruger & Dunning (Unskilled and Unaware of It): Ch. 7

Lateral Reading (University of Washington): Ch. 7

LessWrong (Red Teaming 101): Ch. 8

Library Freedom Project: Ch. 19

Litchi (Drone flight app): Module G

Logic Magazine: Module 9

Malor Books (Burnout: The Cost of Caring): Ch. 12

MAT2 (Metadata Anonymization Toolkit): Ch. 10; Module F

Media Bias Ratings (AllSides): Ch. 7

Metadata: Glossary; Ch. 16, 17

Metadata Investigations (Exposing the Invisible): Ch. 16, 17

Mesh Networks: Glossary; Modules A, E

Mesh++: Module A; Overlaps

Military Survival Manual FM 21–76: Module H

Mindful.org: Ch. 8, 12

Miranda Rights (US Courts): Ch. 13

MoMAR Gallery: Module D

MuckRock (FOIA 101): Ch. 16

Mutual Aid: Glossary

Mutual Aid Disaster Relief: Ch. 1

Mutual Aid Hub: Ch. 10, 11, 12, 13, 14, 15; Module E

NACDL (National Association of Criminal Defense Lawyers): Ch. 14, 15
   Expungement/Record Sealing: Ch. 14, 15

National Immigration Law Center (NILC): Ch. 14, 15
   Community education resources: Ch. 14

National Lawyers Guild (NLG): Ch. 1, 11, 13, 14, 18
   Bust cards: Ch. 13, 14
   Legal observers: Ch. 18
   Mass Defense: Ch. 11, 13, 14

National Police Accountability Project (NPAP): Ch. 13

National Security Archive: Ch. 7

Network Analysis (Graphika/Stanford IO): Ch. 16

Nizkor Project: Ch. 7

Nonviolence International: Ch. 11, 14

NYU Tandon School of Engineering: Modules A, G

ObscuraCam (Guardian Project): Ch. 13, 17

OFAC (Office of Foreign Assets Control): Ch. 15

Open Collective: Ch. 15

Open Research Institute: Module E

Open Source Software: Glossary

Open States Tracker: Ch. 16

OpenStreetMap Foundation: Module G

OpenXR: Module D

Operational Security (OPSEC): Glossary

OsmAnd~: Module E

PACER (Public Access to Court Electronic Records): Ch. 16

Paul Freire Institute: Ch. 11

PBS Frontline (News War): Ch. 7

PBS Moyers Journal (Buying the War): Ch. 7

PEN America (Prison Writing Program): Ch. 19

Permaculture Association: Ch. 12

Photographylife (EXIF Data): Ch. 16

Pi-hole: Module B; Overlaps

Poynter (Fact-Checking): Ch. 7

Press Watchers: Ch. 7

Privacy Guides: Ch. 9

Privacy International: Ch. 12; Modules B, C, D, E, F, H

Proton (Drive, VPN, Mail): Ch. 10, 13, 14; Module B; Overlaps

QAnon (public opinion and research): Ch. 7

QGIS (Geographic Information System): Ch. 16

QR (Quick Response) Code: Glossary

QGroundControl: Module G

Rangzen: Module E; Overlaps

Raspberry Pi: Glossary; Module B

Reboot FM: Ch. 7

Red Scholezine Collective: Module F

RetroShare: Module E, F

Routledge (Teaching to Transgress, All About Love): Ch. 11, 12, 14

Ruckus Society: Ch. 11, 12

Sage Journals (QAnon Unreal): Ch. 7

Science HowStuffWorks: Ch. 9

SecureDrop: Ch. 13

Security in-a-Box (Front Line Defenders & Tactical Tech): Ch. 16, 17; Module H

Signal (Messenger): Ch. 1, 10

SimpleX Chat: Modules E, H; Overlaps

Snopes: Ch. 7

Social Media Verification (Bellingcat): Ch. 16

Solidarity Is (Building Movement Project): Ch. 21

Stanford Internet Observatory: Ch. 16

StoryCorps: Ch. 19

Survival Communications (Tactical Tech): Module E

SWLing Post: Module H

System Jamming (CrimethInc): Ch. 9

Tactical Tech: Ch. 12, 14, 20; Modules B, C, D, E, H

TED (Talks on Courage): Ch. 8

The Atlantic (QAnon article): Ch. 7

The Decision Lab (Confirmation Bias): Ch. 7

The Glass Room (Exhibit/Project): Ch. 9

The Illuminator Collective: Module C

The Laboratory for Aesthetics and Politics: Ch. 20

The Verge: Module D

The Washington Post: Ch. 18

The Onion Router (Tor): Ch. 10, 16, 17; Module B; Overlaps

Theories of Bias (Psychology Today, etc.): Ch. 7, 8

Tipping Point UK: Ch. 21

Tor Project: Glossary; Ch. 10, 16, 17; Module B; Overlaps

Training for Change: Ch. 8, 21

Unity (AR Foundation): Module D

University of Washington Libraries (Lateral Reading): Ch. 7

VeraCrypt: Module F

Virtual Private Network (VPN): Glossary; Ch. 10, 13

Wired Magazine: Ch. 17; Modules A, G, H

Wikipedia (Google Bomb, EXIF): Ch. 9, 16

WonderHowTo: Module 9

Zeno Radio: Module E

Zine: Glossary; Module F

QR Code Reference Pages

Navigate to QR Code Sections

About the QR Codes
The following QR codes are visual representations of web links provided throughout the chapters and modules of this manual. Each QR code corresponds to a URL that is already printed in the text. They are included here for convenience of scanning but are not required to access the resources.

Chapters
Chapter 1: The Spirit of Rebellion
Chapter 2: Historical Mavericks
Chapter 3: The Psychology of Resistance
Chapter 4: The Ethics of Radical Action
Chapter 5: The Myth of the "Good Protest"
Chapter 6: Disobedience in the Age of Surveillance
Chapter 7: Critical Thinking and Skepticism
Chapter 8: Embracing Risk and Uncertainty
Chapter 9: Breaking Boundaries
Chapter 10: Networking with Fellow Mavericks
Chapter 11: Choosing Your Line: Tactical Ethics for Protestors
Chapter 12: Resilience Without Burnout
Chapter 13: Real-Time Rescue: Emergency Legal Tactics and Contacts
Chapter 14: Legal Considerations and Risks
Chapter 15: Funding the Fight: Economics of Resistance
Chapter 16: Knowing More, Risking Less: Tactical Intelligence for Resistance
Chapter 17: Security and Anonymity in Activism
Chapter 18: Being Disappeared
Chapter 19: Education as a Revolutionary Act

Chapter 20: Art as a Weapon

Chapter 21: Sustaining the Spark: A Call to Future Disobedients

Disruption Modules

Module A: Building a Mesh Network

Module B: Raspberry Pi Protest Tools

Module C: Guerrilla Projection Tactics

Module D: AR Activism

Module E: Anonymous Broadcast Messaging in Blackouts

Module F: Zine Warfare

Module G: Drone-Based Messaging

Module H: Bonus Tools

QR Code Reference Pages

Part I – The Why: Foundations of Disobedience

Chapter 1: The Spirit of Rebellion

National War Tax Resistance Coordinating Committee – https://nwtrcc.org

Meshpoint (Mesh networks for crisis response) – https://meshpoint.me

Signal Messenger – https://signal.org

Briar Project (Secure messaging) – https://briarproject.org

National Lawyers Guild "Know Your Rights" – https://www.nlg.org/know-your-rights

Beautiful Trouble (Light Projection tool) – https://beautifultrouble.org/toolbox/tool/light-projection

Mutual Aid Disaster Relief (Resources) – https://mutualaiddisasterrelief.org/resources

QR Code Reference Pages

ACLU – Free speech under attack report – https://www.aclu.org/news/free-speech/free-speech-under-attack-protesters-at-risk

Al Jazeera (Tunisia: cyberwar report) – https://www.aljazeera.com

Chapter 2: Historical Mavericks

Beautiful Trouble (Consequence Scanning) – https://beautifultrouble.org/toolbox/tool/consequence-scanning

OpenDemocracy (Microresistance rituals) – https://www.opendemocracy.net/en/microresistance-political-rituals-power

Beautiful Trouble (Meme Warfare) – https://beautifultrouble.org/toolbox/tool/meme-warfare

CrimethInc (Zine Archive) – https://crimethinc.com/zines

QR Code Reference Pages

Chapter 3: The Psychology of Resistance

Nonviolent Conflict Resource – Strategic nonviolent conflict – https://www.nonviolent-conflict.org/resource/strategic-nonviolent-conflict

APA role play study (cognitive-behavior modification) – https://www.apa.org/pubs/journals/releases/ccp-ccp0669.pdf

Positive Psychology (Anchoring NLP) – https://positivepsychology.com/anchoring-nlp

NCBI – Psychotherapy by reciprocal inhibition – https://www.ncbi.nlm.nih.gov/pmc/articles/PMC3065099

Whistleblowers.org – https://whistleblowers.org

Mental Health First Aid – Self-care plan – https://www.mentalhealthfirstaid.org/external/2019/12/developing-a-self-care-plan

QR Code Reference Pages

Chapter 4: The Ethics of Radical Action

Beautiful Trouble – Escalation Spectrum –

https://www.beautifultrouble.org/toolbox/tool/escalation-spectrum

Electronic Frontier Foundation – Introduction to Encryption –

https://ssd.eff.org/en/module/introduction-encryption

National Lawyers Guild – Legal Observers – https://www.nlg.org/legalobservers/

Yale University Press – Twitter and Tear Gas –

https://yalebooks.yale.edu/book/9780300234176/twitter-and-tear-gas/

CrimethInc – https://crimethinc.com

Hacking//Hustling – https://hackinghustling.org

QR Code Reference Pages

Electronic Frontier Foundation – Surveillance Self-Defense Guide – https://ssd.eff.org

National Lawyers Guild – Know Your Rights and Legal Observer Manual – https://www.nlg.org/know-your-rights/

Chapter 5: The Myth of the "Good Protest"

Media Bias Fact Check – https://mediabiasfactcheck.com

NewsGuard – https://www.newsguardtech.com

Know Your Meme – https://knowyourmeme.com

Canva – https://canva.com

QR Code Reference Pages

CapCut – https://capcut.com

Bot Sentinel – https://botsentinel.com

Hoaxy (Indiana University) – https://hoaxy.osome.iu.edu

CrowdTangle – https://www.crowdtangle.com

Matrix (secure communication) – https://matrix.org

Signal – https://signal.org

InShot (video editing) – https://inshot.com

QR Code Reference Pages

Preview (Instagram content tool) – https://thepreviewapp.com

Chapter 6: Disobedience in the Age of Surveillance

MAT2 (Metadata Anonymization Toolkit) – https://0xacab.org/jvoisin/mat2

ExifTool – https://exiftool.org

Electronic Frontier Foundation – What is Metadata? – https://ssd.eff.org/en/module/what-metada

goTenna Mesh – https://gotenna.com/pages/mesh

Meshtastic – https://meshtastic.org/

QR Code Reference Pages

PiMyLifeUp (Raspberry Pi Wi-Fi Extender Guide) – https://pimylifeup.com/raspberry-pi-wi-fi-extender/

Electronic Frontier Foundation – Operational Security (OpSec Module) – https://ssd.eff.org/en/module/introduction-operational-security

Electronic Frontier Foundation – Activist Privacy & Digital Security Playlist – https://ssd.eff.org/en/playlist/activist-privacy-and-digital-security

Electronic Frontier Foundation – How to Use a Phone Safely at a Protest – https://ssd.eff.org/en/module/how-use-phone-safely-protest

Tails OS – https://tails.net

Wired – Faraday Bags for Digital Privacy – https://www.wired.com/story/faraday-bags-digital-privacy/

QR Code Reference Pages

CNET – Face Paint Can Fool AI Surveillance Systems – https://www.cnet.com/news/privacy/this-face-paint-can-fool-ai-surveillance-systems/

Electronic Frontier Foundation – Surveillance Self-Defense (Main Hub) – https://ssd.eff.org

Wired – Hackers' Delight: Testing Faraday Bags for Digital Privacy – https://www.wired.com/story/faraday-bags-digital-privacy/

Part II – The Who: Becoming a Modern Dissenter

Chapter 7: Critical Thinking and Skepticism

University of Washington Libraries – Lateral Reading – https://guides.lib.uw.edu/research/evaluate/lateralreading

Checkology – https://checkology.org

QR Code Reference Pages

AllSides – Media Bias Ratings – https://www.allsides.com/media-bias/media-bias-ratings

Ad Fontes Media – https://adfontesmedia.com

Your Logical Fallacy Is – https://yourlogicalfallacyis.com

The Nizkor Project – Logical Fallacies – https://nizkor.org/features/fallacies/

InVID Verification Plugin – https://www.invid-project.eu/tools-and-services/invid-verification-plugin/

Google Images (Reverse Image Search) – https://images.google.com

NCBI – Dunning-Kruger Study – https://www.ncbi.nlm.nih.gov/pmc/articles/PMC7757655/

QR Code Reference Pages

Psychology Today – Confidence: The Illusion of Competence – https://www.psychologytoday.com/us/articles/200310/confidence-the-illusion-competence

Data & Society – The Oxygen of Amplification – https://datasociety.net/library/oxygen-of-amplification/

CISA – Disinformation: Stop Its Spread – https://www.cisa.gov/news-events/news/cisa-insight-disinformation-stop-its-spread

Center for Humane Technology – https://centerforhumantechnology.org

Reboot FM – Research: Attention Resistance – https://reboot.fm/research-attention-resistance/

The Decision Lab – Confirmation Bias – https://thedecisionlab.com/biases/confirmation-bias

QR Code Reference Pages

Psychology Today – Confirmation Bias – https://www.psychologytoday.com/us/basics/confirmation-bias

FactCheck.org – https://www.factcheck.org

Snopes – https://www.snopes.com

Poynter – Fact-Checking – https://www.poynter.org/fact-checking/

National Security Archive – Iraq WMD Documents – https://nsarchive2.gwu.edu/NSAEBB/NSAEBB80/iraq02.pdf

CIA – Iraq Survey Group Final Report (2004) – https://www.cia.gov/library/reports/general-reports-1/iraq_wmd_2004/index.html

QR Code Reference Pages

PBS Frontline – News War – https://www.pbs.org/wgbh/frontline/film/newswar/

Press Watchers – Media Failures on Iraq – https://presswatchers.org/2020/06/the-real-story-of-how-the-media-failed-on-iraq/

PBS – Bill Moyers Journal: Buying the War –

https://www.pbs.org/moyers/journal/btw/watch.html

Princeton University Press – Ellen Schrecker's Many Are the Crimes –

https://press.princeton.edu/books/paperback/9780691006001/many-are-the-crimes

The Atlantic – QAnon: Nothing Can Stop What Is Coming –

https://www.theatlantic.com/magazine/archive/2020/06/qanon-nothing-can-stop-what-is-coming/610567/

QR Code Reference Pages

MIT Technology Review – How QAnon Went Mainstream – https://www.technologyreview.com/2020/10/23/1010944/how-qanon-went-mainstream-election/

Pew Research Center – QAnon Public Opinion – https://www.pewresearch.org/fact-tank/2020/09/16/most-americans-have-heard-of-qanon-but-few-have-positive-views-of-it/

Center for Countering Digital Hate – The Disinformation Dozen – https://counterhate.com/research/the-disinformation-dozen/

U.S. House Intelligence Committee – QAnon and Domestic Terrorism – https://intelligence.house.gov/uploadedfiles/qanon_and_domestic_terrorism.pdf

Sage Journals – QAnon and the Emergence of the Unreal (DOI) – https://doi.org/10.1177/14614448211019856

Kruger & Dunning – Unskilled and Unaware of It (DOI) – https://doi.org/10.1037/0022-3514.77.6.1121

QR Code Reference Pages

Chapter 8: Embracing Risk and Uncertainty

Psychology Today – https://www.psychologytoday.com

Greater Good Science Center (Berkeley) – https://greatergood.berkeley.edu

APA Resilience resources – https://www.apa.org/topics/resilience

TED (Talks on courage/risk) – https://www.ted.com

Training for Change – https://trainingforchange.org/training_tools/scenario-drills/

Psychology Tools – https://www.psychologytools.com/resource/grounding-techniques/

QR Code Reference Pages

Beautiful Trouble – https://beautifultrouble.org/tactic/tactic-star/

Electronic Frontier Foundation – https://ssd.eff.org/

LessWrong – https://www.lesswrong.com/posts/Bn8jbmxF7ZRL8KQWa/red-teaming-101

Commons Library – https://commonslibrary.org/using-pre-mortems-to-avoid-campaign-failures/

Activist Security – https://www.activistsecurity.org/

Frontline Defenders – https://www.frontlinedefenders.org/en/resource-publication/security-risk-assessment-planning

Human Rights Connected – https://www.humanrightsconnected.org/activist-toolkit/grounding-and-centering-for-activists/

QR Code Reference Pages

Mindful.org – https://www.mindful.org/mindfulness-and-protesting-how-to-show-up-without-burning-out/

Chapter 9: Breaking Boundaries

Psychology Today – https://knowyourmeme.com/

Electronic Frontier Foundation – https://ssd.eff.org/

Citizen Lab – https://citizenlab.ca/

Beautiful Trouble – Hashtag Hijack – https://beautifultrouble.org/tactic/hashtag-hijack/

Privacy Guides – https://privacyguides.org/

QR Code Reference Pages

Pokemon Go Location Feeder (GitHub) –

https://github.com/ValleZ/PokemonGoLocationFeeder

Science HowStuffWorks –

https://science.howstuffworks.com/innovation/inventions/invisible-ink.htm

QRd – https://qrd.by/tools

Privacy Guides – Tools – https://www.privacyguides.org/tools/

Beautiful Trouble – Fashion as Camouflage – https://beautifultrouble.org/tactic/fashion-as-camouflage/

Frontline Defenders – https://frontlinedefenders.org/en/resource-publication/security-in-a-box

QR Code Reference Pages

Tactical Tech – https://tacticaltech.org/

The Glass Room – https://www.theglassroom.org/

Beautiful Trouble – Hijacking Traditions – https://beautifultrouble.org/tactic/hijacking-traditions/

Tactical Tech – Data and Activism – https://www.tacticaltech.org/resources/data-and-activism/

Exposing the Invisible – Data Shadow – https://exposingtheinvisible.org/en/guides/data-shadow/

GitHub – Maltrail – https://github.com/stamparm/maltrail

QR Code Reference Pages

WonderHowTo – Honeypot Trap for Spam Bots – https://null-byte.wonderhowto.com/how-to/set-up-honeypot-trap-spam-bots-your-website-0175476/

Wikipedia – Google Bomb – https://en.wikipedia.org/wiki/Google_bomb

Beautiful Trouble – Google Bombing – https://beautifultrouble.org/tactic/google-bombing/

Beautiful Trouble – Mock Funerals – https://beautifultrouble.org/tactic/mock-funerals/

HowlRound – https://howlround.com/how-resistance-performs

Beautiful Trouble – Clown Army – https://beautifultrouble.org/tactic/clown-army/

QR Code Reference Pages

CrimethInc – Clowning as Resistance – https://crimethinc.com/2003/07/10/clowning-as-resistance

Beautiful Trouble – Silent Protest – https://beautifultrouble.org/tactic/silent-protest/

Nonviolence International – https://nonviolence.wagingpeace.org/

Logic Magazine – Bureaucracy as Resistance – https://logicmag.io/security/bureaucracy-as-resistance/

CrimethInc – System Jamming – https://crimethinc.com/tools/system-jamming

Beautiful Trouble – Rule Following – https://beautifultrouble.org/tactic/rule-following/

EFF – Censorship – https://eff.org/issues/censorship

QR Code Reference Pages

Beautiful Trouble – Pattern Disruption – https://beautifultrouble.org/tactic/pattern-disruption/

Exposing the Invisible – https://exposingtheinvisible.org/

Beautiful Trouble – Assumption Violation – https://beautifultrouble.org/tactic/assumption-violation/

Tactical Tech – https://tacticaltech.org/

Chapter 10: Networking with Fellow Mavericks

Signal – https://signal.org

Electronic Frontier Foundation – Messaging Module – https://ssd.eff.org/module-categories/messaging

QR Code Reference Pages

CryptPad – https://cryptpad.org

Proton Drive – https://proton.me/drive

ExifTool – https://exiftool.org

MAT2 – https://0xacab.org/mat/mat2

Bitwarden – https://bitwarden.com

KeePassXC – https://keepassxc.org

Authy – https://authy.com

QR Code Reference Pages

Tor Project – https://www.torproject.org

Mullvad – https://mullvad.net

Proton VPN – https://protonvpn.com

Briar Project – https://briarproject.org

goTenna – https://gotenna.com

Mutual Aid Hub – https://mutualaidhub.org

CrimethInc – https://crimethinc.com

QR Code Reference Pages

IPFS – https://ipfs.tech

Secure Scuttlebutt – https://scuttlebutt.nz

Psychological Safety – https://www.psychsafety.co.uk

Harvard Business Review – https://hbr.org/2014/01/building-a-culture-of-candor

Electronic Frontier Foundation – Security Issues – https://www.eff.org/issues/security

Electronic Frontier Foundation – Surveillance Self-Defense – https://ssd.eff.org

Chapter 11: Choosing Your Line (Tactical Ethics)

QR Code Reference Pages

Mutual Aid Hub – https://www.mutualaidhub.org

INCITE! – https://www.incite-national.org

CrimethInc – https://crimethinc.com

Ruckus Society – https://ruckus.org

Albert Einstein Institution – https://www.aeinstein.org

Brian Martin – https://www.bmartin.cc

Paulo Freire Institute – https://www.freire.org

QR Code Reference Pages

Routledge (Teaching to Transgress) – https://www.routledge.com/Teaching-to-Transgress/hooks/p/book/9780415908085

National Lawyers Guild – https://www.nlg.org

Additional Resources:

For further study on creative protest methods and nonviolent strategy, see:

Beautiful Trouble – https://beautifultrouble.org

Nonviolence International – https://www.nonviolenceinternational.net

International Center on Nonviolent Conflict – https://nonviolent-conflict.org

Chapter 12: Resilience Without Burnout

Maslach Burnout Inventory – https://www.maslachburnoutinventory.com

Mutual Aid Hub – https://www.mutualaidhub.org

QR Code Reference Pages

Leaving Evidence Blog – https://leavingevidence.wordpress.com

AK Press (Emergent Strategy) – https://www.akpress.org/emergentstrategy.html

Audre Lorde Project – https://www.audrelordeproject.org

Routledge (All About Love) – https://www.routledge.com/All-About-Love/hooks/p/book/9780060959470

Malor Books (Burnout: The Cost of Caring) – https://www.malor.com/burnout-the-cost-of-caring

AK Press – https://www.akpress.org

QR Code Reference Pages

National Lawyers Guild – Legal Observers – https://www.nlg.org/legalobservers

Permaculture Association – https://www.permaculture.org.uk

Ruckus Society – https://ruckus.org

Additional Resources:

Headspace – https://www.headspace.com

Mindful.org – https://www.mindful.org

Mental Health America – https://www.mhanational.org

QR Code Reference Pages

7 Cups (peer support) – https://www.7cups.com

National Alliance on Mental Illness – https://nami.org

BetterHelp – https://www.betterhelp.com

Part III – The How: Disruption Modules

Disruption Module A: Mesh Networking

goTenna Mesh Manual – https://gotenna.com/pages/gotenna-mesh-user-manual

Wired – https://www.wired.com/2014/10/firechat-hong-kong-usage/

Electronic Frontier Foundation – Secure Messaging Scorecard – https://www.eff.org/pages/secure-messaging-scorecard

Federal Communications Commission – https://www.fcc.gov

QR Code Reference Pages

Medium (M. Fitzgerald) – https://medium.com/@mfitz

goTenna Mesh User Manual – https://gotenna.com/pages/gotenna-mesh-user-manual

goTenna (Mesh Networking Overview) – https://gotenna.com/pages/mesh-networking

Mesh++ – https://meshplusplus.com

NYU Tandon School of Engineering – https://engineering.nyu.edu/news

The Verge – https://www.theverge.com/2017/10/10/gotenna-puerto-rico-hurricane-maria

Disruption Module B: Privacy & Routing with Raspberry Pi

QR Code Reference Pages

Pi-hole – https://pi-hole.net

Tor Project – https://www.torproject.org

Cloudflare (What is DNS?) – https://www.cloudflare.com/learning/dns/what-is-dns/

Federal Communications Commission (Consumer Internet Rules) –

https://www.fcc.gov/consumers

Ofcom (Telecoms Guidance) – https://www.ofcom.org.uk/

Tor Project (Censorship Wiki) – https://community.torproject.org/censorship/

Privacy International – https://privacyinternational.org

QR Code Reference Pages

EFF Surveillance Self-Defense – https://ssd.eff.org

Medium (M. Fitzgerald) – https://medium.com/@mfitz

Pi-hole Docs (Using Tor with Pi-hole) – https://docs.pi-hole.net/guides/misc/tor/using-tor/

Privacy International (Raspberry Pi Setup) – https://privacyinternational.org/guide-step/4341/raspberry-pi-setup-and-run-pi-hole

Opensource.com (Tor Proxy with Raspberry Pi) – https://opensource.com/article/20/4/tor-proxy-raspberry-pi

Tor Project (Overview & How it Works) – https://support.torproject.org/about/overview/

QR Code Reference Pages

Additional Resources:

CryptPad – https://cryptpad.org

Proton Drive – https://proton.me/drive

ExifTool – https://exiftool.org

MAT2 (Metadata Anonymization Toolkit) – https://0xacab.org/mat

Disruption Module C: Guerrilla Projection & Light Tactics

Instructables – Projection Bombing – https://www.instructables.com/PROJECTION-BOMBING/

Opensource.com – Projection Activism – https://opensource.com/article/21/6/projection-activism

QR Code Reference Pages

Electronic Frontier Foundation – Legal Issues – https://www.eff.org/issues/legal

Greenpeace International – https://www.greenpeace.org/

Privacy International – https://privacyinternational.org

The Illuminator Collective – https://theilluminator.org/

Additional Resource:

Beautiful Trouble (Light Projection) – https://beautifultrouble.org/toolbox/tool/light-projection

Disruption Module D: AR Activism

Play Store (Map Marker Pro GPS App) –

https://play.google.com/store/apps/details?id=com.mictale.gpsessentials

QR Code Reference Pages

Clever Podcast (Nancy Baker Cahill Interview) – https://www.cleverpodcast.com/blog/ep-175-nancy-baker-cahill

Adobe Aero – https://www.adobe.com/products/aero.html

Meta Spark AR Studio – https://sparkar.facebook.com/ar-studio/learn/

Unity (AR Foundation) – https://unity.com/features/arfoundation

8th Wall – https://www.8thwall.com/

ZapWorks – https://zap.works/

QR Code Reference Pages

MoMAR Gallery – https://momar.gallery/

The Verge (4th Wall AR Activism) – https://www.theverge.com/2019/08/12/ar-activism-4th-wall

OpenXR Tutorial – https://openxr-tutorial.com/

Privacy International – https://privacyinternational.org

Tactical Tech – Data Activism – https://tacticaltech.org/projects/data-activism

Electronic Frontier Foundation (AR & Legality) – https://www.eff.org/pages/ar-legal-rights

Additional Resources:

Snapchat Lens Studio – https://lensstudio.snapchat.com

QR Code Reference Pages

Spark AR (Meta/Facebook) – https://sparkar.facebook.com

Unity (Main Site) – https://unity.com

Disruption Module E: Anonymous Broadcast Messaging in Blackouts

Rangzen Research Whitepaper – https://arxiv.org/abs/1612.03371

GPS Essentials – https://play.google.com/store/apps/details?id=com.mictale.gpsessentials

Briar – https://briarproject.org

OsmAnd~ – https://osmand.net

QR Code Reference Pages

RetroShare – https://retroshare.cc

Meshtastic – https://meshtastic.org

Survival Communications – Tactical Tech – https://tacticaltech.org/news/survival-communications/

Tactical Tech Survival Guide –

https://survival.tacticaltech.org/sites/survival.tacticaltech.org/files/Digital_survival_book.pdf

Access Now (Internet Shutdowns) – https://www.accessnow.org/internet-shutdowns-2022/

ACLU (BART Pulls the Plug) – https://www.aclu.org/blog/bart-pulls-plug-free-speech

Anwar et al. DOI – https://doi.org/10.1515/popets-2017-0001

QR Code Reference Pages

EFF – https://www.eff.org

FCC – https://www.fcc.gov

Citizen Lab – https://citizenlab.ca/2020/10/routing-around-censorship-circumvention-iran-kazakhstan/

Open Research Institute – https://openresearch.institute

Privacy International – https://privacyinternational.org

SimpleX – https://simplex.chat

QR Code Reference Pages

Tactical Tech Collective – Data Activism – https://tacticaltech.org/projects/data-activism

Zeno Radio – https://zenoradio.com

Disruption Module F: Zine Warfare

Briar Project – https://briarproject.org

Creative Independent (Risograph) – https://thecreativeindependent.com

EFF (Surveillance Self-Defense) – https://ssd.eff.org

ExifTool – https://exiftool.org

MAT2 (Metadata Anonymization Toolkit 2) – https://0xacab.org/jvoisin/mat2

QR Code Reference Pages

goQR – https://goqr.me

OpenKeychain – https://www.openkeychain.org

PDF Association (PDF/A) – https://www.pdfa.org/resource/what-is-pdfa

Privacy International – https://privacyinternational.org

PrivacyTools.io – https://www.privacytools.io/

Red Scholezine Collective – https://redscholezines.net

RetroShare – https://retroshare.cc

QR Code Reference Pages

VeraCrypt – https://www.veracrypt.fr

Disruption Module G: Drone-Based Messaging

Litchi – https://flylitchi.com

QGroundControl – http://qgroundcontrol.com/

FPV (Oscar Liang Guide) – https://oscarliang.com/fpv/

B4UFLY (FAA) – https://www.faa.gov/uas/getting_started/b4ufly

Drone Assist (UK CAA) – https://dronesafe.uk/drone-assist/

QR Code Reference Pages

DJI Mini 2 SE – https://www.dji.com/mini-2-se

DIY Drones – https://diydrones.com

DroneDJ – https://dronedj.com

EFF (Surveillance Self-Defense) – https://ssd.eff.org

FAA Drone Regulations – https://www.faa.gov/uas

FAA Reauthorization Act (2018) – https://www.congress.gov/bill/115th-congress/house-bill/302

Google Earth Outreach (KML guide) – https://developers.google.com/kml/documentation

QR Code Reference Pages

goTenna – https://gotenna.com

Instructables (Drone Payload Drop) – https://www.instructables.com/Drone-Payload-Drop-System/

NYU Tandon School of Engineering – https://engineering.nyu.edu

OpenStreetMap Foundation – https://wiki.openstreetmap.org

Privacy International – https://privacyinternational.org

QGroundControl Docs – https://docs.qgroundcontrol.com

QR Code Reference Pages

Wired Magazine (Best Drones) – https://www.wired.com/story/best-drones/

Disruption Module H: Bonus Tools

Hacking//Hustling – https://hackinghustling.org

HackBlossom – https://hackblossom.org

Hacktivist Field Manual (GitHub) – https://github.com/hacktivist-fm/manual

FCC CB Service – https://www.fcc.gov/general/citizens-band-cb-service

ARRL (Getting Licensed) – https://www.arrl.org/getting-licensed

SWLing Post – https://swling.com

QR Code Reference Pages

Eibispace – https://www.eibispace.de

Practical Survivor (Signal Mirror) – https://www.practicalsurvivor.com/signalmirror

Meshtastic – https://meshtastic.org

Disaster.Radio – https://disaster.radio

OnionShare – https://onionshare.org

Wired (Solar Chargers) – https://www.wired.com/story/best-portable-solar-chargers/

Security in a Box (Encrypted USB) – https://securityinabox.org/en/guide/encrypted-usb/

QR Code Reference Pages

EFF (SSD scripts) – https://ssd.eff.org

ARRL (What is HAM Radio?) – https://www.arrl.org/what-is-ham-radio

EFF (Surveillance Self-Defense) – https://ssd.eff.org

Eibispace (Schedules) – https://eibispace.de/

FAA B4UFLY – https://www.faa.gov/uas/getting_started/b4ufly

OpenKeychain – https://www.openkeychain.org

Google Earth Outreach (KML) – https://developers.google.com/kml/documentation

QR Code Reference Pages

Hackaday (HAM radio) – https://hackaday.com/tag/ham-radio/

GnuPG – https://gnupg.org

Legal Aid Society – https://legalaidnyc.org

Military Survival Manual FM 21-76 – https://archive.org/details/FM21-76

OpenKeychain (GitHub) – https://github.com/open-keychain/open-keychain

SimpleX Chat (GitHub) – https://github.com/simplex-chat/simplex-chat

Privacy International – https://privacyinternational.org

QR Code Reference Pages

SWLing Post (Guide) – https://swling.com/

Tactical Tech – https://tacticaltech.org

Wired – https://www.wired.com

Part IV – Staying Smart, Staying Safe

Chapter 13: Real-Time Rescue

National Lawyers Guild Jail Support – https://www.nlg.org/massdefense

ACLU Protest Tips – https://www.aclu.org/know-your-rights

NLG Bust Card Templates – https://www.nlg.org/bustcards

QR Code Reference Pages

Miranda Rights Basics (US Courts) – https://www.uscourts.gov/about-federal-courts/educational-resources/constitutional-highlights/bill-rights

Community Justice Exchange Bail Funds – https://www.communityjusticeexchange.org/nbfn-directory

ACLU Know Your Rights Guides – https://www.aclu.org/know-your-rights

ACLU Mobile Justice – https://www.aclu.org/issues/criminal-law-reform/reforming-police/mobile-justice

ObscuraCam – https://guardianproject.info/apps/obscuracam

National Lawyers Guild (Mass Defense) – https://www.nlg.org/massdefense

QR Code Reference Pages

ACLU State Chapters – https://www.aclu.org/about/affiliates

First Amendment Lawyers – https://firstamendment.law/

National Immigration Law Center – https://www.nilc.org/

Community Justice Exchange Directory – https://www.communityjusticeexchange.org/nbfn-directory

NLG Bust Cards (Hotline) – https://www.nlg.org/bustcards

ACLU Affiliate Directories – https://www.aclu.org/about/affiliates

QR Code Reference Pages

Proton Drive – https://proton.me/drive

SecureDrop – https://securedrop.org/

Mutual Aid Hub – https://www.mutualaidhub.org/

Mapping Police Violence – https://mappingpoliceviolence.org/

National Police Accountability Project – https://www.nlg-npap.org/

ACLU – https://www.aclu.org

Chapter 14: Legal Considerations and Risks

U.S. Bill of Rights Transcript – https://www.archives.gov/founding-docs/bill-of-rights-transcript

QR Code Reference Pages

Amendments 11–27 Transcript – https://www.archives.gov/founding-docs/amendments-11-27

National Immigration Law Center (NILC) – https://www.nilc.org/

Immigrant Defense Project – ICE Encounter Card – https://www.immigrantdefenseproject.org/icewatch

Immigrant Defense Project – ICE Encounter Card (Spanish) – https://www.immigrantdefenseproject.org/icewatch-spanish

ACLU Immigration Rights Resources – https://www.aclu.org/issues/immigrants-rights

ACLU Affiliate Locator – https://www.aclu.org/about/affiliates

QR Code Reference Pages

NILC – Community Education Resources – https://www.nilc.org/get-involved/community-education-resources/know-your-rights/

ILRC – Worksite Enforcement Toolkit – https://www.ilrc.org/worksite-enforcement-toolkit

Immigrant Legal Resource Center – https://www.ilrc.org/

American Immigration Lawyers Association – https://www.aila.org/

NACDL Record Clearing Guide – https://www.nacdl.org/Legal-Resources/Record-Sealing-Expungement

National Lawyers Guild (Mass Defense) – https://www.nlg.org/massdefense

QR Code Reference Pages

ACLU – https://www.aclu.org/

Electronic Frontier Foundation – https://www.eff.org/

Digital Defense Fund – https://digitaldefensefund.org/

Firestorm Coop – https://firestorm.coop/

ACLU – Know Your Rights – https://www.aclu.org/know-your-rights

Community Justice Exchange – National Bail Fund Directory –

https://www.communityjusticeexchange.org/nbfn-directory

QR Code Reference Pages

Chapter 15: Funding the Fight

Community Justice Exchange – National Bail Fund Directory – https://www.communityjusticeexchange.org/nbfn-directory

Open Collective – https://opencollective.com/

Electronic Frontier Foundation (EFF) – https://www.eff.org/

GoFundMe – https://www.gofundme.com/

Coin Center – https://coincenter.org/

Financial Crimes Enforcement Network (FinCEN) – https://www.fincen.gov/

Internal Revenue Service (IRS) – https://www.irs.gov/

QR Code Reference Pages

Office of Foreign Assets Control (OFAC) – https://home.treasury.gov/policy-issues/financial-sanctions/faqs

Mutual Aid Hub – https://www.mutualaidhub.org/

Digital Defense Fund (DDF) – https://digitaldefensefund.org/

Electronic Frontier Foundation – Atlas of Surveillance – https://atlasofsurveillance.org/atlas

Additional Resources:

Firestorm Coop – https://firestorm.coop/

Immigrant Defense Project (ICE Watch) – https://www.immigrantdefenseproject.org/icewatch

QR Code Reference Pages

Immigrant Legal Resource Center – https://www.ilrc.org/worksite-enforcement-toolkit

NACDL (Expungement resources) – https://www.nacdl.org/Legal-Resources/Record-Sealing-Expungement

NILC (Know Your Rights) – https://www.nilc.org/get-involved/community-education-resources/know-your-rights/

NLG Mass Defense Program – https://www.nlg.org/massdefense

Chapter 16: Tactical Intelligence

SIFT Method (Four Moves) – https://hapgood.us/2019/06/19/sift-the-four-moves/

Bellingcat – Beginner's Guide to Geolocation – https://www.bellingcat.com/resources/how-tos/2014/07/09/a-beginners-guide-to-geolocation/

QR Code Reference Pages

Wikipedia – EXIF – https://en.wikipedia.org/wiki/Exif

Photography Life – What is EXIF Data – https://photographylife.com/what-is-exif-data

Graphika – Bad Reputation (Inauthentic Networks) – https://graphika.com/bad-reputation

Stanford Internet Observatory – Coordinated Inauthentic Behavior – https://cyber.fsi.stanford.edu/news/how-coordinated-inauthentic-behavior-continues-social-platforms

Security in-a-Box (Front Line Defenders & Tactical Tech) – https://securityinabox.org/en/

PACER (Court Records) – https://pacer.uscourts.gov/

QR Code Reference Pages

CourtListener RECAP – https://www.courtlistener.com/recap/

Open States Tracker – https://open.pluralpolicy.com/

EFF – Atlas of Surveillance – https://atlasofsurveillance.org/atlas

MuckRock FOIA 101 – https://www.muckrock.com/about/foia-101/

HOTOSM / OpenStreetMap – https://www.hotosm.org/

QGIS Documentation – https://docs.qgis.org/latest/en/docs/user_manual/index.html

QR Code Reference Pages

Bellingcat – Beginner's Guide to Social Media Verification – https://www.bellingcat.com/resources/2021/11/01/a-beginners-guide-to-social-media-verification/

Amnesty International – Citizen Evidence Lab – https://citizenevidence.org/

Electronic Frontier Foundation – Surveillance Self-Defense – https://ssd.eff.org/

Exposing the Invisible – Metadata Investigations – https://exposingtheinvisible.org/en/guides/behind-the-data-metadata-investigations/

Wardle, C., & Derakhshan, H. (2017). Information Disorder. Council of Europe – https://edoc.coe.int/en/media/7495-information-disorder-toward-an-interdisciplinary-framework-for-research-and-policy-making.html

Chapter 17: Security & Anonymity in Activism

ExifTool – https://exiftool.org/

QR Code Reference Pages

ObscuraCam (Guardian Project) – https://guardianproject.info/apps/obscuracam/

Privacy Guides (Mobile) – https://www.privacyguides.org/en/mobile-phones/

Security in-a-Box (Front Line Defenders & Tactical Tech) –

https://tacticaltech.org/projects/security-in-a-box/

EFF – Surveillance Self-Defense – https://ssd.eff.org/

Freedom of the Press Foundation – Digital Security Guides –

https://freedom.press/digisec/guides/

ACLU – Know Your Rights (Digital Privacy) – https://www.aclu.org/

QR Code Reference Pages

EFF – Face ID and Fingerprints (Biometric Risks) –

https://www.eff.org/deeplinks/2021/07/face-id-and-fingerprints-know-risks-biometrics

EFF – Surveillance Self-Defense – https://ssd.eff.org/

Exposing the Invisible – Metadata Investigations –

https://exposingtheinvisible.org/en/guides/behind-the-data-metadata-investigations/

Freedom of the Press Foundation – Emergency Security Resources –

https://freedom.press/training/

Wired Magazine – Why You Should Turn Off Face ID at Protests – https://www.wired.com/

Part V – For the Future

Chapter 18: Being Disappeared

QR Code Reference Pages

National Lawyers Guild – Legal Observers – https://www.nlg.org/legalobservers

ICE – Online Detainee Locator (ODLS) – https://locator.ice.gov

Forbes – Google to Stop Sharing Location Data with Law Enforcement – https://www.forbes.com/sites/thomasbrewster/2024/12/13/google-to-stop-sharing-location-data-with-law-enforcement

Additional Resources:

ACLU – https://www.aclu.org

Amnesty International – https://www.amnesty.org

Human Rights Watch – https://www.hrw.org

Electronic Frontier Foundation – https://www.eff.org

QR Code Reference Pages

The Washington Post – https://www.washingtonpost.com

Chapter 19: Education as a Revolutionary Act

Popular Education International – https://www.popedint.org

Books to Prisoners – https://www.bookstoprisoners.net

PEN America – Prison Writing Program – https://pen.org/prison-writing

American Association of University Professors (AAUP) – https://www.aaup.org

Library Freedom Project – https://libraryfreedom.org

QR Code Reference Pages

StoryCorps – https://storycorps.org

First Draft – https://firstdraftnews.org

Chapter 20: Art as a Weapon

Beautiful Trouble – https://beautifultrouble.org

Tactical Tech – https://tacticaltech.org

The Laboratory for Aesthetics and Politics – https://thelabla.org

Chapter 21: Sustaining the Spark: A Call to Future Disobedients

Training for Change – https://www.trainingforchange.org

Commons Social Change Library – https://commonslibrary.org

QR Code Reference Pages

Solidarity Is (Building Movement Project – Movement Pantry, Leadership Stool, Ecosystem of Well-Being) – https://www.solidarityis.org/tools-resources

George Mason University – Thriving Activist Toolkit – https://wellbeing.gmu.edu/research/thriving-activist-toolkit

Activist Handbook – Wellbeing Guide – https://activisthandbook.org/wellbeing

Advocates for Youth – Youth Activist Toolkit (PDF) – https://www.advocatesforyouth.org/wp-content/uploads/2019/04/Youth-Activist-Toolkit.pdf

Center for Constitutional Rights – Toolkit for the Movement – https://ccrjustice.org/toolkit-for-the-movement

QR Code Reference Pages

Tipping Point UK / Commons Library – Movement Power Zine – https://commonslibrary.org/movement-power-a-toolkit-for-building-people-power-in-a-time-of-crisis-zine

Modules A–H (Tools & Extended References)

These contain overlaps with the Disruption Modules and additional unique URLs:

goTenna Mesh – https://gotenna.com

Mesh++ – https://meshplusplus.com

Pi-hole – https://pi-hole.net

Tor Project – https://torproject.org

ProtonVPN – https://protonvpn.com

QR Code Reference Pages

OpenKeychain – https://openkeychain.org

SimpleX – https://simplex.chat

GNU Privacy Guard – https://gnupg.org

Rangzen – https://rangzen.org

Drone DIY guides (community repos, not always stable links) – https://www.google.com/search?q=drone+payload+DIY+github

CrimethInc Zine Warfare – https://crimethinc.com/zines

goQR – https://goqr.me

QR Code Reference Pages

www.ingramcontent.com/pod-product-compliance
Lightning Source LLC
Chambersburg PA
CBHW080539030426
42337CB00024B/4803